German pol today

MANCHESTER
UNIVERSITY PRESS

Politics Today

Series editor: Bill Jones

Ideology and politics in Britain today Ian Adams
Political ideology today, 2nd edition Ian Adams
Scandinavian politics today David Arter
US politics today Edward Ashbee and Nigel Ashford
The Politics Today Companion to American government Edward Ashbee and Alan Grant
Pressure groups today Rob Baggott
French politics today David S. Bell
Local government today, 3rd edition J. A. Chandler
Political issues in Ireland today, 2nd edition Neil Collins (editor)
Irish politics today, 4th edition Neil Collins and Terry Cradden
General Elections today, 2nd edition Frank Conley
East Central European politics today Keith Crawford
US elections today (Elections USA, 2nd edition) Philip John Davies
Political issues in America today Philip John Davies and Frederic A. Waldstein (editors)
British political parties today, 2nd edition Robert Garner and Richard Kelly
Spanish politics today John Gibbons
Political issues in Britain today, 5th edition Bill Jones (editor)
British politics today, 6th edition Bill Jones and Dennis Kavanagh
Trade unions in Britain today, 2nd edition John McIlroy
Italian politics today Hilary Partridge
Britain in the European Union today, 2nd edition Colin Pilkington
The Civil Service in Britain today Colin Pilkington
Devolution in Britain today Colin Pilkington
The Politics Today companion to the British Constitution Colin Pilkington
Representative democracy in Britain today Colin Pilkington
German politics today Geoffrey Roberts
European politics today Geoffrey Roberts and Patricia Hogwood
Debates in British politics today Lynton Robins and Bill Jones (editors)
Government and the economy today Graham P. Thomas
Prime Minister and Cabinet today Graham P. Thomas
Political communication today Duncan Watts

German politics
today

Geoffrey K. Roberts

Manchester University Press

Manchester and New York

distributed exclusively in the USA by Palgrave

Published by Manchester University Press
Oxford Road, Manchester M13 9NR, UK
and Room 400, 175 Fifth Avenue, New York, NY 10010, USA
www.manchesteruniversitypress.co.uk

Distributed exclusively in the USA by
Palgrave, 175 Fifth Avenue, New York,
NY 10010, USA

Distributed exclusively in Canada by
UBC Press, University of British Columbia, 2029 West Mall,
Vancouver, BC, Canada V6T 1Z2

British Library Cataloguing-in-Publication Data
A catalogue record for this book is available from the British Library

Library of Congress Cataloging-in-Publication Data applied for

ISBN 0 7190 4960 1 *hardback*
      0 7190 4961 X *paperback*

First published 2000

09 08 07 06 05 04 03 02   10 9 8 7 6 5 4 3 2

Typeset in Photina
by Servis Filmsetting Ltd, Manchester
Printed in Great Britain by Biddles Ltd
www.biddles.co.uk

Contents

List of tables and boxes   vi
Preface   vii
A note on style   xi
Abbreviations   xiii
Glossary   xv

1   The creation of present-day Germany   1

2   The context of politics in reunified Germany   23

3   The development of the political system of the Federal Republic   35

4   The electoral system and electoral politics   50

5   The party-state   76

6   The federal structure   97

7   Chancellor democracy   112

8   Parliamentary politics   131

9   Interest-group politics   152

10 Germany and Europe   167

11 Germany: a 'normal' democracy?   181

Appendix 1: Court cases   200
Appendix 2: Economic, social and political profiles of the Länder   208
Index   215

Tables and boxes

Tables

4.1 Bundestag election results, 1949–98   *page* 51
4.2 Number of parties represented in the Bundestag: 1949–98   55
6.1 The area and population of the Länder, December 1996   99
11.1 Electoral performance of extremist parties, 1990–99   191

Boxes

1.1 Regimes in modern Germany   *page* 1
1.2 The relationship between West Germany and East Germany, 1945–89   18
2.1 Chronology of the reunification of Germany   26
4.1 Surplus seats. A special feature of the German electoral system   52
4.2 Modifications of the electoral system of the Federal Republic, 1949–98   53
5.1 Article 21 of the Basic Law   77
7.1 The election of the federal president: May 1999   114
7.2 Presidents of the Federal Republic of Germany   117
7.3 Chancellors of the Federal Republic of Germany   119
7.4 Governments of the Federal Republic   124
8.1 The Bundestag praesidium, 1998   134
8.2 Committees of the Bundestag, 1998   135
8.3 Allocation of Bundesrat seats and composition of Land governments, May 1999   138
9.1 Trade union membership, 1997   156
9.2 Examples of interest groups registered with the Bundestag   162

Preface

German Politics Today offers an overview of the principal features of the German political system. The sequence of chapters emphasises four important characteristics of Germany's political system: the way in which history, especially twentieth-century history, has shaped the post-Second World War political system; the stability and adaptability of that system, qualities demonstrated in the 1990s by responses to the challenges of reunification; the unusual importance within the political system of legal rules, many of which are derived from the Basic Law (the constitution of the Federal Republic); and the significance of Germany's association with European integration.

The first chapter surveys the historical background of the present-day political system. More than any other western European polity, that of the Federal Republic has been shaped by what has happened in the past. In particular, the Basic Law designed in 1948–49 was a direct response to the failure of Germany's first experiment with democracy – the regime of the Weimar Republic (between 1919 and 1933) – and to the horrors and disasters brought upon Germany, and upon the rest of Europe, by the totalitarian Nazi regime (1933–45) which supplanted the Weimar Republic. But history has affected present-day politics in other ways. Questions concerning the boundaries of the German state (the 'German question') and Germany's proper relations with its neighbours to the east and to the west have been themes recurring through Germany's political history in the nineteenth and twentieth centuries. This chapter also reviews the development of the political system in the first forty years of its existence, and looks at the 'other Germany' – the German Democratic Republic (GDR) – and its significance for the Federal Republic in the period to 1989.

Had this book been written ten years earlier, that first chapter would have sufficed as historical context. In the late 1980s, the post-war division of Germany seemed to be firmly entrenched as part of the 'German question'. A few sentences about the extreme unlikelihood of German reunification occurring in the foreseeable future, and a reference to how the constitutional requirement that reunification remain an ultimate goal for the Federal Republic of Germany (FRG) was incongruent with political reality, as some German politicians themselves were claiming in the 1980s; that would have been sufficient treatment of the division of Germany in an introduction to a textbook on the West German political system.

The fall of the Berlin Wall on 9 November 1989 changed everything. It showed that the future of divided Germany was not predictable. The second chapter therefore provides a brief summary of the momentous events in the GDR from May 1989 (when controversial local elections took place in the GDR, and Hungary began to dismantle its section of the 'iron curtain' – the border with Austria), through what some commentators have called the 'revolution' in the GDR, which certainly included the downfall of the communist regime there, to the processes which resulted in German reunification on 3 October 1990. It also examines the problems of adaptation which reunification had caused: social, economic and psychological adaptation, but of course political adaptation also. Nothing like this has been seen in recent times: the merging of two states within one nation after forty or more years of profound separation.

Chapter 3 examines in some detail the principal influences which have shaped the present-day political system. These include the Basic Law itself and the particular pattern of political institutions to which it gave birth; the Constitutional Court, as responsible both for the interpretation of the Basic Law and for adjudication of controversies concerning its provisions; and a variety of other influences, ranging from the social market economy to political culture, which have shaped and constrained the development of the political system of the Federal Republic.

Chapters 4 and 5 examine the electoral system and electoral behaviour of the Federal Republic, and the features of what is sometimes referred to as the 'party state'. The Federal Republic is more than just a 'party-state', though; it is very much a *federal* republic, and this federal element, while creating an additional set of opportunities for democratic politics, can also often be of considerable importance in political controversies and conflicts which arise. So chapter 6 reviews the structure, operation and political effects of Germany's particular version of federalism.

In chapters 7 and 8 the core institutions of government are analysed. The federal president is head of state and moral leader of the nation, a moral leadership the more efficacious because the president is denied partisan political powers. The office of chancellor is not only the most important position in the political system; it is also the most stable. By 1999, at the time of writing this book, there have only been six chancellors in the first fifty years of the Federal Republic. By comparison, the United Kingdom has had 11 prime ministers since 1945, and the USA 10 presidents since the death of Roosevelt in 1945. The sources of the chancellor's political power, his relationship with his coalition partners, with his cabinet ministers and with the machinery of government, together with the process of policy-making, constitute the subject-matter of chapter 7. The structure and powers of the two legislative chambers, the Bundestag and the Bundesrat, the legislative process, and the role of the elected representative are examined in chapter 8.

Where there is policy-making, and consequently the power to affect – for better or worse, for richer or poorer – the fate of individuals, groups, business enterprises, trade unions or other associations, one can expect to find interest groups at work. The Federal Republic is no exception. In chapter 9 the role of interest groups is examined, together with their opportunities to affect policy, the strategies they adopt and the structure of the more significant interest groups.

Chancellor Kohl, at the time of reunification, promised a 'European Germany'. Chancellor Adenauer, the first chancellor of the Federal Republic, took early steps to ensure that the Federal Republic became embedded in a network of institutions and relationships that linked West Germany to its West European neighbours, especially in the fields of the economy and military security. Chapter 10 charts the path which West Germany took to develop links to 'Europe' over the years, and examines the ways in which membership of European institutions impinges upon the domestic politics of the Federal Republic.

The Weimar Republic was a fragile democracy. The Bonn Republic – in its early years especially – was in many ways a special, one might almost say an 'abnormal', democracy. Today the questions can be asked (questions to which an affirmative answer is anticipated): is Germany now a 'normal' democracy? Has it overcome its past? Has it coped more or less successfully with the special challenges of reunification? The concluding chapter looks at the measures Germany can take in defence of its democratic arrangements ('combative democracy'); the challenges which the polity has faced from extremism and prejudice; the effects of 'new politics' on Germany's democracy; and Germany's changing role in the international system. In this way a balance sheet – provisional, as all such assessments of a country's politics must be – can be attempted, in terms of the qualities of democracy, efficiency and stability of the political system of Germany today.

Deliberately, for reasons of intellectual coherence and restrictions of space, policy sectors such as the economy, social services or foreign affairs are not treated in this book in any detail. To have done so would have meant making a selection of policy areas to cover: the environment? industrial policy? labour relations? And policy-areas can swiftly go in or out of fashion; new issues arise, old issues lose their saliency, so any treatment in 1999 of, say, Germany's defence policy or its policy concerning European monetary union, might in three or four years time have been overtaken by events.

For readers interested in such policy issues, or indeed wishing to study in more depth aspects of Germany's modern political history, the Constitutional Court, electoral behaviour or coalition strategies, many monographs and articles in academic journals are available, and some of the more accessible of these are listed as 'further reading' at the end of each chapter.

Textbooks necessarily have to be divided into chapters according to some logical principle. Politics itself is not so amenable to classification and segmentation. To understand what is going on in an election campaign in Germany, to appreciate why certain policy decisions are taken, to comprehend the sensitivity of sections of the German public to certain social or economic developments (such as the influx of asylum-seekers or the proposed abandonment of the Deutschmark), it may well be necessary for the reader to draw upon material from several of the chapters in this book. Anyway, no textbook can provide all the information necessary to a thorough understanding of day-to-day politics in Germany – or elsewhere. The reader is strongly advised to use three sets of resources to supplement this textbook. History books provide the means to appreciate the historical context in which current political events are occurring. A map of Europe will remind the reader of Germany's central location in Europe, and of how many neighbours (and, so, how many potential problems with those neighbours) Germany possesses: Switzerland and Denmark, Belgium and Austria, Luxembourg and the Czech Republic, the Netherlands, France and Poland. Newspapers, magazines and the broadcast media will provide updates on how politics is developing in the Federal Republic.

Whatever else might be said about Germany, its politics in the twentieth century generally have been extremely interesting, and often have been fateful for itself and for other countries in Europe. To understand its politics, it is necessary to know about its past, its political system and its role in Europe. It is hoped that this book will provide the basis for such an appreciation of German politics today.

This book owes much to the many friends and colleagues in Germany who have provided information, advice and hospitality over many years. Chapters of this book have also benefited from the scrutiny of colleagues in the United Kingdom: Simon Bulmer and David Farrell (Manchester); Patricia Hogwood (Glasgow); Charlie Jeffery (Birmingham); and Thomas Saalfeld (Kent). No responsibility rests with them for any flaws in this book, but I am very grateful for their kind and wise advice.

Geoffrey K. Roberts
Manchester

A note on style

Terms in German have been translated and explained when they have been first used, and most such terms are also included in the Glossary. In a few cases, German terms have been utilised throughout the book, for example for the chambers of the federal legislature (the Bundestag and Bundesrat), for the states which form the Federation (the Länder), and for the parliamentary party group (the Fraktion).

Translations from German sources are the responsibility of the author.

Abbreviations

ADAC	German Motor Club
Alliance '90	*Bündnis '90*: the citizen movement alliance in the GDR
ARD	Arbeitsgemeinschaft der öffentlich-rechtlichen Rundfunksanstalten der Bundesrepublik Deutschland (first television channel)
BDA	Bundesvereinigung der Deutschen Arbeitgeberverbände (Federal Association of German Employers' Organisations)
BDI	Bundesverband der Deutschen Industrie (Federal Association of German Industry)
BP	Bavarian Party
CAP	Common Agricultural Policy (of the EU)
CDU	Christlich-Demokratische Union Deutschlands (Christian Democratic Union of Germany)
COMECON	Council for Mutual Economic Assistance
CSU	Christlich-Soziale Union (Christian Social Union)
DBD	Demokratische Bauernpartei Deutschlands (Democratic Farmers' Party of Germany in the GDR)
DBV	Deutsche Bauernverband (German Farmers' Association)
DDP	German Democratic Party
DGB	Deutscher Gewerkschaftsbund (German Federation of Trade Unions)
DIHT	Deutscher Industrie- und Handelstag (German Chamber of Commerce)
DKP	Deutsche Kommunistische Partei (German Communist Party)
DP	Deutsche Partei (German Party)
DSU	German Social Union
DVP	German People's Party
DVU	Deutsche Volksunion (German People's Union)
EC	European Community
ECSC	European Coal and Steel Community

EDC	European Defence Community
EEC	European Economic Community
EU	European Union
EURATOM	European Atomic Energy Community
FDP	Freie Demokratische Partei (Free Democratic Party)
FRG	Federal Republic of Germany
FVP	Freie Volkspartie (Free People's Party)
GB/BHE	Gesamtdeutscher Block/Bund der Heimatvertriebenen und Entrechteten (All-German Block/Association of Expellees and Those Deprived of Rights) – the Refugees Party.
GDR	German Democratic Republic
Greens	The Greens (official short name for the party: Alliance '90 – the Greens)
KPD	Kommunistische Partei Deutschlands (Communist Party of Germany)
LDPD	Liberal-Demokratische Partei Deutschlands (GDR Liberal party)
MdB	Mitglied des Bundestages (Member of the Bundestag)
MEP	Member of the European Parliament
NATO	North Atlantic Treaty Organisation
NDPD	National-Demokratische Partei Deutschlands (National Democratic Party of Germany: GDR party)
NPD	Nationaldemokratische Partei Deutschlands (National Democratic Party of Germany: party in the FRG)
ÖDP	Ecological Democratic Party
PDS	Partei des demokratischen Sozialismus (Party of Democratic Socialism)
RAF	Red Army Faction
SED	Sozialistische Einheitspartei Deutschlands (Socialist Unity Party of Germany: GDR party)
SPD	Sozialdemokratische Partei Deutschlands (Social Democratic Party of Germany)
SRP	Sozialistische Reichspartei (Socialist Reich Party)
UN	United Nations
WEU	Western European Union
ZDF	Zweite Deutsche Fernsehen (second television channel)

Glossary

Anschluss   Literally: 'connection'. The term refers usually to the annexation of Austria by the Third Reich in March 1938.

Basic Law   The constitution of the Federal Republic of Germany

Bizone   The name given to the linked British and American occupation zones in West Germany which took effect from January 1947.

Bundeskanzleramt   The Federal Chancellor's Office.

Bundestag   The lower chamber of the federal legislature

Bundesrat   The upper chamber of the federal legislature, representing the Länder.

Bundesverfassungsgericht   Federal Constitutional Court

Bundesversammlung   The electoral college which selects the federal president.

Dachverband   A 'peak' or 'umbrella' organisation, the membership consisting of other organisations.

5 per cent clause   The clause in the Electoral Law which requires parties who have not won at least three constituency seats to obtain at least 5 per cent of party list votes in an election in order to be allocated a proportional distribution of seats.

Fraktion   An officially recognised party group in the Bundestag or other legislature in Germany. In the Bundestag, a party needs 5 per cent of MdBs in order to obtain Fraktion status.

'Fundis'   'Fundamentalists': a term applied to the more radical faction of the Greens (see also 'Realos').

Gleichschaltung   The term applied to the nazification of political, economic and social institutions in the Third Reich.

'grand coalition'   A coalition of the two large parties: the Christian Democrats and the SPD. The term is applied especially to the federal coalition 1966–69.

Land (pl. Länder)   The states which together constitute the Federal Republic.

Nazis   The National Socialist Party, led by Hitler, which ruled Germany during the Third Reich, 1933–45.

'new Länder'   The five Länder created in 1990 in the former territory of the
   GDR when Germany was reunified. In fact, these Länder had existed in the
   GDR prior to their abolition in 1952.

Ostpolitik   Literally 'policy towards the east'. The policy towards the USSR
   and countries of the communist bloc in eastern and central Europe
   (including the GDR) initiated by the Brandt government from 1969.

Parteiverdrossenheit   Alienation from political parties.

Politikverdrossenheit   Alienation from the political process.

Politikverflechtung   Co-ordination or linkage of policy (between the federal
   and Land levels, for instance).

'Realos'   'Realists', the more pragmatic faction within the Green party (see
   also 'Fundis').

Rechtsstaat   A state based on the rule of law; a principle of the Basic Law.

Regierungserklärung   Government declaration of its policy for the forthcoming parliamentary period (equivalent to the 'Queen's Speech' in the
   British parliament).

Reich   Empire.

Reichstag   The German lower chamber of the legislature in the Second
   Empire and Weimar Republic.

Richtlinienkompetenz   The power given to the chancellor by Article 65 of the
   Basic Law to set general guidelines for government policy and strategy.

Stasi   The Staatssicherheitsdeinst (state security service) in the GDR, which
   combined various functions including identifying and then eliminating
   dissent and opposition, and conducting intelligence-gathering activities
   against other states, especially the Federal Republic.

Sachverständigenrat   The council of economic experts who report on the economic policies of the federal government and on economic conditions and
   prospects.

Stiftung   A Foundation, generally for charitable, cultural or educational purposes.

'Superwahljahr'   'Super-election year': the term applied to 1994, when the
   Bundestag election took place in the same year as numerous Land and
   local government elections, as well as the European parliamentary election
   and the election of the federal president.

Treuhandanstalt   The trustee agency set up by the GDR parliament in
   preparation for economic and political union with the Federal Republic, to
   transform the state-owned industrial and other economic institutions of
   the GDR to private ownership, or to close them down. It operated from
   1990 to 1994.

Überhangmandate   'Surplus seats': seats additional to the normal number of
   seats in the Bundestag, won by a party because it receives more seats in
   constituencies in a Land than it is entitled to on the basis of its share of
   party list votes in that Land.

Vergangenheitsbewältigung   Overcoming or coming to terms with the past.

The term is applied now to the process of overcoming the Nazi past and of
dealing with the communist dictatorship period in the GDR.

Vermittlungsausschuss   Mediation Committee: joint committee of the
Bundestag and Bundesrat.

Volkskammer   The parliament of the GDR.

Wehrbeauftragter   The commissioner for the armed forces, who receives and
investigates complaints form members of the armed forces and reports to
the Bundestag.

1

The creation of
present-day Germany

Germany before 1949

The Federal Republic of Germany, more than most European democracies, is the product of its past. Its constitution, its political system, its political culture, its policies, even some of its present-day political problems, can be explained comprehensively only by reference to the Weimar Republic, the Hitler regime that supplanted it, and the Second World War which Hitler called into being, as well as the period of the occupation regime that was imposed by the victorious allies at the end of the war.

The historical background to the creation of the Federal Republic of Germany can be divided into five phases. Each phase affected its successors, and certainly the third, fourth and fifth directly affected the political format and many of the policies of the Federal Republic. Each of these phases came to an end when the existing form of political system (the regime) was replaced by a

---

Box 1.1
Regimes in modern Germany

1871	Unification of Germany
1871–1918	Second Empire
1918–19	Provisional republic
1919–33	Weimar Republic
1933–45	Third Reich (Nazi regime)
1945–49	Occupation regime; division of Germany into zones
1949–90	Federal Republic (West Germany only)
1949–90	German Democratic Republic (East Germany only)
1990–	Federal Republic (reunified Germany)

---

new regime. The unification of Germany as the Second Empire (Reich) in 1871, and the way in which that came about, is the first phase. The consolidation of the new German state and its involvement in the First World War, a war which brought with it the end of the Second Empire, is the second phase. The third phase is the foundation, development and downfall of the Weimar Republic. Then came the Third Reich, the period of Nazi rule and the Second World War, which was the product of Hitler's schemes for territorial expansion. The final phase is the four-power occupation regime put in place following Germany's unconditional surrender in 1945, a phase which lasted until 1949.

The Unification of Germany

The territory that later came to be known as 'Germany' consisted before its unification in 1871 of a number of different states, ruled by kings, princes, dukes, even archbishops. These states varied greatly in terms of territorial extent, military power and economic strength. In the eighteenth century, the kingdom of Prussia emerged as the most powerful of these states, though Bavaria and Hanover were also important kingdoms. In this period of conquest and rearrangement of the states of Europe, Napoleon welded together several of these Germanic states within a 'Rhenish League', a grouping of states which then, following Napoleon's defeat, formed the basis for a German confederation created by the Congress of Vienna (1814–15). A customs union (the Zollverein) was established in 1834, facilitating trade among the Germanic states, and there were various manifestations of national feeling prior to 1848, such as the rally of nationalists and radicals at Hambach in 1832, or the composition by Hoffmann von Fallersleben in 1841 of the *Deutschlandlied* (his 'German anthem', 'Deutschland, Deutschland, über alles . . .'), which was officially adopted as the national anthem in 1922. These gave impetus to the cause of German nationalism, which developed apace in the 1830s and 1840s. In 1848, when a wave of revolutionary fervour swept across most of Europe, German nationalists perceived it as an opportunity to press for the creation of a united Germany. At the Frankfurt Parliament (1848–49), convened to discuss the issue of unifying Germany, delegates decided that a unified Germany should be created, though it should not include Austria, a Catholic state whose king was also emperor of the Austro-Hungarian empire, an empire which contained large areas populated by non-Germanic peoples. This Frankfurt Parliament promulgated a constitution for Germany on 27 March 1849, which envisaged a union of German states under an emperor. The next day they elected the king of Prussia as 'emperor of the Germans'. However, that king, Frederick William IV, refused to accept this crown of an imperial Germany, not acknowledging the legitimacy of the popular assembly which wished to convey the title to him. Especially in Prussia, a period of reaction followed, which eroded many of the democratic reforms won in the 1848–49 period, such as freedom of the press and civil liberties. It also terminated, for some years to come, all hopes of the creation of a united German state.

A political crisis in Prussia in 1862 concerning the budget for the military led the king, William I, to appoint Otto von Bismarck as his new prime minister. Bismarck utilised a political dispute in the Danish border provinces of Schleswig and Holstein to expand Prussia's military strength in a war with Denmark (1863–64), and to develop its alliances with other north German states. A quarrel with Austria and her allies arising from the settlement of the Schleswig-Holstein crisis resulted in a war in 1866 against Austria, in which Prussia was victorious. This ended any possibility of Austria, rather than Prussia, exercising hegemony within what was later to become Germany. In 1867 a North German Confederation was created, led by Prussia, which also had special treaties of friendship with south German states. A dispute with France about dynastic matters swiftly led to a war between France and Prussia (supported by its north and south German allies) in 1870. The successful prosecution of this war offered Bismarck the opportunity to translate Prussia's alliances with other German states into a more integrated political arrangement: the creation of the Second Empire, with the king of Prussia, William I, proclaimed as its emperor on 18 January 1871. In this way, a unified German state was at last created, and created by Bismarck's policy of uniting the various states of Germany by 'blood and iron' (i.e. through military alliances and the joint prosecution of war) rather than by the rhetoric of liberal-nationalists in the Frankfurt Parliament.

The Second Empire was not very much more than a confederation of member-states (the Länder). The royal rulers of component states such as Bavaria, Württemberg and Saxony (and of course Prussia, by far the largest and most powerful of the member-states) retained their thrones and many privileges. Bavaria, for instance, retained special rights relating to its postal services, beer taxes and – in time of peace – control of its army. Each of the 25 component states retained its own form of franchise for election of its own parliaments. These states were represented in the Bundesrat (though Prussia dominated in this upper chamber of the legislature, as it did in the elected lower chamber, the Reichstag). Bismarck realised that creating a united German state was one thing; integrating its peoples so that they became 'Germans', rather than considering themselves primarily to be Bavarians, Saxons or Prussians, was something else entirely. In a period when these states were coping with the tensions of rapid industrialisation, coupled with the exodus of populations from rural areas to the towns and cities, with the growth of literacy and the spread of radical political ideas to members of the working class, Bismarck tried to ensure that no rival political force would counter his efforts at political and social integration. In particular, he instituted repressive policies against the Catholic church (the Kulturkampf) and the socialists (the Socialist Laws), seeing international Catholicism and international socialism as potential loyalties which could be rivals to the feelings of German nationalism that he wished to foster among the people. In this aim, Bismarck's policies eventually were successful, after he himself had left office. By August 1914, when the First World War started, it could be said that feelings of German nationalism certainly were prominent indeed!

The Second Empire set about expanding its military and economic power. This brought it into conflict with a number of its European neighbours and encouraged several of them to enter into a set of mutually protective alliances. In turn, Germany wanted to prevent itself becoming encircled by potential enemies, so it, too, entered into alliances, particularly with the Austro-Hungarian empire and Italy. By 1914, rivalry among the principal European powers had created a situation in which war was likely. The assassination of the heir to the Austrian throne, Archduke Ferdinand, in Sarajevo in June 1914 created a situation which drew Russia and Germany, then France and Britain, into a European war in August – a war that expanded to become the First World War. After years of virtual stalemate on the western front, then the collapse of the Russian military following the 1917 Bolshevik revolution, and the decision by the USA to enter the war against Germany, the German western front was decisively breached in Autumn 1918, and an armistice took effect on 11 November 1918.

Germany's defeat was relatively sudden and, especially for Germany's civilian population, entirely unexpected. They had suffered deprivation during the war as a result of the Allied blockade of sea routes upon which much of Germany's foreign trade depended. They had believed the propaganda of their military-directed government that victory and territorial gains would be the outcome of the war and a recompense for their sufferings. Many families had lost sons and fathers in the war of attrition on the western front (in total, Germany lost 1.8 million dead during this war, more than any other combatant country). The closing days of the war saw riots and demonstrations in several parts of Germany, mutinies by the military, and agitation by communists who wanted Germany to follow Russia's example and engage in its own communist revolution. The Social Democrats proclaimed a republic in Berlin on 9 November. Germany's emperor, Kaiser Wilhelm II, fled to Holland and then abdicated – as did many other royal rulers in Europe – later that month. The chaos within Germany accompanying the end of the war was utilised by the communists to try to impose a system of workers' councils. The new Social Democrat-led provisional government had to use the military to combat this revolutionary attempt. The assassinations in January 1919 of Rosa Luxemburg and Karl Liebknecht, the two leading figures of the abortive 1918–19 communist revolution, signalled the end of that attempt. Elections went ahead on 19 January 1919 for a constituent assembly, which was to draw up a new, republican, constitution for Germany, meeting in the small, relatively peaceful, town of Weimar rather than in the capital, Berlin, which was a centre of continued political unrest. The hope was that this new constitution would establish, for the first time in Germany, a truly democratic form of government.

The Weimar Republic

The product of the deliberations of the National Assembly was the Weimar constitution, signed on 11 August 1919. This constitution has been blamed by many analysts for the failure of the Weimar regime to survive for longer than 14 years. Certainly it appeared to be a democratic constitution. It was based on an electoral system of extreme proportional representation, which allowed numerous, often very small, political parties to obtain representation in the legislature (the Reichstag). This, in turn, meant that it was difficult for governments to be formed, since coalitions often had to consist of several parties, any one of which could abandon the coalition on a whim and bring down the government. Indeed, 20 different governments were formed before Hitler was invited to become chancellor in 1933. Of these, only four lasted longer than a year, and four lasted less than three months. The president of the republic (who was elected directly by the people) possessed the right to use emergency powers, which enabled him and his government to by-pass the Reichstag. Though the constitution provided for civil liberties and a form of constitutional court (the Staatsgerichtshof), these were not very efficacious in protecting the rights of citizens or the inviolability of the constitution itself. Though still a federal state in its structure, the political system of the Weimar Republic severely restricted the former powers of the Länder, so they could not act as bastions of democracy once the Republic itself was threatened.

But the Weimar regime faced greater problems than the content of its constitution. First, though the constitution was formally very democratic, Germany lacked convinced democrats. On the left, the communists wanted their version of republicanism to prevail, with a system of soviets (workers' councils) rather than what they saw as a bourgeois parliamentary regime. On the right, a mixture of opponents of the regime preferred either the restoration of the monarchy or else a non-monarchical but authoritarian regime less open to popular control and less influenced by political parties than the Weimar political system would be. This left the Social Democrats, the Catholic Centre party and the liberal German Democratic Party – the so-called 'Weimar coalition' – as the enthusiastic supporters of the regime. The bureaucrats, the military (what was left of it in its reduced form after the Versailles Treaty had been signed, see below), the judiciary, the universities, large sections of the press, commerce and industry, sections of the Protestant churches, all were suspicious of, or downright opposed to, the new democratic and republican regime.

Second, the politicians in office in 1919 had had to sign the Versailles Treaty (the peace treaty after the First World War), with no opportunity to negotiate milder terms. For this, they and their new regime were blamed by the German people and especially by their political enemies. The terms of that treaty, involving losses of territory on the western and eastern borders of Germany, severe restrictions on the size and structure of the military, payment of heavy reparations to the victorious powers (just as France had had to pay reparations to Prussia in 1871), and admitted acceptance of guilt for starting the war, all rankled with many Germans. Agitators on the extreme right – including a young ex-corporal called Adolf Hitler – claimed (correctly) that German troops had not been defeated on German soil, and therefore they asserted (falsely) that surrender must have been the result of the activities of traitors on the home front; in other words, that German troops had been 'stabbed in the back'. Such agitators opposed fulfilment of the terms of the Versailles Treaty, though they were generally not very open about what the consequences for Germany might be of such a policy of 'non-fulfilment'. For many Germans, 'the constitution and the treaty were both seen as embodying alien principles, imposed on Germany by the victorious West' (Pulzer, 1997, p. 102). Certainly the Versailles Treaty gave ammunition to populist rabble-rousers for the lifetime of the Weimar Republic. Pre-eminent among these populist groups was the National Socialist Workers' Party – the Nazis – who, from small beginnings in the early 1920s, gained increasing numbers of votes once the economic depression struck Germany from 1929 onwards.

Even this may not have mattered so much had the new republic not been challenged by crises within and outside its borders. In Germany itself, the end of the war had resulted in large-scale unemployment, affecting, among other groups, many former professional soldiers and sailors, unemployed because of the Versailles Treaty limitation on the size of the military. Production took time to get back to anything like peacetime normality. The need to meet annual demands, especially from France, for reparations payments and to service the public debts that had built up during the war (debts which were to have been repaid from the reparations that Germany, had it been victorious, would certainly have demanded of its defeated opponents) all added to the economic fragility of post-war Germany. Political unrest took many forms, including a semi-serious attempt by a military group to take over the state – the 'Kapp putsch' in March 1920 – and assassinations of politicians, the most prominent of whom was Walther Rathenau, the liberal Foreign Minister of the Republic, murdered in 1922. These added to the problems that the new government had to face. In 1923 problems in the Ruhr mining area concerning coal production earmarked to meet French reparations demands, the occupation of the Ruhr and parts of Baden by the French and resistance by workers to that French occupation, led to a period of hyperinflation. That same year, Hitler tried to institute a *coup* in Munich, to take over the government of Bavaria. The attempt failed, and Hitler was imprisoned for a while, during which time he started to write his famous political testament: *Mein Kampf* (My Struggle). Even when these early problems had been resolved, resentments remained, and street clashes between rival political groupings of the left and the right were indicative of an unsettled, and intolerant, political atmosphere.

Externally, Germany was slowly readmitted as a 'normal' member of the international political system, including in 1926 admission to membership of the new League of Nations (an institution intended to resolve international conflicts before resort to war became necessary).

Despite these crises, eventually all might still have gone well for the new Republic, had not the world economic depression occurred in 1929. Germany, heavily indebted to other countries and especially to the USA, was forced to repay these debts, and this led to the closure of factories, the decline of foreign trade, and rapidly increasing unemployment. In such a climate, it became even more difficult to find a government that would be stable and effective in dealing with the situation. After the failure of the two short-lived governments of von Papen and Schleicher, which had ruled in effect by decree from June 1932, President Hindenburg was persuaded in January 1933 to give the responsibility of government to Adolf Hitler as chancellor. This marked the end of the Weimar Republic.

The Nazi period and the Second World War

The one name everyone associates with Germany's history is that of Adolf Hitler. He and his Nazi party imposed totalitarian political control within Germany, and set about expanding Germany's borders and extending its conquests before and then during the Second World War. That war brought devastation and division – but also, ironically, an effective democracy – to Germany.

The Nazi party constituted one of the problems challenging the Weimar Republic (see above), but for many Germans Hitler was perceived as a welcome alternative to the Weimar system, associated as that regime was with ineffective government and economic distress. The Nazi party experienced an astonishing upsurge in electoral support, membership, resources and media attention. The Nazis were encouraged by many on the right of the political spectrum who had never been able to tolerate a democratic republic in Germany (and especially one in which social democrats and communists could be so influential), readily financed by business interests who hoped that Hitler would revive the economy and emasculate the trade unions, and supported by more and more voters – especially liberal and Protestant conservative voters who had lost faith in the ability of their parties to rescue the economy and integrate society.[1]

Expectations that Hitler would be constrained in his exercise of political power by the non-Nazis who constituted a majority in his cabinet, proved fatally misplaced. Politicians who believed this, including President Hindenburg and his conservative associates, such as von Papen and Hugenberg, the media tycoon (both of whom were members of Hitler's cabinet), did not appreciate the extent of Hitler's political skills or his ambitions. Hitler called a general election for March 1933. During the campaign, the Reichstag building was set ablaze. This gave the Nazis an excuse to refuse the communists – blamed by the Nazis for the fire[2] – the right to take their seats in the newly elected legislature. This made it easier for Hitler to force through his Enabling Act on 23 March 1933, a law which gave him and his party more or less total power in Germany.[3] Trade unions were banned on 2 May 1933, and other parties (some of which had already voluntarily dissolved themselves) were prohibited on 14 July 1933. In this way, a one-party state was swiftly created. The death of Hindenburg in August 1934 allowed Hitler to take over the role of head of state as well as head of government. By manipulation of the leadership of the army, Hitler was able to force the military to become his loyal instrument, rather than remain a 'neutral' agency in the service of the state. Hitler developed an internal security system under the management of Heinrich Himmler (the SS: Schutzstaffel – protective bodyguard), which set about the elimination of any remaining internal threats to Hitler's rule.

Under Nazism, the society and economy of Germany underwent extensive change. The policy of *Gleichschaltung* (nazification) meant that all social institutions – whether associated directly with the state or not – were subjected to Nazi ideas and control. The civil service, the military, the judiciary, education, organised labour (the free trade unions having been abolished), even the Protestant churches, along with clubs and societies of all kinds, were penetrated by Nazism. Many people supported Hitler's ruthless policies aimed, first, at discrimination against Jews, then at the elimination of the Jewish population in Germany, a population which served as a handy scapegoat for the perceived ills and failings of the Weimar Republic. The economy was subjected to Nazi control in all its aspects. Thanks to a combination of a revival in world trade after the depression, public works schemes initiated by the Nazi regime (such as the construction of the motorway system), and a programme of rearmament, unemployment declined, the economy flourished and Hitler got the credit.

Hitler had gained public support in the period of the Weimar Republic as much for his denunciations of the Versailles Treaty and his populist promises to rectify the 'injustices' of that treaty, as for anything else he and his party stood for. The reparations payment and military limitation clauses of the treaty were repudiated by Hitler. He made plans to repossess territories lost by Germany under the terms of the treaty. First Hitler sent troops into those areas of the Rhineland which had been demilitarised under the treaty – on a Sunday (8 March 1936), knowing that the British and French governments would be slow to react at a weekend, and claiming anyway that Germany was only reasserting sovereignty within what was its own territory. This move produced admonition but no action from the French or British governments, so Hitler's next moves were to institute compulsory military service, conclude an alliance (the Axis pact) with Italy, then, in March 1938, to annex Austria, the so-called *Anschluss*, a move also expressly prohibited under the Versailles Treaty. The Sudetenland area of the newly created state of Czechoslovakia was Hitler's next target. His manipulation of a crisis among the German-speaking population of that border region almost led to war with Britain and France in 1938, under their treaty obligations with Czechoslovakia. A meeting of Chamberlain, Daladier, the French prime minister, and the Italian dictator Mussolini with Hitler in Munich on 29 September 1938 produced reassurances from Hitler that Germany had no further plans for territorial expansion, so Britain and France accepted his annexations in Czechoslovakia. War was prevented, though the further dismemberment of Czechoslovakia was not. On 1 September 1939 Hitler invaded Poland. This time, though, Britain and France were not prepared either to negotiate further with Hitler or to accede to his demands. On 3 September 1939 Britain and France declared war on Germany.

At first, the war went Germany's way. Poland was swiftly defeated and occupied. Then France, Belgium, Luxembourg, the Netherlands, Denmark and Norway fell to German invasions. Italy joined the war as Germany's ally. Only Switzerland, the Irish Republic, Sweden, Portugal and Spain escaped invasion, being neutral countries, several of which could offer valuable services or supplies to Germany. A threatened invasion of Britain was delayed (permanently, as it turned out) by the 'Battle of Britain' in the summer of 1940, which prevented Germany acquiring the air supremacy it needed to protect the English Channel crossing for the army. The German campaign of submarine warfare, aimed at choking off supplies for the United Kingdom, also failed once US aid was provided and more effective measures of defence of convoys, including air coverage of much of the Atlantic, were developed.

Hitler made a fatal error. In June 1941 he invaded the Soviet Union. The German army failed to make sufficient progress in that campaign in either 1941 or 1942 before the harsh Russian winters closed in on them. In the winter of 1942–43 the German army was first halted, then defeated and forced to surrender at Stalingrad. Meanwhile, in December 1941 the USA had entered the war following the Japanese attack on the US naval and air base at Pearl Harbor, in the Hawaiian islands, and in Autumn 1942 the German advance in North Africa, intended to lead to the capture of the Suez canal and the middle eastern oilfields, was repulsed by the British army and its allies in the battle of El Alamein. This period of late 1942 and early 1943 was the turning-point in the war. In 1943 the western allies announced their policy of unconditional surrender as an essential condition for ending the war. The Italians overthrew Mussolini (Hitler's fascist ally) and declared war on Germany. The allies landed in Italy, to begin an attack on Hitler's empire from the south. The military forces of the Soviet Union made gains on Germany's eastern front. In June 1944 British, American and Canadian troops landed in Normandy, to begin the liberation first of France, then of the other countries of western Europe conquered by the German military. On 11 September 1944 the western allied forces crossed the border into Germany itself. On 26 April 1945 the western and Soviet armies had linked up on the river Elbe. On 30 April 1945 Hitler committed suicide and on 7 May 1945 the war in Europe came to an end with the unconditional surrender of all German forces.

The occupation period in West Germany[4]

One lesson learnt by the western allies and the Soviet Union from the experience of the peacemakers at the end of the First World War was that a defeated
Germany this time should be totally occupied, until such time as a peace treaty
could safely be signed with a democratic German state. So, as a result of decisions taken at wartime conferences in Teheran (1943), Moscow (1944) and
Yalta (1945), the allied powers put into effect an occupation regime for
Germany, based on the division of Germany into four zones. The British took the
north-west, with its valuable coal-mining and steel-producing area of the
Ruhr; the USA had the south-west area, including Bavaria, Hesse and part of
what is now Baden-Württemberg; the French occupied an area in the south
bordering the river Rhine;[5] the Soviet Union occupied eastern Germany. The
capital, Berlin, was subjected to special four-power administration, though it
was located entirely in the Soviet zone. These arrangements for the immediate
future of Germany were also confirmed at the Potsdam conference in July
1945.

The common principles upon which all the allies agreed were that Nazism in
all its forms was to be eliminated; re-education for democracy was to be imposed
on the German people; and those parts of Germany's industrial capacity that
could be used for military production were to be dismantled. It soon became
apparent that strains between the western allies and the Soviet Union which
had become visible during the war, based on ideological differences between
liberal democracy and communism, as well as on issues of strategy (such as the
timing of the allied invasion of western Europe), and which were again apparent at the Potsdam conference once the war in Europe had ended, were now
greater than ever. This meant that the intention to treat Germany as a single
economic unit, agreed by the wartime conferences, came to nothing. Disputes
about the rights of the Soviet Union to claim plant and machinery located in
the western zones as reparations, the status of Berlin, Marshall Plan aid for
Germany (see below), control of the issuance of occupation currency and other
matters led to the breakdown of four-power control of Berlin and to the *de facto*
creation of two separate Germanies, one in the east, the other in the west. An
attempt by the Soviet Union to blockade western access to Berlin in 1948,
caused by disputes about currency reform and intentions to create a provisional
West German state, failed because of the success of the allied airlift of supplies.[6]
Then the Federal Republic came into existence in western Germany, and a
German Democratic Republic – in effect, already a communist regime – was
established in eastern Germany.

In West Germany, the allies had permitted political parties and other associations such as trade unions to be formed at local level as early as summer and
autumn 1945. Like German press and broadcasting enterprises, these had to
be licensed by the occupying power, to ensure that they were being led by non-
Nazi, reliably democratic persons. Licences were given to the re-emerged Social

Democratic Party (SPD) and Communist Party (the KPD), whose leaders had been in exile during the war, parties that could swiftly resurrect their networks of local party organisations that had existed before 1933; to the Christian Democrats, who had created a new, cross-denominational Christian party (the Christian Democratic Union (CDU), in Bavaria the Christian Social Union (CSU)), and to the pre-war Catholic Centre party; and to the liberals, who in most areas had succeeded in linking together in a single party, which in 1948 became the Free Democratic Party (FDP). A small number of other parties also received licences, such as the Bavarian Party (BP), the German Party (DP) and the right-wing Socialist Reich Party (SRP). Local elections were held from 1946, and then regional elections took place for Länder parliaments, whose first important task was to draft constitutions for their Länder. In this way, local democracy became swiftly re-established in the western zones.

Social and economic, as well as political, institutions were denazified, including universities and schools, local and regional public-service bureaucracies, the police and the judiciary. Trials of war criminals (those that took place in Nuremberg being the most prominent) and procedures for denazification of the whole population were put into effect. Physical reconstruction was also important. Bomb damage throughout the war and destruction (by the Nazis as well as by the allies) during the closing days of the war had destroyed homes, factories, roads, railways, harbours, hospitals, shops and schools. Some of the major cities, like Frankfurt, had retained only half their pre-war population and less than half of homes in some cities were still habitable. Shortages of personnel and materials during the war had meant failure to undertake routine maintenance of things like sewers, water and power supply. All this meant that an enormous task of clearance, reconstruction and repair had to be undertaken. Social reconstruction was also important. Families had been separated during the war; prisoners of war and demobilised troops were now returning home; refugees flocked from the eastern zone and from parts of Germany now under Polish or Soviet Union rule; former concentration camp victims or inmates of forced labour camps were liberated, and looked for shelter or a way to get home. Food and medical supplies were in short supply. The extremely cold winter of 1946–47 intensified the suffering of the German people, and gave further impetus to the black market that was the scourge of every German town and city. The occupation authorities were blamed for this economic misery, and the prospect of some revival of Nazism – or of a turn to communism as a remedy – seemed to increase.

Three innovations changed this situation. On 1 January 1947 the US and British zones were fused to form 'Bizonia', to remove economic barriers between those two zones and encourage greater economic independence in that area (France joined the scheme in April 1949). Within this 'bizone', an Economic Council was instituted in June 1947, consisting of 52 representatives chosen by the Land parliaments. This was thus the first cross-zonal representative assembly of the West Germans themselves. Second, in June 1947 US

Secretary of State George Marshall announced a generous aid scheme, later called the 'Marshall Plan', to encourage economic recovery in Europe. By the end of 1948 Marshall Plan aid was flowing into West Germany, producing economic revival. Third, an economics professor who was a member of the Economic Council, Ludwig Erhard, implemented his plan for currency reform in the western zones. On 20 June 1948 a new 'Deutschmark' replaced the existing currency, based at first on an equal allocation of Deutschmarks per head, in two instalments, supplemented by ration cards for goods such as textiles. This scheme, by substituting a currency in which people had confidence for one that had become almost worthless, made the black market redundant, encouraged producers to supply goods to the shops and stimulated workers to work more regularly and for longer hours once they were being paid in a hard currency. These measures together laid the foundation for what later became known as the German 'economic miracle' – the rapid rise of West Germany to a leading position among western economies.

The occupation, with its economic costs and its political problems, was a strain on the western powers. Pressure increased for the release to civilian life of the troops involved in the occupation, and calls became more vocal, especially by the US public, for withdrawal from what was a thankless task. However, the intensification of the 'cold war' between the western allies and the Soviet Union (symbolised by the Berlin blockade) compelled the allies to remain in West Germany and, indeed, to strengthen their military presence. It was realised that the burden of the occupation could be lightened by giving the West Germans a form of self-rule. At the London conference in 1948 of the USA, Britain, France and the Benelux countries, a decision was taken to move towards the establishment of a provisional West German state. Plans were drawn up for such a state, plans which were then relayed to the prime ministers of the western Länder at a meeting in Frankfurt. Their acceptance of these plans led to the creation of the Parliamentary Council to draft a constitution for this West German state.

The Parliamentary Council, which commenced its proceedings in Bonn on 1 September 1948, consisted of sixty-five delegates, selected by the Land parliaments in proportion to the strength of party representation in those parliaments. The Christian Democrats and SPD each had twenty-seven representatives, the FDP had five, the DP, Centre Party and KPD each had two. After long discussion and negotiation, involving the occupation authorities and interest groups such as the churches and trade unions, as well as the parties themselves, the Basic Law was promulgated on 8 May 1949. After acceptance by the Länder parliaments,[7] this Basic Law came into effect on 23 May 1949, deliberately called a 'Basic Law' rather than a 'constitution', to emphasise that it was a document for a provisional and temporary political system, pending German reunification. (The content of the Basic Law is described in chapter 3.)

The Federal Republic

The first elections to the Bundestag took place on 14 August 1949. A coalition government, comprising Christian Democrats, the FDP and the DP, was formed under the chancellorship of Konrad Adenauer. Theodor Heuss, the leader of the FDP, was elected as the first federal president shortly before the Bundestag met for the first time.

Adenauer soon established a form of government in which the chancellor was unquestionably dominant; this came to be known as 'chancellor democracy' (see chapter 7). He set about ensuring the security and prosperity of the new republic by linking it to European and western collective institutions, such as the North Atlantic Treaty Organisation (NATO), the Council of Europe and the European Coal and Steel Community (ECSC), later the European Economic Community (EEC) (see chapter 10). This necessarily affected the chances of eventual reunification, since it would render more difficult the design of any alternative to the division of Germany which would be acceptable to the Soviet Union and to the new regime in the GDR. Adenauer negotiated with the western allies concerning the lifting of remaining restrictions on the sovereignty of the Federal Republic. These were removed by the Paris agreements of October 1954. The Korean war (1950–53) gave impetus to West German exports, but also led to a debate about the rearmament of the Federal Republic, to reduce the burdens on the former occupation powers, involved as they now were with the supply of troops to the United Nations (UN) force in Korea. Rearmament was of course an extremely delicate issue within the Federal Republic itself, given the calamities that the Second World War had brought upon Germany and the widespread mood of rejection of militarism, so Adenauer's plans were opposed strongly by left-wing parties and politicians, as well as by large sections of the public. After a first international scheme (the European Defence Treaty) was rejected by the French National Assembly in August 1954, an eventual solution was found which involved membership of the Federal Republic in NATO.

Adenauer's firm style of government, together with his authoritarian manipulation of his own party and the continuing electoral weakness of the SPD, allowed his coalition to win the election in 1953 with an increased majority. After a quarrel with the FDP resulted in that party (though not its ministers) withdrawing its support from the government in 1956, Adenauer and the Christian Democrats won an overall majority in the 1957 election, so Adenauer did not need the FDP in his government anyway. Adenauer's personal popularity, boosted by increasing prosperity resulting from Erhard's successful 'social market economy' policies as Minister of Economics, was responsible for this extraordinary electoral success. However, in 1959 the SPD changed its image and identity at its Bad Godesberg congress, by abandoning its Marxist-based class image and adopting a more modern, less ideologically confined programme and political approach. This made it a more potent rival to the CDU-CSU. Nevertheless, despite this improvement in the electoral fortunes of the SPD, Adenauer formed a government (with the aid of the FDP) after the 1961 election, though he promised to retire before the next election, a promise he fulfilled in 1963. He was then aged 86. The 'Adenauer era' had set a pattern for West German politics and for the external relations, prosperity and internal values of the Federal Republic, a pattern that his successors would not be able easily to change, even should they so wish.

Erhard succeeded Adenauer as chancellor, and won the 1965 Bundestag election, but lacked both the leadership skills and the popular appeal of his predecessor. An economic recession put even his famed 'economic miracle' at risk, and when in 1966 the FDP left the coalition after trying to force Erhard to amend his budgetary plans, Erhard was thrown aside by his party, which entered into a 'grand coalition' with the SPD (but without the troublesome FDP) under the chancellorship of Kurt-Georg Kiesinger. This government, lacking any substantial opposition within the Bundestag, was able to introduce measures to deal with the economic situation and with the wave of radical political activity on the streets and in the universities which had arisen. It was able to take first, faltering, steps towards contacts with eastern European countries (see below). However, few politicians or voters wanted this rather unnatural government of the two major parties to continue after the 1969 election.

In that 1969 Bundestag election, thanks to the narrow failure of the radical right-wing National Democratic Party (NPD) to gain the 5 per cent of votes needed for representation, the small FDP (that had itself only received just under 6 per cent) was able to select which of the two major parties it would ally with in government. In fact, though never making this preference absolutely explicit, the campaign of the FDP had contained several indications that it would try to form a coalition with the Social Democrats; and that is what occurred. Willy Brandt, Foreign Minister in the 'grand coalition' and formerly lord mayor of West Berlin, became chancellor; Walter Scheel, the FDP leader, became Foreign Minister. The change of government, the first in terms of one party relinquishing the chancellorship to its rival, marked the end of the 'postwar' phase of the Federal Republic, and the commencement of its status as a 'normal' democracy, a regime that had overcome crises but which had, unlike the Weimar Republic, been strengthened rather than weakened by them. This new government tried to implement the radical programme of reform which both parties had promised in their electoral programmes. Certainly its efforts to abandon the old rejective policy regarding contacts with the communist bloc countries were successful. The new policy of the Brandt coalition became known as the Ostpolitik, resulting in treaties with the USSR and Poland, and a treaty-like agreement with the GDR, as well as a four-power treaty concerning Berlin (see below).

Domestic policy was of less interest to Brandt, and less was achieved in terms of internal reform. In any case, the small majority that the government had achieved in 1969 was eroded, especially because of the *Ostpolitik*, as dissidents from the coalition parties who could not accept the new policy towards East Germany and Eastern Europe went over to the opposition. Chancellor Brandt barely survived a constructive vote of no confidence in 1972 (see chapters 4 and 7), though his coalition did then increase its majority in the 1972 Bundestag elections. A scandal concerning an East German spy in Brandt's entourage led in 1974 to Brandt's resignation, and his replacement as chancellor by Helmut Schmidt. At about the same time, Scheel resigned (to become federal president), and Hans-Dietrich Genscher became Foreign Minister and leader of the FDP.

The new Schmidt government had to cope with a number of challenges. These included: the economic effects of the oil crisis; the continuation of the 'cold war' despite the progress towards detente made by Brandt and Scheel; terrorism, especially from a group calling themselves the 'Red Army Faction' (RAF); and a new political force – environmentalism – which by 1980 had started to use elections and the formation of a political party as one of its political strategies. The Schmidt government won the 1976 election (though Helmut Kohl, the CDU chancellor-candidate, secured a remarkable 48.6 per cent for his party), but soon after this the coalition showed signs of wear and tear. Many thought it would not hold together for the 1980 election. However, the Christian Democrats selected the CSU leader, Strauss, as chancellor-candidate. Because the FDP would under no circumstances consider supporting Strauss, whom it regarded as its arch-enemy since the time of the 'Spiegel affair',[8] the SPD–FDP coalition remained intact and won the 1980 election also. Nevertheless, increasingly left-wing tendencies became apparent in the SPD, tendencies found even more visibly among its grass-roots organisations, who had power within the SPD through the annual party conference. This meant that, despite Schmidt's own more centrist policy positions, the FDP was not happy within the coalition. The FDP feared that the unpopularity of the SPD, indicated by opinion polls and Land elections, might well make the FDP unpopular too. Attempts by the FDP – as in 1966 with Erhard – to insist on the adoption of its own more market-oriented policy positions concerning public expenditure and taxation were unsuccessful, and in September 1982 the FDP left the government. On 1 October 1982 the FDP supported the Christian Democrats in a constructive vote of no confidence against Chancellor Schmidt. This motion was carried, and Helmut Kohl became chancellor in Schmidt's place.

The new government, having come to power because of the FDP's change of coalition partner, realised that it should obtain an electoral mandate. So it contrived to get the federal president to dissolve the Bundestag a year and a half before the next Bundestag election normally should have occurred. An election took place in March 1983, which provided the new government with a safe majority. Though Genscher remained in office as Foreign Minister to provide a guarantee of continuity of the foreign policy of the Federal Republic, economic and social policy underwent a change of direction in favour of retrenchment, reduction of the public sector deficit and encouragement for business through tax measures and other provisions. The Kohl government went on to win a further period in office in the election of January 1987.

The 'Other Germany'

Even before the unconditional surrender of Germany in May 1945, the Soviet Union sent a group of German communists (who had spent the war in exile in Russia) into areas of eastern Germany to set up local administration and to prepare the way for the Soviet occupation regime. Though the Soviet Union, like the western allies, allowed the formation of political parties within its zone of occupation, it showed blatant favouritism towards the KPD (the Communist Party of Germany) in terms of supply of resources such as newsprint and office space, for instance. Within the Soviet zone, a campaign developed in late 1945 and early 1946 to join the two working-class parties – the KPD and the slightly stronger SPD – into a single party. This fusion took place in April 1946, creating a new party – the Socialist Unity Party (Sozialistische Einheitspartei Deutschlands (SED)). Promises of parity of treatment of members of the KPD and SPD within the SED, made during the fusion campaign, were soon ignored by the Soviet Union, and the SED became, in effect, a communist party. A liberal and a christian democratic party were allowed to continue in being (the Liberal-Demokratische Partei Deutschlands (LDPD) and the CDU), but in 1948 two 'puppet' parties were created by the occupation regime; the Demokratische Bauernpartei Deutschlands (DBD, a farmers' party) and the National-Demokratische Partei Deutschlands (NDPD, a party for ex-soldiers and rehabilitated members of the Nazi party). The purpose of these new parties was to draw support to them from those who otherwise might support the LDPD and CDU. To ensure the subservience of these other parties, two other measures were taken by the Soviet occupation regime. Party leaders and officials who refused to agree to Soviet and SED policies were removed from office, and other members purged (sometimes involving their imprisonment and even execution). A 'bloc party' system was created, by which at all elections seats would be allocated in advance of polling day to the parties – and to other organisations such as the trade union and youth organisation, both of which were under the control of the communists – according to a quota system, and voters would vote for or against a single joint list of approved candidates. In this way, party competition was eliminated and a communist hegemony was ensured.

The creation of the Federal Republic by the western powers in 1949 was swiftly imitated by the Soviet Union (as it had earlier imitated the currency reform of 1948 in its zone). On 7 October 1949 a constitution for the new German Democratic Republic came into effect. The harshness of the communist regime and the austerity produced by the socialist economic system, with its collectivisation and reliance on central planning, meant that many inhabitants of the GDR fled to the Federal Republic. The implementation of more demanding work targets set by the government led to an uprising by workers in East Berlin on 17 June 1953. Though this was soon crushed by the intervention of Soviet troops, it indicated the level of dissatisfaction with the regime, and was used by the Federal Republic as a propaganda weapon against the GDR regime. Until reunification, the anniversary of 17 June was a national holiday in the Federal Republic, and streets in West Germany were named for that date. The continued loss of its population to the west through migration led the GDR regime in 1961 to erect the Berlin Wall, which divided that city in two, and to construct a well-guarded frontier fence the entire length of the German–German border. This produced more stability within the GDR, as people realised that they had to adapt to the regime rather than try to migrate from it. However, draconian measures of internal security continued to be imposed, and the standard of living fell further and further behind that of the Federal Republic.[9] A few people still tried to flee to the west, some at the cost of their lives. Others, imprisoned for dissidence or for attempts to leave the GDR without permission, were 'purchased' by the Federal Republic as 'political prisoners', when the GDR needed to obtain convertible currency, but deliberately becoming a political prisoner in this way was a painful and uncertain strategy for escape.

The GDR became increasingly integrated into the Soviet bloc, through its membership of East European economic and military collective institutions – the Council for Mutual Economic Assistance (COMECON) and the Warsaw Pact. The GDR was among those states in the communist bloc most supportive of the USSR (prior to Gorbachev's reforms, that is). Its leaders enthusiastically supported Soviet action in putting down the Hungarian uprising in 1956–57, and in combating the reformist trend in Czechoslovakia (the 'Prague Spring' of 1968). The change of leadership in the GDR from Ulbricht to Honecker in 1971, which many hoped would signal a more pragmatic, perhaps even a more liberal, leadership style, failed to make much difference to the domestic or foreign policies of the GDR, though the 'Basic Treaty' between the two states was signed in 1972 (see below).

A key factor in shaping those policies was, of course, the relationship between the GDR and the Federal Republic. At first, reunification seemed to be a development which was merely being postponed by the 'cold war' and the creation of two German states, each integrated into one of the rival blocs. The GDR regime, like the Federal Republic, at first officially accepted that reunification would eventually occur, though its vision of a reunified Germany was that of a socialist republic. The steps taken by Adenauer and the western allies to link the Federal Republic firmly to the west, including plans for West German rearmament, put pressure on the Soviet Union and the GDR. Offers by Grotewohl, the GDR prime minister, in 1950 and 1951 to agree to a plan for reuniting Germany, even, if necessary, with free elections, were unacceptable

Box 1.2
The relationship between West Germany
and East Germany, 1945–89

30 August 1945	Allied Control Council to co-ordinate government in Germany held its first meeting.
20 March 1948	USSR abandoned its participation in the Allied Control Council, which thereafter failed to convene again.
16 June 1948	USSR withdrew from the Four Power Military Administration meetings, which co-ordinated occupation government in Berlin.
23 June 1948	USSR began the blockade of West Berlin by land and inland waterway.
26 June 1948	Allied airlift of supplies to West Berlin commenced.
12 May 1949	USSR lifted the blockade of West Berlin.
24 May 1949	The Basic Law came into effect, creating the Federal Republic of Germany.
7 October 1949	The constitution of the GDR came into effect, creating the German Democratic Republic.
10 March 1952	The 'Stalin Note' sent to the western allies proposed a scheme for reunification of Germany and peace treaty negotiations.
25 March 1952	The western allies, with the assent of the Adenauer government, rejected the Stalin Note.
9 December 1955	Announcement by the Federal Republic of the Hallstein Doctrine, by which the Federal Republic refused to have diplomatic relations with any state that had diplomatic relations with the GDR.
12 August 1961	The Berlin Wall was erected, sealing off East Berlin from West Berlin.
19 March and 21 May 1970	Meetings in Erfurt and Kassel took place between Chancellor Brandt and the GDR prime minister, Stoph.
3 September 1971	The four occupying powers signed the Berlin Agreement, which improved contact between East and West Berlin, recognised the *status quo* concerning the position of West Berlin in relation to the Federal Republic, and regulated the relations between the two parts of the city.

Box 1.2 (*cont.*)

21 December 1972	The Basic Agreement between the Federal Republic and the GDR was signed.
27 August 1987	The Basic Paper concerning ideology and collective security, negotiated by representatives of the SED and SPD, was published.
7–11 September 1987	State visit of Erich Honecker, party chief of the GDR, to the Federal Republic of Germany.

---

to the Adenauer government, who demanded that all-German free elections should precede any conference on the constitution of a reunited German state, a condition which the communist party in the GDR dare not accept. In 1952, Stalin sent a note to the western powers offering a reunified Germany based on free elections and a peace treaty with the allies, though on condition that reunified Germany would be a neutral state, not one tied to NATO, and that it conceded permanently to Poland the territory to the east of the Oder-Neisse boundary, territory under Polish administration since 1945, and which had been largely purged of its Germanic inhabitants. These terms, even if it were conceded that they were meant in earnest by Stalin, were unacceptable to Adenauer and his western allies. Adenauer anyway suspected the Soviet Union's intentions in making such an offer. Instead, Adenauer's government developed a policy of isolation towards the communist bloc. This led to the 'Hallstein doctrine', which stated that – with the single exception of the Soviet Union[10] – no country that had diplomatic relations with the GDR could also enjoy such relations with the Federal Republic. The intention was to deny to the GDR international legitimacy, by compelling especially third world countries needing aid from and trade with the Federal Republic to accept that such benefits carried a political obligation also. Domestically, too, a policy of non-recognition was carried to extreme lengths: references were made to 'the so-called German Democratic Republic', for instance, and the media also generally referred to the GDR as 'middle Germany' (eastern Germany to them being the lost territories to the east of the Oder-Neisse border). The official constitutional position of the Federal Republic, based on the wording of the Basic Law, was that the GDR could not be 'foreign' to the Federal Republic; it was a part of Germany under – temporary – foreign control. This also meant that all citizens of the GDR had an automatic right to citizenship of the Federal Republic.[11] The Federal Republic also maintained that it, and it alone, had the right to speak for, and represent, all Germans (the *Alleinvertretungsanspruch*), since it was the only democratic and legitimate sovereign successor-state in Germany.

Not until the period of the 'grand coalition' was there a slight thawing of this policy of the Federal Republic. The Kiesinger government undertook limited contacts with some of the states of the Soviet bloc. But it was the *Ostpolitik* of the Brandt government that introduced a radical change in relations between the two German states. After well-publicised but not very fruitful talks between Brandt and Stoph (the then prime minister of the GDR) in Erfurt and Kassel in 1970, a treaty-like agreement was signed in November 1972 (it could not be called a 'treaty' because the Federal Republic did not see it as an agreement with a foreign power). This agreement accepted the renunciation of force in relations between the two states, and the integrity of existing borders, points that had been covered also in the Moscow Treaty between the Federal Republic and the USSR in 1970. It regulated a variety of other matters, such as the free access of journalists from one German state within the territory of the other, and enabled both German states to join international organisations such as the UN. The Federal Republic ensured, in annexes to the treaty itself, that its own fundamental position concerning eventual reunification of the two parts of Germany was preserved.

This agreement and its implementation regulated relations between the GDR and the Federal Republic in a more pragmatic manner than had been the case prior to 1969. Trade was expanded on the basis of increased loans by the Federal Republic to the GDR, as well as generous hard-currency payments by the Federal Republic for things like postal services and transit routes to West Berlin. Personal and commercial contacts, though mainly those of West Germans visiting the GDR, also increased considerably. By the mid-1980s, the idea of eventual German reunification appeared to be totally unrealistic. Indeed, some left-wing politicians suggested that the Federal Republic should face that fact, remove from its constitutional order all reference to eventual reunification and formally accept the validity of the Oder-Neisse border with Poland as permanent and legitimate. Honecker was invited to visit West Germany, and, after several delays because of objections by the USSR, made what amounted to a state visit in 1987. Also in 1987, the SPD held a meeting with representatives of the SED, as a result of which a joint paper was produced identifying the ideological similarities and differences between the two parties. The relations between the two German states appeared to have reached a condition of mutual tolerance and the GDR and the Federal Republic seemed to have found a modus vivendi capable of persisting for many years to come.

Notes

1 Hitler's electoral support is analysed in Falter (1991). The votes received by the Nazis in Reichstag elections in the last years of the Weimar Republic were: 1928 2.6 per cent; 1930 18.3 per cent; July 1932 37.4 per cent; November 1932 33 per cent; 1933 43.9 per cent. In the presidential election in 1932 Hitler received 36.8 per cent in the second ballot.
2 There have been various theories about who actually caused the Reichstag fire. There is strong evidence that it was not the Nazis themselves, as many have

supposed, but rather that von Lubbers, the Dutch communist caught and tried for the crime, could have in fact managed to lay the fire single-handedly (Backes, 1990). However, what is indisputable is that the Nazis utilised the fire for political advantage. It was important for the Nazis not to prohibit the Communist Party from participating in the election: that would have meant that their voters would have voted for other left-wing parties. Instead, Hitler banned the elected communist legislators from taking their seats, thus invalidating the votes they received.

3 The Enabling Act gave Hitler's government, for a period of four years, the power to make laws without the legislature being required to agree to them. This required a two-thirds majority, because it changed the constitution. With the Communist Party representatives excluded, only the Social Democrats voted against this law, so Hitler had a majority of 444 out of 538 votes in favour.

4 The occupation period in East Germany is treated later in this chapter.

5 The French zone included southern parts of Baden and Württemberg, and the area that is now Rhineland-Pfalz. France had also been given the administration of the Saarland, an important coal-mining and steel-producing region on the French border, but this was outside the arrangements for the occupation zones. The Saarland eventually became part of the Federal Republic on 1 January 1957. This followed a referendum in 1955 in which its people rejected a plan (the Saar statute) by which the Saarland would be governed by a commissioner, in effect as part of France.

6 The blockade of surface routes was lifted on 6 October 1949.

7 Except for Bavaria, whose Land parliament voted against approval, though Bavaria did agree to abide by the majority decision of the other Länder.

8 The 'Spiegel Affair' occurred in 1962. The weekly news magazine, Der Spiegel, published a critical report on the performance of German armed forces in a NATO exercise. Strauss, the Defence Minister in Adenauer's government, initiated a series of actions which resulted in copies of the magazine being confiscated and its editorial staff being arrested. Challenged in the Bundestag concerning his responsibility for these illegal instructions, he prevaricated and attempted to both justify the actions and clear himself of blame. Adenauer, pressed to dismiss Strauss, eventually agreed to reshuffle his government, and Strauss (but also some other ministers) were omitted from the new government. The FDP was among the most vocal critics of Strauss's actions, and in 1965 refused to agree to his being included in the Erhard coalition government.

9 Of course, comparison of living standards is a controversial matter. East Germans enjoyed a fairly constant supply of staples, at heavily subsidised and stable prices: bread, milk, and other basic items of groceries, housing, public transport, cultural activities and books. However, items such as coffee, chocolate, washing machines, television sets or motor cars were very expensive and of poor quality compared to western products. Medical care, nurseries for babies and infants of working mothers (and most mothers were in employment), sporting facilities and other forms of social provision were also made readily available, free of charge or at only nominal cost.

10 Adenauer made a visit to Moscow in 1955, which resulted among other things in the release of thousands of German prisoners of war still in Soviet hands. It was obvious that the Federal Republic could not avoid – even had Adenauer so desired – having diplomatic relations with the Soviet Union, since that country had been one

of the major victors in the Second World War and exercised rights over Berlin, and a peace treaty which would have abolished that special position of the USSR had not yet been concluded.

11 It also meant that, when the Federal Republic became a member of the EEC, in effect the GDR was a member as well – at least in terms of goods exported to the Federal Republic, since the Federal Republic refused to treat such exports as coming from outside Germany (as stated in the 1957 Protocol to the Treaty of Rome on Internal German Trade). This situation did make it easier, once economic and monetary union, then political reunification, occurred in 1990, for East German territory to become part of the European Union. It was regarded merely as a member-state (the Federal Republic) undergoing enlargement, not as a new member-state being admitted.

References

Backes, U. (1990) 'Objektivitätsstreben und Volkspädogogik in der NS-Forschung. Das Beispiel der Reichstagsbrand-Kontroverse', in U. Backes, E. Jesse and R. Zitelmann, (eds), *Die Schatten der Vergangenheit. Impulse zur Historisierung des Nationalsozialismus*, Frankfurt (Main) and Berlin, Propyläen.

Falter, J. (1991) *Hitler's Wähler*, München, Verlag C.H. Beck.

Pulzer, P. (1997) *Germany 1870–1945. Politics, State Formation and War*, Oxford, Oxford University Press.

Further reading

Berghahn, V. (1987) *Modern Germany: Society Economy and Politics in the Twentieth Century*, Cambridge, Cambridge University Press.

Crawley, A. (1973) *The Rise of West Germany*, London, Collins.

Glees, A. (1996) *Reinventing Germany. German Political Development since 1945*, Oxford, Berg.

Golay, J. (1958) *The Founding of the Federal Republic of Germany*, Chicago, Chicago University Press.

Merkl, P. (1963) *The Origins of the West German Republic*, Oxford, Oxford University Press.

Nicholls, A. (1997) *The Bonn Republic. West German Democracy 1945–1990*, London, Longman.

Pulzer, P. (1995) *German Politics 1945–1995*, Oxford, Oxford University Press.

Pulzer, P. (1997) *Germany 1870–1945. Politics, State Formation and War*, Oxford, Oxford University Press.

2

The context of politics
in reunified Germany

When a state has recently lost or gained a large amount of territory, it can be expected that its political arrangements will be affected in consequence. The loss of Bangladesh by Pakistan, Russia after the break-up of the Soviet Union, or the Czech Republic after Slovakia's independence, are examples. Should Korea, Cyprus or Ireland ever become united countries, or should a separate northern state ever form in Italy, of course political arrangements would have to be adapted to accommodate such changes. It is therefore important, in understanding the present-day political arrangements of the Federal Republic of Germany, to appreciate how the reunification of the two parts of Germany came about, and what the effects of such reunification have been. The events of the fateful years 1989 and 1990 which led to reunification can be examined in three phases: the downfall of the old regime; the period of adjustment and transition to a democratic regime in the GDR; and the process and consequences of reunification itself.

The decline and fall of the communist regime in the GDR

Though there had been various expressions of dissent during the lifetime of the GDR, and especially in the 1980s, the regime had never had much difficulty in dealing with any form of opposition. The internal security apparatus (especially the Stasi: the secret police), political control, by means of the 'block system' of parties,[1] non-competitive elections and the penetration of loyal communists to key positions in all economic and social institutions, the use by the regime of the educational system and censorship to impose communist ideology on the people, harsh punishment of political offenders, restrictions on the importation of ideas and on the entry of individuals to the GDR itself at its closely guarded borders (only western radio and television broadcasts avoided the heavy hand of the regime), all served to limit expressions of dissent and more especially the reporting of such dissent in the media. It was therefore extremely unusual and

23

unexpected when in May 1989 a group of dissidents co-ordinated a campaign of observation of the GDR local elections, to try to shame the regime into admission of the true statistics both for turnout and for those voters who had rejected the official list of candidates. The failure of the regime to break with its practice of manipulating election results to meet pre-set targets (targets that were, as in other communist states, improbably high) led to an outburst of protest by dissidents, their supporters and foreign sympathisers, and to a series of monthly demonstrations to mark the election fraud.

Another event in May and June of 1989 was also of great importance in pre-cipitating the outbreak of protest which grew during the summer and early autumn of 1989. Hungary, hitherto an ally of the GDR within the communist camp, decided to remove restrictions on travel across its border with Austria. As Hungary was a favourite holiday destination for GDR families, many of them there at the time took advantage of this development to flee to the west. Others sought refuge in western embassies in Prague and Budapest, and these would-be emigrants – after long and delicate negotiations – were eventually allowed to travel to the Federal Republic. This exodus of GDR citizens prompted others within the GDR to demonstrate in favour of reforms and civil rights including the right to travel to the west on a return ticket, rather than emigrating permanently. 'We're staying here' was one of their slogans. The most important of such dem-onstrations took place every week in Leipzig. Despite arrests and beatings of dem-onstrators by the Stasi, more and more people joined in these demonstrations (eventually totalling some 300,000 in Leipzig alone). In October, official celebra-tions marking the fortieth anniversary of the foundation of the GDR led to other demonstrations and protests. The presence of Gorbachev at those celebrations was seen by many as a sign of hope, since his reforms in the Soviet Union and his declared policy of non-intervention in the affairs of other communist states (including Hungary and the GDR) had encouraged many people to join in public protests, and had led some to form political organisations, such as New Forum, to serve as structures within which a dialogue about reform could take place.

The ruling elite in the GDR refused to make any concessions. They regarded Gorbachev's reform policies as mistaken and dangerous; and anyway certainly as inappropriate for the GDR. They considered any concession to be a sign of weakness and a signal for revolution. They refused to give official registration to New Forum or other new groupings, claiming that they were at best superfluous, at worst hostile to the state. However, since the GDR's economic situation was clearly nearing crisis, and since too repressive a response to dissi-dents (along the lines of the ruthless Chinese response earlier that year to student demonstrators in Tiananmen Square) would provoke economic sanc-tions from the Federal Republic and other western states, the rulers of the GDR were in a dilemma. The absence from workplaces of teachers, nurses, doctors, factory workers, engine drivers, shop assistants, entertainers and others who had escaped to West Germany during the summer holidays could not be con-cealed from their colleagues or shrugged off as being of no importance. A first response was to persuade Honecker (the party leader) and two of his senior colleagues to resign their offices; they were the 'old guard', most implacable in opposition to reform. Egon Krenz, a more youthful but not necessarily more liberal member of the party elite, replaced Honecker. As party leader, Krenz gave the task of heading the GDR government to Hans Modrow, seen by many as a 'reform communist' who might emulate Gorbachev's liberal policies in the GDR. Still the protests and demonstrations continued. Half-hearted promises of concessions (on foreign travel, for instance) failed to lessen the pressure on the regime. A more far-reaching policy regarding the right to travel to the west was announced at a press conference on 9 November 1989, but in such a confused and ambiguous manner that it unintentionally seemed to indicate that East Germans could travel to West Germany immediately. Hundreds rushed that evening to the Berlin Wall and, under pressure from the crowds, in the confusion the guards opened the borders. The fall of the Berlin Wall could be taken as signalling the fall of the regime – and, as it turned out, the imminent end of the existence of the GDR as a separate state.

Krenz tried unavailingly to regain control of the situation. He forced his party colleagues to resign with him from the Politburo (the effective ruling body in the GDR) on 3 December, and the now leaderless communist SED party called a special party congress a few days later to consider its future. It decided on a compromise: it would not dissolve itself, but would instead amend its name to SED-PDS (PDS: Party of Democratic Socialism; PDS became the sole name of the party from February 1990). It retained the wealth, property, staff and organisational networks of the old SED, but introduced an entirely new form of party leadership, modelled on the structures of West German democratic parties rather than on the old Communist Party of the Soviet Union. Gregor Gysi was elected as the chairman of the SED-PDS. The block parties hastily disassociated themselves from the SED-PDS and broke up the block party system, in order to act autonomously. New parties and other political groupings were being formed, and these joined together to create a 'Round Table', at which they could discuss with the SED-PDS and the former block parties what steps could be taken to deal with the political crisis and to introduce a more democratic form of regime. This Round Table, modelled on others organised elsewhere in the former Soviet bloc and, for instance, locally in Dresden, agreed that proper democratic and competitive elections for the legislature (called the Volkskammer, People's Chamber) should be held in May 1990 as a basis for a new form of regime. Under pressure of events (including a rapidly deteriorating economic situation) in the New Year this election date was brought forward to 18 March 1990.

The transitional regime

The Volkskammer election on 18 March 1990 resulted in a victory for the 'Alliance for Germany' (an electoral grouping of the Christian Democrats and

Box 2.1
Chronology of the reunification of Germany

5 May 1989	Hungary commenced dismantling its fortified border barriers with Austria.
7 May 1989	Local elections in GDR, which led to protests and demonstrations.
4 September 1989	First demonstration held in Leipzig following a prayer meeting at St Nicholas church.
9 September 1989	New Forum founded.
7 October 1989	Fortieth anniversary of founding of GDR, marked by official celebrations and by protest demonstrations.
18 October 1989	Resignation of Honecker from party and state leadership positions. Egon Krenz appointed leader of the SED in place of Honecker.
7 November 1989	Resignation of GDR government
8 November 1989	Resignation of Politburo of SED.
9 November 1989	Opening of Berlin Wall for GDR citizens.
13 November 1989	Hans Modrow elected by Volkskammer as new GDR prime minister.
28 November 1989	Kohl's ten-point plan for moving towards German reunification.
3 December 1989	Krenz resigned as leader of the SED.
7 December 1990	First meeting of the Round Table took place.
8–9 December 1989	At a special congress of the SED, Gysi was elected as leader of the reformed party.
15–16 December 1989	SED changed its name to SED-PDS at a continuation of its special party congress.
28 January 1990	Modrow and the Round Table agreed to bring forward the date of the Volkskammer election to 18 March; it had been originally scheduled for 6 May 1990.
18 March 1990	Volkskammer elections took place; the Christian Democrat-led 'Alliance for Germany' won most seats and went on to form a coalition government under its leader, de Maizière.
18 May 1990	Treaty on monetary, economic and social union of the GDR and the federal Republic was signed.
1 July 1990	Treaty on monetary, economic and social union came into effect.
31 August 1990	Treaty of reunification was signed.
3 October 1990	Reunification of Germany.
14 October 1990	First elections for the Land parliaments of the 'new Länder' took place.
2 December 1990	First Bundestag election in reunified Germany took place. First post-reunification city-wide election in Berlin took place.

smaller allied parties). The leader of that electoral alliance, Lothar de Maizière, became prime minister of a coalition government which included the Liberal electoral alliance and the Social Democrats. The campaign had come to be dominated by hopes of early economic and monetary union with the Federal Republic, then eventual reunification of the two German states, rather than by demands for political reform within the GDR. This meant that the new government was regarded very much as a transitional, caretaker government, whose task it was to ameliorate the economic crisis if it could, but to negotiate speedily the terms and timing of, first, economic and monetary union, then of political fusion. Many in both the Federal Republic and the GDR, as well as in other western European countries, were concerned that a backlash in the Soviet Union could destabilise the Gorbachev regime, and consequently make acceptance by the USSR of reunification much less likely.

Economic and monetary union was instituted from 1 July 1990. The currency of the GDR was replaced by the Deutschmark.[2] The laws and conditions that governed economic transactions and production in the Federal Republic (above all, the rules of a free market) replaced the centralised, planned and politically controlled economy of the GDR; and the West German social security network which constituted the second pillar of the 'social market economy' alongside the free market was also introduced to the GDR. To administer the huge task of transferring the various state-owned industries and commercial enterprises to private ownership, as required by the Treaty on Economic and Monetary Union, the Volkskammer agreed to the creation of a trustee agency (called the Treuhandanstalt). This agency would sell whatever enterprises could be sold, would attempt to reconstruct others with a view to finding a purchaser, and would close down those which were clearly never going to be viable in a competitive environment. As time passed, so it became clear that many of the industrial and commercial undertakings in the 'new Länder' were unprofitable, uncompetitive and in need of investment for modern plant and for clearing-up the sites to meet environmental and health and safety standards. The demands of East German employees for wage levels equal to those of West Germans meant that costs of production of items such as Trabant cars or Praktica cameras would be higher than could ever be covered by income from their sale. When the Treuhandanstalt finally terminated its activities in 1995, instead of the predicted large surplus garnered from sales of state-owned businesses, the Federal Republic had to cover a substantial deficit, arising from the costs of running the Treuhandanstalt itself, the financial burden of subsidising firms until they could be sold and the failure to attract purchasers for many of the undertakings at any price.

Meanwhile negotiations were being conducted at two levels to prepare for reunification. It would have been difficult, perhaps impossible, for the two German states to reunite without the consent of the four former occupying powers. For one thing, officially there had not yet been a peace treaty to end the Second World War, so the allies all retained certain rights within Germany, and especially in Berlin. A series of conferences took place in 1990, involving representatives of the governments of the two German states and of the four allied powers – the so-called 'two-plus-four' talks. These conferences produced a number of decisions which were equivalent to a peace treaty, and which accepted – under conditions – the right of the Germans themselves to determine their political future. In particular, the Soviet Union was persuaded to drop its opposition to a reunited Germany remaining a member of NATO. Gorbachev, the Soviet Union leader, was rewarded for this concession by generous compensation payments to meet the costs of the USSR withdrawing its military forces stationed in the former GDR over a period of three years, and then resettling in the Soviet Union. Another issue was settled at these talks: the acceptance by the Federal Republic of the validity of the Oder-Neisse border between Poland and Germany and therefore the acceptance that Germany, once reunited, would have no unresolved territorial claims.[3]

The other negotiations were bilateral, between the governments of the GDR and the Federal Republic. These talks produced a draft treaty of reunification. This draft treaty was debated by the two legislatures. After controversial matters had been eventually settled, such as the electoral system to be employed for the first post-reunification Bundestag election, and how to treat the very different types of abortion legislation that existed in East and in West Germany, the treaty was approved which, on 3 October 1990, created a reunified Germany within the constitutional and institutional framework of the Federal Republic.

Integrating the two parts of Germany

> Uniting Germany was the easy part. The real challenge is to unite the Germans.
> (McElvoy, 1992, p. 244)

At the start of 1990, there had been three possible options available as modes of linking the two German states. The idea of a confederation, in which both states would retain their identities and separate political systems, though mooted by Chancellor Kohl in his ten-point plan on 28 November 1989, was soon perceived as unrealistic and unsatisfactory. The Basic Law contained as its final provision Article 146, which would have involved the termination of both German states (and of the Basic Law itself) when a reunified Germany was created, under some new constitution. There were two important drawbacks to using this scheme. It would involve the creation of a constitutional assembly of some kind, and long deliberation by that assembly to draft a new constitution. This would take far too long, when monetary union had already created the basis of a single economic space, when the political and economic situation of the GDR required that some swift resolution of the transitional situation be implemented, and when the people of the GDR wanted reunification – and immediately. The other reason was that the population of the Federal Republic saw no reason why they should lose their Basic Law (which had served them very well over a period of forty years), and many in the GDR were also comfortable with the idea of adopting that system. So instead another provision of the Basic Law was employed, Article 23, which allowed for parts of Germany not yet within the Federal Republic to become part of that state, and had been used to bring the Saarland into the Federal Republic in 1957. This involved the rapid re-creation of the Länder in the GDR, Länder which had been abolished in 1952. This was a necessary step, since the Federal Republic was a federal state, and the GDR would have been too large to be absorbed within the Federal Republic as a single Land.[4] Elections for the parliaments of those 'new Länder', parliaments which would have the task of creating constitutions for their Land, took place on 14 October 1990. Berlin, which became a reunited city through German reunification, held an election for its city assembly (the equivalent of a Land parliament) on the same day as the Bundestag election, 2 December 1990.

The employment of Article 23 avoided the need to create a totally new constitution for reunited Germany. However, it did involve certain consequential changes to the Basic Law. The preamble, which had originally referred to reunification as an obligation for Germans in the future, now was amended to confirm that the Germans had achieved reunification by free self-determination. Article 23 had lost its purpose and its original wording was deleted (since it was now accepted that there were no other parts of Germany which could later accede to the Federal Republic).[5] Article 146 was changed to recognise that the Basic Law was now applicable to the entire German people following reunification, though provision remained in that Article for a new constitution to replace the Basic Law as an option at some time in the future. Article 5 of the Reunification Treaty provided for the possibility of further changes to the Basic Law at some period after reunification had occurred. The procedures and the changes to the Basic Law which resulted are described in chapter 3.

The reunification of Germany, though a complicated political procedure, was relatively simple compared to what followed: the task of creating one society from two diametrically different political, social and economic systems. One expert claimed: 'It would be far easier for the FRG to merge with Belgium than with the GDR' (Dönhoff, 1993, p. xiv), since the main difference would have been language, but the economic, social and political system differences would have been far smaller.

The easiest task was political integration. The party system remained relatively unchanged from that which already existed in the Federal Republic. The Bundestag election in December 1990 had shown that the only party from the GDR that had any chance of winning seats in the parliament was the PDS, and they had only obtained seats in that election because of the special, one-time-only rule that parties must win 5 per cent in either West Germany or East Germany to qualify for a proportional distribution of seats (see chapter 4).

Otherwise East German political parties had either merged with their West German counterparts in 1990 (the SPD, Liberals, CDU and – just after the election – the Greens) or else had no prospect of winning seats on their own. The citizen movement groups first became officially a political party (Alliance '90), then merged that new party with the Greens in 1993. True, there were signs of discontent within the parties, and in the Bundestag from East German politicians in all parties, who believed that the interests of the 'new Länder' were being neglected by the more numerous and far more experienced West German politicians. Some of the discontent concerning the outcome of reunification was channelled through the PDS, which became a hybrid party trying to retain an uncompromising left-wing identity, but seeking also to represent the 'losers from reunification' in East Germany.

The Bundestag was increased in size to 656 seats (compared with 498 prior to reunification) to accommodate the 'new Länder' and Berlin. The Bundesrat also increased in size (see chapter 8). But that was basically the extent of post-reunification political change in terms of institutional structures.

One important political issue did cause controversy, though did not divide politicians either on simple East–West lines or by political party affiliation. This was the issue of whether Bonn should remain the seat of government or whether Berlin – the capital city in every other respect – should also be the centre of government. Those against the choice of Berlin pointed to the misfortunes that Germany had suffered when the Prussian capital was also Germany's capital; claimed that Bonn had proven to be a tranquil and attractive location as centre of government, and one which had come to symbolise the success of the post-war West German democratic system; noted that Berlin was on the eastern margin of the country at a time when the core of the European Union was located to the west, north and south of the Federal Republic; and pointed to the enormous costs which would be involved in relocating and providing residences for civil servants, and building new ministries, in what was already an overcrowded city. The proponents of Berlin (which of course included almost all East German members of the Bundestag) argued that Berlin was always intended to be the capital and seat of government of reunited Germany, that the change would symbolise the new beginning for the 'new' Federal Republic, that the metropolitan character of Berlin was more suited to a capital city and seat of government than the provincial and relatively small Bonn, and that the choice of Berlin would do much for both the economic prosperity and the morale of the citizens of the 'new Länder'. After lengthy and vociferous campaigning by both sides, a vote was taken in June 1991 in the Bundestag, which produced a small majority in favour of Berlin (337:320).

Economic integration has proved to be the most contentious aspect of reunification. Because of the necessary closure of many factories and other enterprises by the Treuhandanstalt, because new owners of business enterprises purchased from the Treuhandanstalt reduced their workforce to make those enterprises competitive, because East German employees and the West

German trade unions which now represented them insisted on rapid equalisation of wage levels in the two parts of Germany without regard for the
differences in productivity that still remained, unemployment in the 'new
Länder' soared after reunification and, though it has declined from its highest
levels, remains much higher than unemployment in West Germany.[6] Post-
reunification investment in utilities and public services has been high in East
Germany (the telephone network required replacing and expanding; the roads
system and the railways were in generally poor condition; housing required
considerable renovation and improvement, for example). Private sector investment, however, has not matched expectations. Chancellor Kohl airily spoke of
'flourishing landscapes' appearing in the 'new Länder', but West German and
foreign investors have found it more profitable to invest in the Czech Republic
or Hungary, or in Ireland or Portugal, or even further afield, and have found,
additionally, that such investment usually involved less bureaucracy.

Economic problems have caused problems of social integration also.
Unemployment has especially affected women, who, in the GDR, were usually
employed even when they had young children; the widespread provision by the
state of child-care facilities made this easy. Now these women were among
the first to be made redundant, and anyway child-care facilities became expensive or were not available. The system of subsidies of basic goods and services
(bread, milk, meat, bus fares, rented accommodation, cinema tickets, sports
club facilities) was quickly wound down after reunification, and East Germans
have found it hard to adjust to western prices and western competition. The particular mode of reunification chosen (Article 23, see above) meant that almost
all the changes and adjustments necessary to merge two political systems and
two societies had to be made by East Germans, rather than West Germans.
Citizens in the 'new Länder' were presented with new systems of education
(and university education); a new tax regime; competition in services such as
insurance, where previously the state-sponsored provider had had a monopoly;
a bewildering range of choice of newspapers and magazines, of shops, of
brands of food and drink, of television programmes, of holiday destinations.
Security of tenure of East Germans in their homes suddenly disappeared in
many cases, when West Germans, successors to East German residents who
had owned flats and houses confiscated by the GDR, but who were now legally
entitled to reclaim that property, raised rents or gave notice to quit to tenants,
many of whom had been there for years. This need for wide-ranging adjustment (equivalent to an emigrant arriving in a new and unfamiliar country),
together with economic insecurity, a standard of living still usually below that
which a comparable West German citizen could expect and a feeling that West
Germans still perceived 'Ossies' (East Germans) as inferior, has made what some
have called the 'wall in the head' as big an obstacle to integration as the Berlin
Wall itself was from 1961 until 1989.

A further cause for resentment for East Germans was the problem of
'overcoming the past' (*Vergangenheitsbewältigung*, see also chapter 11). This

involved, for example, political purging of members of the SED and the block parties, as well as others, from positions of responsibility as judges, teachers, professors, civil servants and members of the military. To some degree, this was essential: lawyers familiar only with the Marxist-Leninist mode of arguing and presenting cases (where the good of the party took priority over the legal rights of the individual), professors who had lectured on Marxist-Leninist philosophy or the strange kind of 'statist' economics that was the ideological basis of the GDR's planned economy, officers in an army that had been trained to regard the Federal Republic in particular, and the western powers in general, as the enemy, and which anyway was being disbanded, were clearly going to be unsuited to their professions in the reunified Federal Republic. Another problem was the large numbers of individuals (some politically prominent in the newly democ-ratised GDR, others with international reputations as writers or musicians, for instance) who had served as informers for the Stasi. When the Stasi files were made available for public inspection from 1990 onwards, many people found that family members, friends or workplace colleagues had been spying on them for years. This introduced a mood of mutual distrust and recrimination into East German society. The prosecution of border-guards and their commanders because they had shot and attempted to kill would-be escapers, trials of SED pol-iticians for electoral fraud in relation to the 1989 local elections, and the pros-ecution of prominent politicians and others, including Honecker himself,[7] for corruption and other misdeeds (misdeeds that also contravened GDR law) also added to this feeling by some in the GDR that West Germany had 'won' the ideo-logical war, and was imposing revenge on the communist 'losers'. Others, though, compared it to denazification after the Second World War. They saw the process as a vital stage in clarifying what had really happened in the GDR and as a necessary preliminary to the establishment of a democratic political culture in the 'new Länder'.

The East Germans were not the only ones with cause to grumble about the outcome of the reunification process. West Germans found that they had to meet most of the costs of reunification by increases in the national debt and tax surcharges and the cost of subsidies required to keep the 'new Länder' running. Because of low employment levels and lack of profitable commercial enter-prises, the tax product of the 'new Länder' was far too small to meet the admin-istrative and other costs of providing all the services (such as policing, education and road maintenance) that every Land had to supply within the federal system (see chapter 6). The costs of pensions and unemployment benefit for East Germans was another form of financial burden, since recipients had not paid contributions or taxes to the Federal Republic. So a number of indirect taxes were increased, and income tax and other taxes had temporary 'solidar-ity' surcharges placed on them – which affected all Germans, but cost the wealthier West Germans relatively more.[8]

So the reunification of Germany is important to an understanding of the German political system for two reasons. It has changed the size of the Federal

Republic and affected its political institutions. It has also affected the political agenda, so that new problems (but also new opportunities) have arisen since 1990. Each of the remaining chapters of this book will reflect those changes.

Notes

1 The 'block system' of parties was an arrangement by which the various political parties co-ordinated their activities under the leadership of the SED, and presented a joint list of candidates, with predetermined allocation of seats, for local and national elections. No other parties were permitted. This arrangement meant that, in effect, the SED controlled the other parties, could veto elections of their officers and control their membership recruitment, and had a permanent majority on councils and in the Volkskammer.

2 The rate of exchange was, broadly, 1:1 for savings and incomes (wages, salaries, pension payments), but 2 GDR Marks exchanged for 1 DM for other purposes. This was a generous, if economically precarious, exchange rate for East Germany, since it made wage levels in the GDR uncompetitive with those in West German, as productivity was so low in the GDR. However, had the exchange rate been closer to the previously prevailing grey market rates (of between 7 and 10 East German Marks for 1 DM) employees in the GDR would have all migrated to West Germany, to earn higher wages there.

3 This is in contrast to the situation of the Federal Republic prior to reunification. The state goals of the Federal Republic included not only reunification, but also, at least formally, claim to the territories given in 1945 to Poland and the USSR to administer.

4 Though in terms of population, it would have matched North Rhine-Westphalia. As one Land, it would only have had five votes in the Bundesrat (or six under the reformed allocation of votes that followed reunification). The five 'new Länder' were allocated a total of nineteen votes: more than North Rhine-Westphalia, Bavaria and Baden-Württemberg added together. (The composition and voting system of the Bundesrat are dealt with in chapter 8.)

5 Though a small minority of politicians wanted, unavailingly, to retain that Article as a way for former territories to the east of the Oder-Neisse line to be included at some future date.

6 The rate of unemployment in the Federal Republic at the end of 1997 was 12.7 per cent. In West Germany it was 11 per cent, but in the 'new Länder' it was 19.5 per cent, with a range between 18.4 per cent (Saxony) and 21.7 per cent (Saxony-Anhalt). In West Germany, the Land with the highest rate of unemployment was Bremen (16.8 per cent). Berlin had an unemployment rate of 17.3 per cent. (*Statistisches Jahrbuch für das Bundesrepublik Deutschland, 1998*, 1998, pp. 123–4). For comparison, the unemployment rate in the Federal Republic in 1989 was only 7.9 per cent. No comparison can be made with the GDR before 1990, since unemployment officially did not exist; it was disguised by measures such as severe over-staffing in many enterprises. One illustration of this is the foreign service of the Federal Republic which employed a total of 7000 staff, but had a population of 62 million; the smaller GDR – which had diplomatic relations with far fewer countries anyway – had 14,000 employees, but a population of only 17 million (Dönhoff, 1993, p. xv).

7 Honecker himself eventually escaped a trial first by fleeing to Russia, then pleading ill-health. He went to Chile, and died there of cancer in 1994.
8 Chancellor Kohl in 1990 had insisted that reunification could be achieved without additional taxes, a claim which his political opponents used against him later.

References

Dönhoff, M. (1993) 'Foreword', in H. Kurz (ed.), *United Germany and the New Europe*, Aldershot, Edward Elgar.
McElvoy, A. (1992) *The Saddled Cow*, London, Faber & Faber.
Statistisches Jahrbuch für das Bundesrepublik Deutschland, 1998 (1998) Wiesbaden, Statistisches Bundesamt.

Further Readings

Dennis, M. (1988) *The German Democratic Republic: Politics, Economics and Society*, London, Pinter.
Flockton C. (1996) 'Economic management and the challenge of reunification', in: Smith, G., Paterson, W. and Padgett, S. eds., *Developments in German Politics 2*, Basingstoke, Macmillan.
Fulbrook, M. (1991) '"Wir sind ein Volk"? Reflections on German unification', *Parliamentary Affairs*, 3: 389–404.
Glaessner, G-J. (1992) *The Unification Process in Germany. From Dictatorship to Democracy*, London, Pinter.
Glaessner, G-J and Wallace, I. (eds) (1992) *The German Revolution of 1989: Causes and Consequences*, Oxford, Berg.
Hancock, M. and Walsh, H. (eds) (1994) *German Unification. Processes and Outcomes*, Boulder, CO, San Francisco and Oxford, Westview Press.
Joppke, C. (1993) 'Exit and voice in the German revolution', *German Politics*, 3: 393–414.
Kurz, H. (ed.), *United Germany and the New Europe*, Aldershot, Edward Elgar.
Kvistad, G. (1994) 'Accommodation or "cleansing": Germany's state employees from the old regime', *West European Politics* 4: 52–73.
McElvoy, A. (1992) *The Saddled Cow*, London, Faber & Faber.
Osmond, J. (1992) *German Reunification: A Reference Guide and Commentary*, Harlow, Longman.
Roberts, G. (1991) '"Emigrants in their own country": German reunification and its political consequences', *Parliamentary Affairs*, 3:373–88.
Schmidt, M. (1992) 'Political consequences of German unification', *West European Politics*, 4: 1–15.
Wiesenthal, H. (1998) 'Post-unification dissatisfaction, or why are so many East Germans unhappy with the new political system', *German Politics*, 2: 1–30.

3

The development of the political system of the Federal Republic

The Basic Law

The political system of the Federal Republic is very much affected by its constitutional foundations. The steps that led to the convening of the Parliamentary Council which drafted the Basic Law have been described in chapter 1. The content of the Basic Law reflected several influences on the delegates to the Parliamentary Council. Most obviously, as with many constitutions (such as that of the French Fifth Republic), there was a determined concern to avoid the errors and flaws of Germany's previous democratic constitution; in this case that of the Weimar Republic. The occupation powers themselves, in various ways, influenced the Basic Law. They had their own preconceptions about what the Basic Law should contain, based on their interpretations of the weaknesses of the Weimar system and on their desire to ensure that a democratic system took firm root in West Germany, and reflecting their pride in their own systems of government. The delegates to the Parliamentary Council were affiliated to political parties, and these parties had their own agendas, concerning the structure of the federal system, the composition of the upper chamber, and the sources and allocation of state finances between the federal and Land levels of government for example. Interests such as those of the churches, the trade unions and civil servants also made their wishes known to the Parliamentary Council. The Länder, which after all possessed already functioning political systems and from whose legislatures the delegates to the Parliamentary Council had been assigned, also had an interest in many of the decisions that the Parliamentary Council would take, since these would affect their own powers and competences, as well as their financial resources.

What emerged, then, in the document which the Parliamentary Council promulgated on 23 May 1949,[1] was a temporary constitution for a provisional West German state – the Federal Republic of Germany. The preamble to the Basic Law emphasised that it was only temporary, and called on the whole German people to bring about the unity and freedom of Germany. This temporary quality of the Basic Law was emphasised again in its final provision, Article 146: 'This Basic Law loses its validity on the day that a constitution comes into force which has been accepted by the German people by their free decision.'

Nevertheless, though intended as a temporary measure, the drafters had designed a constitution with care and concern about detail. Indeed, the success with which they had done this is indicated by three later developments: the fact that the Basic Law lasted, in essence unchanged, until the reunification of Germany forty-one years after its promulgation; that it was widely admired and sometimes imitated beyond Germany itself (the new democratic constitutions of Portugal (1976) and Spain (1978), for instance, were influenced by the Basic Law); and that it seemed to be regarded by many East Germans, as well as by the vast majority of West Germans, as a suitable constitution for the enlarged Federal Republic following the act of reunification on 3 October 1990.

The Reunification Treaty in 1990 did contain provisions which altered the Basic Law, but these were limited to what could be seen as necessary consequences of the reunification process: changes in the votes given to the Länder in the Bundesrat, for instance, and the abolition of the now redundant provisions of Article 23 concerning accession of other parts of Germany to the Federal Republic. Article 5 of the Reunification Treaty provided for an opportunity for more comprehensive revision of the Basic Law within a two-year period following reunification. This revision process would also be able to deal with those areas of law where major differences remained between the law in East Germany still applicable to the 'new Länder', and the law as it was in the pre-reunification Federal Republic (on topics such as abortion), issues which had been left unresolved for a transitional period. The Bundestag and Bundesrat decided in November 1991 to create a Joint Constitutional Commission, consisting of thirty-two members from each chamber, to consider amendments to the Basic Law. Realising that any amendments which they might propose in their report would require a two-thirds vote in favour in each chamber in order to be incorporated into the Basic Law, members of the Commission were cautious in their proposals for constitutional changes. The Commission took evidence from experts and submissions from the Länder parliaments (the governments of the Länder were already represented in this revision process by the Bundesrat members of the Commission). It produced its report in October 1993. In November 1994 the amendments agreed by the Bundestag and Bundesrat on the basis of the report of the Joint Commission took effect.[2]

Four guiding principles run through the Basic Law as key motifs. The first is the absolute protection of individual rights, enumerated in the very first Articles of the Basic Law (Articles 1–19). These range from equality before the law and equality of men and women (Article 3) to freedom of belief and conscience (including the right to conscientious objection to military service) (Articles 4 and 12(a)), freedom of association (Articles 8, 9) and free choice of profession (Article 12). This prominence of individual rights in the Basic Law is in contrast to the Weimar constitution, which buried such rights in the middle of the document, and which did not give them such transparency or emphasis, and which therefore made it easier for these rights to be ignored in the Weimar Republic and abolished by the Hitler regime which followed. This prominence given to individual rights in 1949 was indicative of the priority afforded to basic rights by the framers of the Basic Law. The second motif is then stated in Article 20: that the Federal Republic is a democracy, in which all state authority emanates from the people, and which – a provision that is often overlooked – provides since 1968 an explicit constitutional right to resistance by the individual if anyone seeks to overthrow the constitutional order and if other means of countering such an overthrow are lacking.[3] The third motif is the federal basis of the state (Article 20). This, like the catalogue of individual rights, forms an unamendable feature of the Basic Law (Article 79), since the framers of the Basic Law wished to protect its key elements against amendments which would undermine the democratic and decentralised nature of the regime. The fourth motif, the rule of law, is not expressly stated in any single Article, but is mentioned indirectly in several: e.g. Articles 3, 19, 20, 28. These guiding principles all, in theory anyway, contribute to a constitutional basis that would make the introduction of a dictatorship impossible – at least, impossible without abandonment of the Basic Law first.

Following the preamble and the enumeration of individual rights, the Basic Law then deals with provisions concerning the state, its federal structure and its relations with other states. Article 20 (as mentioned above) is concerned with the source of state power and the rule of law. Article 21 is very important and is unusual among West European constitutions. It is concerned with the role and functions of political parties, and the provision that they must be democratic (see also chapter 5). Article 23 listed the Länder of Germany within which the Basic Law had immediate validity, but went on to state that: 'In other parts of Germany it will come into effect following their entry' (to the Federal Republic). This provision was utilised in the case of the Saarland, which joined the Federal Republic on 1 January 1957. Later it came to be of supreme significance at the time of reunification, because this procedure (and not that contained in the more radical Article 146, which would have involved the total replacement of the Basic Law by some new constitution) was selected as the mode by which the reunification of Germany was effected. After reunification, the original wording of Article 23 lost its purpose, since there no longer remained any part of the historic territories of Germany which could in future legitimately seek to join the Federal Republic. Instead, under the terms of the Treaty of Reunification, Article 23 in its original form was abolished.[4] Article 24 expressly provides for the transfer of sovereignty to international organisations, for the furtherance of collective security and the development of a peaceful order in Europe and the world. This has enabled the Federal Republic to become a member of international institutions such as the EEC (as it then was) and NATO (see chapter 10). Article 26 prohibits the preparation by the Federal Republic for an aggressive war. Article 28 requires that the constitutional order in the Länder must conform to the republican, democratic and social principles of the Basic Law itself. A lengthy Article 29 provides procedures for restructuring the federal system to ensure that the Länder are of suitable size and capability to fulfil the functions laid on them by the Basic Law (for further details, see chapter 6).

The next sections of the Basic Law deal with the institutions of government. Articles 38–48 are concerned with the structure and method of election of the Bundestag (though it must be noted that in Article 38 only general principles concerning an electoral system are offered; the Basic Law does not go into details concerning the features of the electoral system, such as the 5 per cent clause, see chapter 4). They also provide guarantees for the independence of the Members of the Bundestag (MdBs) e.g.: Article 38 confirms that MdBs are only responsible to their own conscience, and Article 46 provides for their immunity from penalties for their actions undertaken as Members of the Bundestag. Articles 50–53 are concerned with the functions and structure of the Bundesrat. Articles 54–61 deal with the election and obligations of the federal president. Articles 62–69 describe the composition and responsibilities of the government, including the election of the chancellor (Article 63) and the chancellor's responsibility for setting general guidelines for the government: the *Richtlinienkompetenz* (Article 65), as well as provisions for the constructive vote of no confidence (Article 67: see chapter 7) and the dissolution of the Bundestag following a failure of the government to obtain a vote of confidence, a provision which proved to be of great importance in 1972 and 1982 (Article 68).

Articles 70–91 are concerned with the division of powers between the federal level of government and the Länder, with the enumeration of areas where they have concurrent powers, and areas where they must act in concert. (These provisions are examined in more detail in chapters 6 and 7.) Article 79 provides for procedures for the amendment of the Basic Law (see below).

Articles 92–104 provide the constitutional basis for the judiciary and the system of courts. Article 93 lists the matters with which the Federal Constitutional Court (Bundesverfassungsgericht) is to be concerned, and Article 94 deals with the composition of the Constitutional Court and the way in which its judges are to be selected (see below). Article 97 provides for the independence of the judiciary.

Articles 104–115, one of the lengthiest and most detailed sections of the Basic Law, provide constitutional foundations for state finances, including the division of taxation revenues between the federal and Land levels of government and the principles under which budgets (for both the federal and Land governments) should be structured.

Articles 115(a)–115(l) describe the special arrangements which come into force in a state of emergency (termed in the Basic Law a 'state of defence': *Verteidigungsfall*). These Articles were introduced as a constitutional amendment by the 'grand coalition' government in 1968. Such a state of emergency can be declared to exist by the two chambers of the legislature. It provides for the chancellor to assume the role of commander-in-chief of the military, for the creation of a legislative council (two-thirds of its members being MdBs, the remaining one-third drawn from the Bundesrat (Article 53(a))), the possible postponement of scheduled elections and similar matters.

The remaining Articles have a miscellaneous quality. They include a definition of who is a 'German' for the purposes of the Basic Law (Article 116), the incorporation of Articles from the Weimar constitution concerning relations between the church and the state (Article 140), provision for the federal government to deal flexibly with issues arising from reunification, such as abortion law and property rights (Article 143), the method of ratification of the Basic Law by two-thirds of the legislatures of the Länder (Article 144), and the self-termination of the Basic Law when a 'proper' constitution for the whole German people became available (Article 146). After reunification, this concluding Article was reworded to take account of the completion of German reunification, but still holds open the possibility for a new constitution to be adopted.

Article 79 lays down the procedures for amendment of the Basic Law. With the exception of those provisions of the Basic Law declared to be unamendable (the federal basis of the state, the participation of the Länder in the legislative process, and the essential aspects of the freedoms incorporated in Articles 1–20), the Basic Law can be amended by votes of two-thirds of the MdBs and two-thirds of the votes of the Bundesrat being cast in favour of the change. In fact there have been numerous amendments, ranging from minor corrections or additions (such as the lowering of the voting age to 18 in 1970) to more substantial alterations (such as adaptive provisions in 1956 when the Federal Republic was allowed to have responsibility for its own defence, the emergency powers provisions of 1968, and the changes consequent upon reunification in 1990). However, even the more significant of these amendments have not affected the essential characteristics of the Basic Law.

The Federal Constitutional Court

The Basic Law has been adapted over the years by process of amendment. It has also been adapted by judicial interpretation, the task of the Federal Constitutional Court.

Though provision for a constitutional court was made in the Basic Law (Articles 92–94), it was not until the passage of the Federal Constitutional Court Act in 1951 that the Court could be founded. This law established detailed provisions concerning the organisation and operation of the Court. That same year, the Court commenced its work in the south-west city of Karlsruhe.

The Constitutional Court is organised into two senates, each responsible for particular types of cases might come before the Court. In this way, the Court can handle more cases than if it were required to meet (as does the US Supreme Court) in plenary session for every case, and the judges can develop a degree of expertise concerning types of cases. Each senate consists since 1962 of eight judges (reduced, in stages, from the original establishment of twelve on each senate). The president of the Court presides over the first senate; the vice-president presides over the second senate. The president also presides on those occasions when the Court meets in plenary session to decide on a dispute concerning allocation of a case to a particular senate, to discuss the Court's budget and to decide on administrative issues. The Court controls the appointment and management of its own staff, through its own director, equivalent to the top civil servant in a ministry.

Judges are chosen by the two houses of the legislature (and then formally appointed by the federal president). Each house chooses half the judges, who serve for a twelve-year non-renewable term or to the retirement age of 68, should that occur before the twelve-year term is completed. The Bundestag and Bundesrat alternate in selecting the president and vice-president of the Court.[5] The Bundestag delegates its selection duties to a special committee, consisting of twelve MdBs selected proportionally to the strength of the parties in the Bundestag. At least eight members of this committee must vote in favour of a nomination for it to be successful. Informally, there is a convention that a particular vacancy will be in the gift of a particular party, provided that the person nominated is broadly acceptable to the other members of the committee. The Bundesrat votes on nominations in plenary session. Again, a two-thirds vote is needed to elect a judge. Party and Land interests come into play in the case of Bundesrat nominations (Kommers, 1997, pp. 21–2). Most judges chosen have some identifiable connection to a political party; only a minority have been non-party. 'In reality, the actual process of judicial selection is highly politicized' (Kommers, 1997, p. 22).

Many judges of the Constitutional Court are appointed from the judiciary from other courts (including Land courts). However, some are selected from professors of law at universities; their published books and papers will have given them prominence, and will have indicated to those responsible for nominating judges the range of their expertise and their attitudes to the constitution. Some judges – even some presidents of the Court, such as Ernst Benda (previously federal Minister of the Interior; president from 1971 to 1983) and Jutta Limbach (formerly Minister of Justice in Berlin; president from 1994) – will come from the ranks of politicians, though normally will have held some political office which has had a close association with the law and its administration.

Because of the large number of cases submitted to the Court by the public, a filtering system is in operation. Few such cases progress to a full hearing by the Court. Depending on how the number is calculated, commentators have suggested that only between 1 and 3 per cent of those cases submitted are considered formally by the Court (Kommers, 1997, p. 15; Ismayr, 1997, p. 435). Most complaints sent to the Court are rejected as inadmissible. Others are given preliminary consideration by a committee of three judges. Only if at least one of the three decides that the case merits further consideration will it go to the appropriate senate.

The cases that are decided by the Constitutional Court include complaints from individuals concerning their constitutional rights (where lower courts have failed to satisfy the complainant); requests by the federal government or a Land government, or by at least one-third of the membership of the Bundestag, for the Court to rule on a point of constitutionality after the passage of legislation, but without a case having been brought before the courts arising from that legislation (abstract review); complaints that a law is in fact unconstitutional in a particular instance, and where a case has been brought before a lower court in consequence of this (concrete review); and disputes either between federal political institutions or between the federal government and Land governments concerning, for example, division of constitutional authority. The Court also has other functions, such as the declaration that a political party is unconstitutional, or action on a request to remove from office a judge from a lower court on constitutional grounds (Article 98 (2)).

Many of the decisions that the Court has made have had direct significance for the institutions and processes of the political system. A selection of the more important of these cases (some of which are referred to also in appropriate chapters of this book) are summarised in Appendix 1. Other cases, while not themselves having a direct effect on the political system, nevertheless have been important in their own right, demonstrating that the constitution itself is supreme law within the German political system, and affecting the rights of individuals, the scope of authority of institutions and the social and moral basis of the state. Here, too, a selection of such topics and cases is provided in Appendix 1.

So the Constitutional Court can be seen to be one of the most important of the political institutions of the Federal Republic. It enjoys considerable respect among the public and among politicians. The history of Germany before 1949 means that issues of the constitutionality of political institutions, policies and procedures, and the protection of the rights of individuals, are especially sensitive matters in the Federal Republic. So the Court's protective concern, extending far beyond that found in the USA or in other West European countries with constitutional courts, is understandable in the light of such history. Nevertheless, the Constitutional Court has not been without its critics. Such criticism has mainly focused upon two developments, which are in fact related.

On the one hand, there has been, say the critics, a tendency for politicians to misuse the Constitutional Court in two ways. Politicians have been too ready to submit legislation to the Constitutional Court as a way of avoiding difficult political decisions; for example, on party financing, on abortion law, and on property rights following German reunification. This tendency fits in with the view that Germany's political culture shies away from an adversarial style of politics, whether between parties or within parties, favouring consensus politics instead, and that the Kaiser's famous statement in 1914: 'I see no parties; I see only Germans' still has some echo in the suspicion held by many Germans of party-based politics and their preference for the certainties of the law.

Further, politicians have not hesitated to use the Constitutional Court as a 'third chamber of the legislature' when in opposition, as a means of reversing legislation proposed by the government and passed by the legislature by use of that government's majority. The Court is then called into play in a final attempt to invalidate the policies of the government. The appeal in 1973 by the CSU-governed Land of Bavaria against the constitutionality of the 'treaty' between the Federal Republic and the GDR can be seen as an example of this.

On the other hand, the Court itself has been criticised for its readiness to accept cases as matters for judicial resolution where the point at issue is 'political' as much as legal, and to go beyond merely pronouncing a verdict on the constitutionality of legislation by attaching guidelines to its decisions; guidelines which, in effect, act as the basis of alternative legislation. Judicial restraint concerning 'political' cases, a doctrine of the US Supreme Court, is not found at Karlsruhe (von Beyme, 1998, pp. 113–14). This can be seen, for instance, in the Danish minority case (1954), where the Court suggested that Schleswig-Holstein could make a special electoral rule by which parties representing national minorities in Land elections would not need to obtain 5 per cent of the vote before qualifying for seats, in the party finance decision of 1966 where the level of vote-share which qualified for reimbursements from the state proposed in the legislation was criticised by the Court, which suggested what it considered to be a more appropriate level (see Appendix 1, 1C), in the electoral rules case in 1990, concerning the electoral system to be employed in the first all-German election following reunification (see Appendix 1, 2G), or in the Maastricht Treaty decision of 1993, where restrictive conditions for transfers of sovereignty to institutions of the European Union within the principles of democracy as stated in the Basic Law were emphasised by the Court (see Appendix 1, 1F). With reference to another series of cases, those concerned with the constitutionality of aspects of university admissions policies in the 1970s, the proposals of the Court went so far as to practically amount to substitute legislation, leading one expert to claim that: 'the Constitutional Court has transformed itself into a veritable ministry of education' (Kommers, 1997, p. 289).

Influences affecting the development of the political system

The pre-history and history of the Federal Republic (chapter 1), the process of reunification (chapter 2), the content of the Basic Law and the interpretations of the Basic Law by the Constitutional Court (discussed in this chapter) are all topics necessary for an understanding and appreciation of the present-day political system and political processes of the Federal Republic. They are not in themselves sufficient, though. Other influences have shaped the present-day democratic system by which the Federal Republic is governed. One of the most significant of these, the relations between the Federal Republic and

'Europe' (its neighbours individually, and institutions of European co-operation and integration more generally), provides the subject-matter of chapter 10. Other influences directly concerned with political institutions, such as the role of political parties (chapter 5) or political leadership (chapter 7) will be considered in other chapters In this chapter, the economy, the division of Germany and the 'cold war', and political culture will be examined as among the most important contextual influences on the development of the political system.

The economy of the Federal Republic

The economy is certainly one of the more important of these other factors. The concept of the social market economy as an economic system was developed by Ludwig Erhard on the basis of economic ideas put forward by economists such as Müller-Armack. Measures to establish a social market economy were implemented when Erhard was responsible for economic policy on the Economic Council and, after the 1949 Bundestag election, when he served as Economics Minister in the Adenauer government. The social market economy attempts to cultivate a free market economy, in terms of limiting regulations and controls that would obstruct the working of the free market, though accepting regulations aimed at the removal of hindrances to the operation of competition, such as anti-monopoly legislation. It combines this emphasis on the free market with the institutionalisation of a set of welfare and social provisions by – or under the sponsorship of – the state and with recognition of the social responsibilities which ownership of property entails. Once the currency reform of 1948 had put in place the Deutschmark as a stable, reliable currency an 'economic miracle' developed in the Federal Republic: unemployment fell, production and productivity increased, stimulated by increased demand due to the Korean war, prices remained fairly stable and, thanks to the social market economy, industrial relations were generally peaceful and co-operative.

The independent status of the Bundesbank (German central bank) was an important contributory factor in sustaining the prosperous condition of the West German economy. Set up under the Bundesbank Act of 1957 (in conformity with Article 88 of the Basic Law) to replace the Bank of the German Länder, which had acted as a central bank since 1949, the Bundesbank had as its first priority the protection of the stability of the currency, primarily by means of seeking to secure low rates of inflation. Though nominated by the government, the president of the Bundesbank enjoys a high degree of independence from political pressures during his term of office, and the Bundesbank has often opposed by public statements and through policy decisions economic and financial policies of the federal government (e.g. concerning the terms of economic and monetary union between the Federal Republic and the GDR in 1990). The creation of a European central bank in connection with the introduction of the European single currency project has had the effect of severely diminishing the importance of the Bundesbank within the German political system.

Not until the mid-1960s did a first serious set-back to this economic progress occur. However, fears then that the economic situation could lead to another Nazi take-over, as had occurred in the period 1929–33, in fact proved groundless. The recession and the associated increase in unemployment which began under Erhard's chancellorship did provide receptive audiences for the propaganda of the recently founded extreme right-wing NPD, enabling that party to win representation in several Land parliaments between 1966 and 1969. Nevertheless, the NPD failed to obtain the 5 per cent of votes necessary to enter the Bundestag in the 1969 federal election, and declined rapidly in terms of electoral support and membership thereafter, as the economic situation improved. The period of the 'grand coalition' (1966–69) did, though, see some amendments made to the system of economic management. A number of new government committees concerned with matters such as financial planning were created, and earlier a Council of Economic Advisers (Sachverständigenrat) had been founded under a law of 1963 with the task of publishing an annual report on the state of the economy and its probable future development. These reports have often contained views critical of government policy, and provide a basis by which the opposition and the public can assess the extent to which the economic policies of the government take account of expert opinion.

The prosperity of the Federal Republic can therefore be seen as an important factor in producing a stable democratic system, a system which came to attract increasing support. Though, in the first fifteen years or so of the lifetime of the Federal Republic, citizens were primarily concerned with the private sphere and with working hard to establish a comfortable home life, from the mid-1960s they also then participated in democratic politics at levels found in other West European democratic states. The fact that the Federal Republic had come to acquire the leading economy in Europe, and one of the strongest economies in the world, gave people confidence and pride. It encouraged them to engage more freely in political participation, whether of an orthodox kind (such as becoming a member of a political party), or more exotic types of activity such as joining citizen initiative groups or engaging in activities of one of the new social movements concerned with opposing nuclear weapons or nuclear power-stations, with feminism, with environmental protection or with 'third world' causes, for example.

The oil crises in the 1970s, global recession in the 1980s and the high costs of reunification in the 1990s have all damaged the image of the German economy as a model for other countries. At times extreme right-wing parties have had limited local or regional successes at elections by manipulating fears of economic uncertainty and by blatant opposition to foreign residents who – claim those parties – might constitute an economic burden to the Federal Republic. Nevertheless, no such radical party has ever obtained sufficient votes to enter the Bundestag since the early years of the Federal Republic, and the democratic system itself has not been threatened, even if there has been a growing alienation of some voters from politics in general and from mainstream political parties in particular (see chapters 5 and 11).

The division of Germany and the 'cold war'

To establish and then foster a democratic political system in Germany after the problems of the Weimar Republic and the horrors of the Nazi era and the Second World War would have been a difficult task anyway. To have to do so in an environment of international politics where Germany itself was divided and where that division represented also the division of Europe into two warring ideological camps added a special degree of difficulty. The 'cold war', already manifest within Germany during the period of the Berlin blockade, was one reason why the Federal Republic came to be established in 1949 as a provisional state. Had there been better relations between the western occupying powers and the USSR, there might well have been no need for the creation of a West German temporary state, and the occupying powers could have worked together towards the creation of a united German state instead. The intensification of the 'cold war' then meant that the Federal Republic had to make a contribution to its own defence and to that of the rest of western Europe against a possible Soviet invasion. This issue of the defence of West Germany led to debates on rearmament, and to an upsurge of popular protest, which caused the SPD to be accused by the Christian Democrats of being sympathetic to communism because of the SPD's opposition to rearmament. It also led to membership of NATO for the Federal Republic.

External security was one major concern of successive governments; internal security was another. Anti-Nazism of course made West German politicians and the general public especially sensitive to issues such as xenophobia, anti-Semitism, the dangers of aggressive war and over-mighty claims of the state in relation to the civic rights of the individual or the autonomy of social institutions. Anti-communism made them suspicious of anything that seemed to call into question the official line on the 'illegitimate' status of the GDR, sensitive to the perils of state control of social services or economic planning, the tenets of Marxism or pacifism. A number of measures taken in the name of 'combative democracy' (see chapter 11), such as the prohibition by the Constitutional Court of the KPD in 1956, or the 'radicals decree' of 1972, however justified these might have been in terms of constitutional law, must be understood within this context of anti-communism and the 'cold war'. Espionage and counter-espionage (and dramas such as the resignation in 1974 of Brandt from the chancellorship, following discovery of an East German secret agent employed on his staff) also had an effect on the development of the political system.

As long as Germany remained divided into two states, and as long as those two states represented diametrically opposed ideological systems, problems concerning the identity and future of 'Germany' persisted. These problems included matters of high policy (such as the claim of the Federal Republic to represent 'all Germans', or its possible membership of international institutions such as the United Nations Organisation), but also matters of day-to-day concern at the level of the family; visits to relations in the GDR, for instance. A special ministry existed from 1949 until reunification. This was called the Ministry for All-German Affairs until 1969, then the Ministry for Inter-German Relations, a change of name indicative of the change of policy of the Brandt government at the time. This ministry was concerned with matters affecting relations between the Federal Republic and the GDR. The federal budget included items of some considerable size for the subsidisation of West Berlin, for regional aid to economically disadvantaged areas close to the GDR border, for payments to the GDR for such things as use of its roads for transit traffic between the Federal Republic and West Berlin, as well as for the subsidies involved in financing inter-German trade. The division of Germany and the 'cold war' gave – though to a declining degree from the 1960s onwards – a polit- ical role to refugees from the GDR and from other parts of what had been the German state prior to the Second World War. The development of policy towards the Soviet Union and its satellite states, and especially towards the GDR, forms an important part of the history of the international relations of the Federal Republic, and had important consequences for domestic politics as well. The erosion of the majority of the Brandt government between 1969 and 1972 because of that government's more pragmatic policy towards eastern Europe, and the unsuccessful first use of the constructive vote of no confidence in 1972 which that loss of a majority caused, are examples of how the political system could be affected by issues arising from the division of Germany.

Political culture

The political culture of the Federal Republic has, of course, influenced the development of the political system. Three stages can be identified in the shaping of the political culture of the present-day Federal Republic.

The first stage, extending from 1945 to about 1965, was marked by a toler- ation of democratic politics, even a readiness to vote in elections, but an unwill- ingness to take an active role in political life. Almond and Verba's renowned study of the political cultures of five countries included the Federal Republic. They found that West Germans had attitudes towards politics that rejected assumptions that the ordinary citizen could, or should, become involved in pol- itics, whether by joining a political party or less formally by approaching politi- cians or office-holders in order to argue a case about something or press for a decision on some matter in which the citizen had a personal interest. Respondents also had the attitude that such involvement in politics would be inefficacious. Politics itself, politicians and political institutions were not held in high esteem. Almond and Verba termed this a 'subject political culture',

marked by a high degree of passivity, in contrast to the more participant political cultures of, say, the USA and Britain at that time (Almond and Verba, 1965,
pp. 312–13, 362–3). Of course, all this has to be seen against the background
of the German population's experiences of the Weimar Republic, the Third
Reich, the Second World War and the occupation regime instituted at the end
of the war. Such passive attitudes suited Adenauer, who was able to govern in
a patrician, even authoritarian, style without much criticism from the electorate, and without much need to explain and defend his decisions in the mass
media or in election campaigns.

The period of the 'grand coalition', with its student demonstrations, its left-
wing 'street politics', the rise of an extremist right-wing party (the NPD) and
the lack of an effective parliamentary opposition (leading to the concept of
'extra-parliamentary opposition'), made domestic politics newsworthy to a
degree not previously seen in the Federal Republic. This period of minority political action and involvement can be seen as a transitional period between the
first and the second stages for the political culture of the Federal Republic. In
1969 the 'grand coalition' was replaced by a coalition government of the SPD
and the Free Democrats. The FDP had changed their political orientation to one
far less conservative than when they had been a coalition partner for Adenauer
and Erhard. This meant that there was now a government that sought to
encourage political participation and the greater application of democracy in
all kinds of political, social and economic institutions; in political parties, universities, schools and business firms, for example. By the end of the 1960s West
Germans had in any case come to be more confident that their political system
was stable and effective.

The second stage of the development of political culture, from 1969 to
1989, can be seen as one of 'normalisation'. More and more West Germans
claimed to be 'interested in politics'; they joined political parties in increasing
numbers; they were willing to participate in politics in a variety of ways; and
they had a more positive attitude to politicians and political institutions. By the
late 1970s the political culture of the Federal Republic could be regarded as
very similar to that of other West European democracies. Indeed, the Federal
Republic was in advance of most other West European countries in the degree
to which some citizens adopted 'post-materialist' attitudes and values. This led
them to engage in activities of 'new social movements' (see above and chapter
11) and produced the Green party, which from 1980 contested Bundestag as
well as Land elections, and came to be – in electoral terms, anyway – the most
successful environmentalist party in western Europe.

The third phase of the development of political culture dates from German
reunification in 1990. Both the act of reunification itself and the problems of
integration which then followed, as well as the addition to the population of the
Federal Republic of some 16 million new citizens, citizens who had been social-
ised within an authoritarian communist regime, could not but have had an
effect on the political culture of the Federal Republic. It is too early to assess

what lasting differences to the political culture will result from reunification. In any case, some changes which have become evident recently, such as a withdrawal from orthodox modes of political participation and a decline in electoral participation, were evident in the 'old' Federal Republic even before 1990, so cannot be said to have been caused by reunification. There is now, not surprisingly, a visible East German–West German divide in political attitudes and political behaviour. Some East Germans, resentful that the prosperity of the former Federal Republic has not spread rapidly enough to the 'new Länder', have less supportive attitudes than most West Germans towards the political system in particular and towards parliamentary democracy in general. They reveal different patterns of voting than in West Germany, a significant minority of voters support their own Party of Democratic Socialism, they are less ready to join or be active in political parties and significant numbers of individuals at times seem more receptive to the propaganda of extreme right-wing, usually very xenophobic, political organisations.

With the exception of this post-reunification east–west social divide – though that is a large exception – it can be claimed that Germany's political culture is now more homogeneous than ever before. The old north–south distinction in the former Federal Republic has diminished, as have the denominational differences related to religion that were partly the cause of that north–south divide. The main religious division in politics now seems to be between those who attend church frequently, of whatever denomination, and those who do not (the secular voters). Social class divisions are not as significant politically as they were twenty or thirty years ago. There is on the other hand a significant difference between those, of whatever social class, employed in the private sector and those in public sector occupations, in terms of their political attitudes and likely electoral behaviour. The political integration of the two parts of reunited Germany seems to be the only remaining problem in relation to the political culture of the Federal Republic and its effects on the development and performance of the political system.

Notes

1 The Basic Law was accepted by the Parliamentary Council on 8 May 1949 by 53 votes to 12. 6 delegates from the CSU, and 2 each from the Centre Party, the German Party and the KPD voted against acceptance. The military governors approved it on 12 May. It was then ratified by Land parliaments (only the Bavaria Land parliament voted against it).
2 These changes to the Basic Law included extensions of Article 3 concerning gender equality and removal of disadvantages for disabled persons; the elevation of environmental protection to a goal of the state (Article 20(a)); changes to Articles 72, 74 and 75 concerning the competence of the federal government in areas of concurrent powers; and changes to Articles 76, 77 and 80 concerning legislative procedures. Changes concerning adjustment of the political system to the requirements of the

Maastricht Treaty on European Union (in particular a new Article 23, see Chapter 10) had already been adopted in December 1992.

3 The provisions of this Article went some way towards removing the moral dilemma which had faced some Germans during the Third Reich, where resistance, especially by the military who had sworn an oath of loyalty to Hitler himself, was regarded as treason, however much it might otherwise have been justified.

4 A new version of Article 23 was then used to accommodate the adjustment of the political system of the Federal Republic to provisions of the Maastricht Treaty (1992) regulating the European Union (see chapter 10).

5 The qualifications for a Constitutional Court judge are that the judge be at least forty years old, be qualified as a voter for Bundestag elections and have passed the examinations for the office of judge. Judges must not hold legislative or executive office, whether at Land or federal level, nor during their term as a Constitutional Court judge are they permitted to carry out any other professional duties (except those of a professor of law at a German university). At least three of the eight judges on each senate must be selected from serving judges from federal courts.

References

Almond, G. and Verba, S. (1965) *The Civic Culture. Political Attitudes and Democracy in Five Nations*, Boston, Little, Brown (paperback edition).

von Beyme, K. (1998) *The Legislator: German Parliament as a Centre of Political Decision-Making*, Aldershot, Ashgate.

Ismayr, W. (1997) 'Deutschland', in Ismayr, W ed. *Die politischen Systeme Westeuropas*, Opladen, Leske & Budrich.

Kommers, D. (1997) *The Constitutional Jurisprudence of the Federal Republic of Germany*, 2nd edn, Durham, NC, and London, Duke University Press.

Further reading

Berg-Schlosser, D. and Rytlewski, R. (eds) (1993) *Political Culture in Germany*, Basingstoke, Macmillan.

Goetz, K. (1996) 'The Federal Constitutional Court', in Smith, G., Paterson, W., and Padgett, S. (eds), *Developments in German Politics 2*, Basingstoke. Macmillan.

Gunlicks, A. (1995) 'The New German Party Finance Law', *German Politics*, 1: 101–21.

Kommers, D. (1997) *The Constitutional Jurisprudence of the Federal Republic of Germany*, 2nd edn, Durham, NC, and London, Duke University Press.

Landfried, C. (1988) 'Judicial Policy-Making in Germany: the Federal Constitutional Court', *West European Politics*, 3: 50–67.

Ress, G. (1994) 'The Constitution and the Maastricht Treaty: Between Cooperation and Conflict', *German Politics*, 3: 47–74.

4

The electoral system and electoral politics

The principles of the German electoral system

The German electoral system is a key feature of the political system. Some understanding of its detailed aspects is necessary for an appreciation of how the party system and the system of government work. Even some of the neglected provisions of the electoral system, such as 'surplus seats' (see Box 4.1), may at times affect significantly the composition of the Bundestag, and hence influence the range of possible coalition governments that can be formed.

The four most important defining features of the German electoral system can be summarised as follows:

1 Every citizen who has reached the age of eighteen is entitled to vote. Each voter has two votes. The 'first' vote is for a constituency candidate. There are 328 single-member constituencies, in which the candidate with the most votes wins the seat (as happens with elections to the House of Commons or the US House of Representatives). The 'second' (party list) vote is for a list of candidates presented by a party in the Land in which the voter resides (for example, the SPD in Hamburg, or the Greens in Saxony). It is this party-list vote which determines the total allocation of seats among the parties. Once the votes have been counted, each party has a total allocation of seats based on its share of the 'second' votes.[1] A party receives additional list seats to add to the number of constituency seats it has won, and so obtains its total allocation (see Table 4.1).[2] For example, the Christian Democrats (CDU-CSU) in 1998 received list votes entitling it to an allocation of 245 seats and won 112 constituencies. They were thus allotted 133 list seats. However, if they had won only 90 constituencies they would have been allotted 155 list seats, to make up the total of 245 seats. If they had won 120 constituencies, their total would still have been 245 seats, because the party would only have been alloted 125 list seats.

2 The electoral system is defined by the Electoral Law of 1956 (with amendments in later years), and is not defined in detail in the Basic Law. The Basic

Table 4.1 *Bundestag election results, 1949–98*

	Turnout	CDU-CSU	SPD	FDP	Greens	PDS	Other
			(percentages)				
1949	78.5	31.0	29.2	11.9			27.9
1953	86.0	45.2	28.8	9.5			16.7
1957	87.8	50.2	31.8	7.7			10.3
1961	87.7	45.3	36.2	12.8			5.7
1965	86.8	47.6	39.3	9.5			3.6
1969	86.7	46.1	42.7	5.8			5.4
1972	91.1	44.9	45.8	8.4			0.9
1976	90.7	48.6	42.6	7.9			0.9
1980	88.6	44.5	42.9	10.6	1.5		0.5
1983	89.1	48.8	38.2	7.0	5.6		0.5
1987	84.3	44.3	37.0	9.1	8.3		1.4
1990	77.8	43.8	33.5	11.0	5.1	2.4	4.2
1994	79.0	41.4	36.4	6.9	7.3	4.4	3.6
1998	82.2	35.1	40.9	6.2	6.7	5.1	5.8

Sources: Schindler, 1983, pp. 29, 31; Veen, 1998, p. 16.

The 1998 Bundestag election:

	Votes (%)	Total seats allocation	List seats	Constituency seats
SPD	40.9	298	86	212
CDU-CSU	35.4	245	133	112
Greens	6.7	47	47	–
FDP	6.2	43	43	–
PDS	5.1	36	32	4
Total		669[a]	341	328

Note: [a] includes thirteen 'surplus seats', all won by the SPD.

Law only prescribes five general principles which the electoral system must possess: that whatever electoral system is used should be 'general, direct, free, equal and secret' (Basic Law Article 38).

3 The electoral system is a completely proportional system, modified only by two special features: first, the requirement that a party obtains either at least 5 per cent of 'second' votes or 3 constituency seats in order to qualify for a distribution of list seats;[3] and the possibility of 'surplus seats' being created (see Box 4.1).

4 There are no by-elections in the German electoral system.[4] If a Member of the Bundestag dies in office, or retires for any reason, the seat is filled from the next available candidate from the Land list of the party of the deceased or retired MdB. This applies equally whether the vacant seat belonged to an MdB elected in a constituency or one elected from the party list.

Box 4.1
Surplus seats. A special feature of the German electoral system

Surplus seats (*Überhangmandate*) exist when a party wins more constituency seats in a Land than its total proportional allocation of seats for that Land. Since constituency seats cannot be 'taken away' from a party, it has to retain these. Since it would be wrong to penalise other parties by reducing their entitlements in that Land, they retain their allocation of list seats.

For example, in Brandenburg in 1998, the SPD won 43.5 per cent of 'second' votes, which would have entitled it to nine of the twenty seats available. The SPD won all twelve constituency seats (three more than its entitlement), so the total number of seats was increased by three to twenty-three in that Land. The CDU won five list seats; the PDS won four; the Greens and the FDP each won one list seat.

In most Bundestag elections there have been a small number of such seats (between one and six), but in 1994 there were sixteen such additional seats, and in 1998 there were thirteen surplus seats (all won by the SPD).

Surplus seats arise from several causes, including below average turnout in a Land; constituency seats of below average size population, resulting in more such seats than should equitably exist in the Land; split voting, giving the larger parties more constituency votes than the share of list votes – and thus total seats – that they receive.

Consequently no changes occur in the relative strengths of the parties in the Bundestag between elections, except those caused by individual MdBs withdrawing from their Bundestag party group (Fraktion), perhaps to join another Fraktion.

How did this system come into existence?

The present-day electoral system owes its origins to three sources. First, the electoral system selected by the Parliamentary Council in 1949 for use in the first Bundestag election was influenced, like the Basic Law itself, by the preferences of the western occupying powers. The British wanted to include an element of direct constituency representation, while the Americans and the French favoured proportional representation. Second, various electoral systems already existed in the Länder of the western zones of occupation (these had also been influenced by the preferences of the occupation authorities), and these electoral systems had been utilised to elect Länder legislatures, so many of the delegates from those legislatures who were members of the Parliamentary Council would wish to select an electoral system similar to those with which they were already familiar.[5] Third, there was a desire on the part of many politicians in the Parliamentary Council to employ an electoral system based on proportional representation in order to give several parties representation in the Bundestag and because such a system seemed fairer and more democratic than the constituency-based system used in the United Kingdom and the USA. Of course, others blamed proportional representation for the weakness and collapse of the Weimar Republic, so they argued against using a proportional representation electoral system in the post-war Federal Republic. The decision whether or not to support a proportional representation system, of course, also depended on how politicians calculated their chances in coming elections. Where a party was very strong, like the Christian Democrats in North Rhine-Westphalia, or the Social Democrats in Hamburg and Bremen, there was sympathy for a British-style system. Where parties were weaker, they were more ready to support a proportional representation system of election, as did small parties such as the Communist Party and the Centre party.

In the end, a compromise system was chosen for the 1949 election, one which, with small variations, has been in use ever since. A special variant was used for the 1990 Bundestag election, because of the circumstances of that

---

Box 4.2
Modifications of the electoral system of the Federal Republic, 1949–98

1949   Single vote: counting for a constituency candidate and the party list of that candidate. 242 candidates elected from constituencies; 158 from party lists. Parties received an allocation of list seats if they obtained either a constituency seat or 5 per cent of the total votes cast in any Land (but only received an allocation of seats in those Länder where they received at least 5 per cent or had won a constituency seat).

1953   The two-vote system was introduced, making split-voting possible. Size of the Bundestag was increased to 484 seats, so that equal numbers of MdBs were elected in constituencies and from Land lists (242 in each case). To qualify for an allocation of list seats, a party had to win a constituency seat or secure 5 per cent of list votes calculated for the whole of the Federal Republic (not on a Land basis, as in 1949).

1956   The qualification for allocation of list seats was raised to three constituency seats as an alternative to 5 per cent in the Federal Republic.

Other changes:
• The number of seats in the Bundestag was increased to 494 for the 1957 and 1961 elections; to 496 for elections from 1965 to 1987 inclusive; to 656 for the elections from 1990 to 1998 inclusive. A decrease to 598 seats for the election in 2002 and for elections after that date has already been agreed and made law. These numbers do not take account of any surplus seats.
• The Hare-Niemeyer formula replaced the d'Hondt system for allocating list seats from 1987 onwards (see note 1).

Source: Schindler, 1987, pp. 18–19, 46.

post-reunification election[6] The system is also used, with some variations, for Land elections. Some Länder retain the single-vote electoral system, for instance; some have only list seats; some have five-year rather than four-year electoral periods, and so on.

The effects of the electoral system on the party system and on government

The electoral system, though a system based on proportional representation, has certainly not produced the multi-party system predicted by pessimists in 1949 and later. The 5 per cent qualification for seats was introduced in 1949 because of fears that an unrestricted system of proportional representation would lead to another 'Weimar Republic' situation, with numerous parties having seats in the legislature and unstable, multi-party governing coalitions resulting from that. Though this 5 per cent requirement has not been solely responsible for this avoidance of multi-party politics, certainly the number of parties represented in the Bundestag dropped sharply in the 1950s once the 5 per cent qualification was calculated on a federal, rather than a Land, basis (see Table 4.2). Whereas ten parties (and three non-party candidates) were represented in the 1949 Bundestag (counting the CDU and CSU as one party), only six had seats in 1953, four in 1957 and just three from 1961 until 1983, when the Greens won Bundestag seats for the first time. The only other West German party from 1961 until reunification in 1990 to obtain at least 3 per cent of the vote was the radical right-wing party, the National Democrats, which won 4.3 per cent in 1969, but afterwards declined to under 1 per cent. Since reunification, the PDS has also entered the Bundestag. However, it did so in 1990 only because of provisions in a special version of the electoral system used just for that election, and in 1994 was helped by the 'three constituencies' alternative to the 5 per cent requirement. In 1998 the PDS qualified for seats because it obtained over 5 per cent of list votes. Other than the West German Greens in 1990 (who won only 4.7 per cent in western Germany, and thus failed to win seats, even though the East German Greens were represented in the Bundestag), the only party not to obtain seats at a Bundestag election since reunification and yet secure at least 2 per cent of list votes was the Republican party in 1990 (2.1 per cent).

Small parties have sometimes retained their representation in the Bundestag thanks to a feature of the electoral system called split voting. This is possible because there is no requirement that a voter should vote for the list of the same party as that of the constituency candidate chosen by the voter. Of course, most voters are loyal: they vote for a candidate of the party whose list they have also voted for. But two different types of 'split voting' may occur. First, voters supporting a small party, like the Greens or the Free Democrats, know that the constituency candidates of those parties have little or no hope of winning the constituency seat.[7] So instead they may choose another constituency candi-

Table 4.2 *Number of parties represented in the Bundestag: 1949–98*

Years	Parties
1949	10 (plus three non-party MdBs)
1953	6
1957	4
1961–80	3
1983–87	4
1990–98	5

Source: Schindler, 1983, pp. 34–9.

date from a different party, one with more prospect of winning the constituency seat; perhaps a candidate from the major party with which the small party is likely to be an ally in coalition. Second, sometimes voters who really support one of the large parties may vote for the constituency candidate of the party they realy prefer, but vote for the list of a small party. They do so to ensure that that small party gets above the 5 per cent barrier and so qualifies for Bundestag seats, perhaps because it would thus be available as a potential coalition partner for the larger party (see below).

The electoral system affects the type of government which the Federal Republic possesses. On the one hand, because the system is one of proportional representation of parties, which makes it difficult for one party by itself to win an overall majority of seats, invariably there is a coalition government and, for the past forty years, a coalition government consisting of only two parties (counting the CDU and CSU as a single party). Only once, in 1957, has a party managed to win an absolute majority of Bundestag seats, and even then Adenauer as chancellor chose to bring the small German Party (DP) into coalition with his Christian Democratic party. There is evidence from surveys that many German voters positively dislike the idea of one-party government, equating it with government in the Nazi period or the communist regime of the GDR, and that on occasion loyal supporters of the large parties will 'split' their vote and support a smaller allied party to avoid giving too much power to one party alone and to try to bring about a coalition government (see above). On the other hand, the restrictions imposed by the 5 per cent qualification for list seats has, for much of the period prior to reunification, limited the number of parties in the Bundestag to three or four, and thus has enabled coalitions to be formed of just two parties. Even since reunification, the fact that five parties have seats in the Bundestag has so far not prevented two-party coalitions from being able to govern with an overall majority. Such coalitions (in contrast to the multi-party governments of the Weimar Republic, the French Fourth Republic, or post-war Italy) tend to be very stable, especially because that stability is reinforced by other institutional structures (see chapter 7).

What the German electoral system had not done until the 1998 Bundestag election was to compel changes of government to occur. There have been four changes of government since 1949 (disregarding adjustments within coalitions, but where the chancellorship has remained with the same party). Those of 1966 (the formation of a 'grand coalition' between the Christian Democrats and Social Democrats) and 1982 (the replacement of the SPD–FDP coalition by a Christian Democrat–FDP government) occurred in mid-term. The change of government in 1969 from the 'grand coalition' to a coalition between the SPD and FDP occurred following a Bundestag election, but this was not the necessary outcome of that election: other options were available.[8] Only in 1998 did the electorate use the electoral system to compel a change of government, from the Christian Democrat–Free Democrat coalition to a coalition between the SPD and the Greens. So it can be said that the functions of the electoral system have been more concerned with adjusting the balances among the strengths of the parties than with changes of government.

Reform of the electoral system

In general, the Germans are content with their electoral system. The electoral system is relatively simple to operate for the voter, and the calculation of results is easy to understand. The level of invalid votes is low: since 1972 normally just over 1 per cent (in 1998 1.6 per cent of constituency votes and 1.3 per cent of second votes were invalid, for example), which indicates that voters do not find the system particularly difficult to use.

However, there is evidence at every election that large numbers of the electorate do not realise that the 'second' vote (the vote for the party list) is the important vote. For example, a survey published a few weeks before the 1998 Bundestag election found that only 43 per cent of respondents in western Germany, and only 36 per cent in the 'new Länder' of eastern Germany, identified the party-list vote as the vote which is decisive in determining the allocation of seats among parties (*Focus*, 24 August 1998, p. 31). This allows small parties to rely on voters' misperceptions in order to appeal for 'second' votes as though they were somehow less value than 'first' votes, and so perhaps achieve more list votes (and hence seats) than would otherwise have been the case. It has been proposed that the votes should be reversed: that the party list vote should be called the 'first' vote, the vote for a constituency candidate the 'second' vote, to prevent such misperceptions, or that the votes should simply be called the 'candidate' and 'party list' votes.

There have only been two periods when significant reform of the electoral system seemed likely to occur. In 1956 Adenauer became impatient at the constraints imposed on his actions by the necessity of coalition government with the FDP, and especially exasperated by opposition of the FDP to his proposals for dealing with the Saarland issue.[9] He therefore floated the idea of changing the electoral system by introducing what was called the *Grabenwahlsystem*, so called because it would introduce a 'trench' (*Graben*) between the allocations of constituency and list seats, a separation which did not exist under the electoral system used in the 1953 elections. This proposed system would allocate list seats without taking into consideration any constituency seats a party had won; in other words, it would have been proportional only with respect to that half of Bundestag seats allocated from party lists. This system would have affected the FDP especially, since it won few constituency seats, and so it would have its number of seats reduced by about half (and the CDU-CSU would benefit by increasing its seats, thus very probably ending its reliance on the FDP as a coalition partner).[10] The FDP managed to prevent this change occurring, by switching from a coalition with the CDU to a coalition with the SPD in the largest Land, North Rhine-Westphalia, as a warning to what could also happen in Bonn. The FDP later did withdraw from the coalition in Bonn. The scheme for separating the calculation of the two types of vote was dropped, and the existing system, with a few modifications, was retained (see Box 4.2).

The second occasion when radical reform of the electoral system was debated was during the 'grand coalition'. In 1966 the FDP had again with-drawn from a coalition government with the Christian Democrats, and this withdrawal had led to the formation of the 'grand coalition' between the CDU-CSU and SPD. One of the agreed policies of this coalition was to examine the electoral system, with a view to amending it in such a way that government stability (by which was meant single-party governments with secure major-ities) would be enhanced. A commission of experts recommended adoption of a system very like the 'first-past-the-post' British system. However, the SPD then calculated that, as they had never up to that time won more constituency seats than the Christian Democrats, this new system could condemn them to perma-nent opposition, so might not be such a good idea. A majority of the public seemed to be opposed to a change to a majority system.[11] As the 1969 election approached, the scheme for reform was quietly abandoned.

From time to time experts criticise features of the system: the near certainty that major parties will have to depend on smaller parties to form coalition governments; the unfairness of the three-constituency alternative to the 5 per cent requirement (one party with 4.9 per cent would win no seats; another party could obtain, say, only 2.9 per cent but by winning three constituency seats, would then receive a share of list seats as well); and the two-vote system that allows for split voting. More recently, the disproportionalities produced by 'surplus seats' have been a target for criticism, especially in the 1994 Bundestag election, where these additional seats increased the majority for the governing coalition from two seats to ten.[12] However, most politicians – especially those of the FDP and the Greens – and the general public seem satisfied with the present system, which does combine proportional representation with barriers against the entry of a host of small parties to the Bundestag and with provision for con-stituency representation also.

Electoral politics

How does the electoral system work in practice? Clearly it affects candidate selection, election campaigns and of course the outcome of elections.

Candidate selection

Because there are two 'routes' by which candidates can be elected – the constituency contest and the party list – so there are two different forms of candidate selection. In both cases, procedures are regulated by the Electoral Law.

The process of selection of constituency candidates is very similar to that which occurs in Britain. A constituency selection committee for each party makes a choice among prospective candidates.[13] In cities which contain several constituencies (such as Hamburg, Munich or Cologne) the Electoral Law allows for a single process of selection for all the constituencies at once, by a city-wide committee.

List candidates are selected by either the congress of the Land party, or a special meeting of delegates of all the party organisations in that Land. Normally, the party's Land Executive will make recommendations to the meeting concerning nominations for the most hopeful places on the list (including the top five places – the only candidates whose names will be printed on the section of the ballot paper containing the list). Normally these recommendations will have taken into account representation of the various interests within the Land party. These could include, for example, regions within the Land (for Baden and for Württemberg within Baden-Württemberg, for instance, or Bremen and Bremerhaven for Bremen Land lists); rural and urban areas of the Land; balance between religious denominations (in the CDU); trade union representation (in the SPD); as well as generational and gender representation. So any changes made by delegates to these nominations from the Land Executive, or even changes to the recommended ordering of the names which might be made at the selection meeting, could disturb that balance and cause bitter internal conflicts in the selection meeting. Nevertheless, such changes do occur occasionally.

Various factors affect the likelihood of any particular list candidate being elected. First, candidates can be nominated for both a party list and a constituency seat. In the 1998 Bundestag election 41 per cent of all constituency candidates were also placed on a party list (Statistisches Bundesamt, 1998a, p. 19). So once it is known on election night which candidates from the list have been successful in constituency contests, their names are removed from the list and all the other candidates move to higher positions on the list. In the 1998 Bundestag election for example, in Bavaria nine list candidates were elected from the CSU list, but the ninth of these candidates had been originally placed nineteenth. This was because ten candidates with higher places on the list had won constituency seats. In Rhineland-Pfalz the five successful SPD list candidates had been originally placed in positions 7, 9, 11, 12 and 14. In the same Land the eight successful CDU candidates elected from the list were originally placed as number 1 (Helmut Kohl, defeated in his constituency by an SPD challenger), 3–5, 7–8 and 10–11, because candidates originally given places 2, 6 and 9 had been elected in constituencies. In Lower Saxony in 1998 the successful CDU candidates from the list had been placed in positions 1, 4–15 and 17–23. A number of these candidates had been defeated in their constituencies, including the top candidate, Rita Süssmuth, the president of the Bundestag prior to its dissolution (Statistisches Bundesamt, 1998b, pp. 206–17).

Second, although each Land gets a fixed number of constituency seats, allocated in advance on the basis of population, the total number of seats for each Land is affected by relative turnout. Theoretically, each Land should normally have as many list seats as constituency seats. However, a Land with a higher than average turnout will normally receive more list seats, one with below average turnout fewer list seats, than its allocation of constituency seats. Any 'surplus seats' that need to be created will complicate this equation still further. In 1998 the average turnout in the Bundestag election was 82.2 per cent. Hesse, with 84.2 per cent turnout, had only twenty-two constituency seats but twenty-five list seats; Mecklenburg-Vorpommern (80.3 per cent turnout) had nine constituency seats, but only five list seats, and that was after adding 2 'surplus seats', and Saxony (turnout 81.6 per cent) had 21 constituency seats, but only 16 list seats.[14] So a candidate from the SPD list who would have been elected if turnout had been average in a particular Land might just miss out on election if turnout in that Land was below average. Instead, a candidate from that same party would be elected in a Land which had an above average turnout.

Third, somewhat perversely, if a large party increases its vote-share in a Land by a significant amount (compared to the previous election), it may find that its share of list seats actually declines compared to the previous election. This is because an increase in vote-share of, say, 4 per cent in a Land may result in victory in an extra 20 per cent of constituencies, leaving a need for fewer list seats to make up the total allocation of seats for the party in that Land. Thus the SPD in Lower Saxony won only eight list seats in 1998, because it had so many constituency victories, whereas in 1994, with far fewer constituency victories, it had won fourteen list seats. Similarly, in North-Rhine Westphalia the SPD had twenty-six list seats and forty constituency victories in the 1994 Bundestag election, on 43.1 per cent of the votes cast in the Land. In 1998, it increased its vote-share to 46.9 per cent in that Land, but was allocated only nineteen list seats (because it won fifty-three constituency seats). Indeed, where a party performs especially well it will win all the constituency seats in that Land, but qualify for no list seats whatsoever (as the SPD did in six of the Länder in the 1998 Bundestag election).

So calculation of the likelihood of a particular candidate winning a list place is a difficult and chancy business. The existence of list candidates does have two other important effects. It means that candidates who contest constituencies may be 'insured' against defeat by occupying a list place more or less guaranteed to be successful. Had such a system of 'insuring' candidates on regional lists been in operation in Britain, Patrick Gordon Walker, the designated Foreign Secretary in the new Labour government, would not have been excluded from the House of Commons in 1964 because of his defeat in his constituency, and the Conservatives would have retained Chris Patten (1992) and Michael Portillo (1997) as MPs, despite defeats in their constituencies. Second, it means a party can 'balance' its Bundestag contingent. For instance parties can ensure (through use of list places) that more women are elected than would have been the case had list places not been available (see chapter 8), and candidates with connections to interest groups (business, agriculture, trade unions, the professions) are elected by being allocated high places on the list.

Election campaigning

In one sense, election campaigning in Germany can be regarded as a process which begins as soon as the last Bundestag election is over. Certainly campaign planning commences many months, sometimes as much as a year, in advance of the Bundestag election date. Schedules for the activities of the leading personalities are drawn up; public relations and advertising firms are hired to plan the production of the campaign; poster sites are booked; election programmes are drafted; party political broadcasts are designed. However, the so-called 'hot phase' of the campaign is concentrated into the six weeks or so leading up to election day. It is in this period that the public becomes aware of the campaign.

Because the important vote is the party-list vote, rather than a vote for a well-known local personality in the constituency, campaigning is dominated by emphasis on the party 'image' and the personality of the chancellor-candidate or, for small parties, leading national personalities in the party, such as Gysi for the PDS or, in the 1980s, Genscher and Lambsdorff for the FDP (though the Greens, because they seek to downplay the importance of prominent politicians for ideological reasons, have only recently made use of the popularity of a few of their better known politicians in campaigning).

Campaigning in Germany has come to rely mainly upon four methods of communication with the voter. First, the election is 'news', so parties attempt to capitalise on this by creating 'newsworthy' events, and in this way obtain exposure on television, radio and in the press. Ministers will hold press conferences, chancellor-candidates will meet with prominent foreign statesmen, candidates will attend exhibitions or sporting events, open new buildings, meet with representatives of particular groups such as young people; the disabled; single parents; owners of small businesses; wine-growers: and all this will be publicised well in advance so that media coverage can be obtained. Interviews and staged 'debates' for television, radio or the press are another, similar, means of obtaining media exposure. Second, party political broadcasts (allocated, as in Britain, roughly in proportion to a party's proven electoral strength) are utilised as 'commercials' to emphasise the merits of the party's leaders or the benefits that would accrue from its policy proposals. In the 1990s, campaign broadcast 'spots' have been purchased by some parties on commercial radio and television stations. These broadcasts are brief, and so only simplified messages, often in the form of repeated slogans, are used to persuade the voter. Third, poster coverage is used, to a greater extent than in Britain. National poster campaigns, using street hoardings, sites at railway stations, or advertising spaces on buses and trams, are supplemented locally by posters drawing attention to local candidates. Fourth, press advertising is used, sporadically, but again more extensively than in Britain. Such advertisements will appear in most of the national daily papers, and probably the regional press and weekly magazines as well. Public rallies are still staged from time to time (though only the most prominent politicians can attract crowds to such meetings now), and there are street information stalls, where the local candidate and party helpers will attempt to engage potential voters in conversation, and passers-by will be given leaflets, balloons, plastic shopping bags and other items bearing the party slogans.

Leaflets and other publicity materials will be delivered through the letter-box, but generally the house-to-house canvassing so customary in British election campaigns will not be attempted. One reason is the prevalence in German urban areas of flats rather than houses, so the privacy of the doorstep dialogue is less feasible. Other reasons are the lesser emphasis placed on local candidates in the Bundestag election campaigns, the political culture of Germany, which does not encourage such personalised approaches, and the fact that memories of what the unannounced 'knock on the door' has meant in Nazi Germany or in the GDR are still potent. In recent election campaigns, the main parties increasingly have used computer technology for campaign purposes. The parties tend to spend heavily on campaigning. In 1994, the CDU and SPD each had a budget of DM70 million; the CSU's budget was DM14 million; the FDP allocated about DM10 million; the Greens only had DM4.9 million for their national campaign; the PDS devoted DM8 million to the Bundestag campaign.[15] Parties are able to spend these sums because of generous party financing legislation, which has awarded them considerable sums of money from the national budget (see chapter 5).

Occasionally, the main parties agree to an election campaign treaty (*Wahlkampfabkommen*), which regulates matters such as the starting date for poster display and other forms of publicity, fair treatment of rival parties during campaigning, limits on campaign expenditures and the formation of a neutral tribunal to adjudicate on alleged breaches of the agreement. Such treaties are also sometimes arranged locally, and may include agreements not to display any posters on highways in the constituency, for instance.

Bundestag elections: 1949–98

The 1949 election resulted in both major parties: Adenauer's Christian Democrats and Kurt Schumacher's Social Democrats, receiving about 30 per cent of the votes. Though there was some talk of the creation of a 'grand coalition' involving the Christian Democrats and the SPD (which would have been very difficult to construct because of major disagreements between those parties, particularly on economic policy), Adenauer formed a coalition with the liberal FDP and the DP. Ten parties in total had seats in the Bundestag.

In 1953, seventeen parties contested the election but only six parties won Bundestag seats. Adenauer's popularity, as well as the successes of the government's economic policy and its strategy of linking the Federal Republic to western alliances, enabled the Christian Democrats to increase their vote-share to 45 per cent, whilst the SPD vote-share remained static. The Adenauer government continued in office, bringing into the coalition ministers from the Refugees' party in addition to the FDP and DP, which had been members of the previous coalition. This arrangement provided Adenauer with a two-thirds majority, enough to guarantee amendment of the Basic Law if necessary.

The 1957 election followed a crisis within the coalition in 1956, which had led to the departure of the FDP from the government. The FDP contested the Bundestag election without any firm indication of which major party they would seek to join with in coalition. However, this 'open to both sides' strategy proved irrelevant. Adenauer, at the height of his electoral popularity, secured an overall majority for his party. He did include the DP in a coalition government, though, to increase his overall majority. The SPD increased its vote-share slightly. Only four parties had seats in the Bundestag.

In the 1961 election campaign the FDP indicated their preference for a coalition with the Christian Democrats, but towards the end of the campaign announced a condition: that Adenauer be replaced as chancellor. This tactic was responsible for securing the FDP its greatest ever vote-share – 12.8 per cent – and, because the CDU-CSU vote-share declined from over 50 per cent in 1957 to 45 per cent in 1961, the FDP was needed to form a coalition. However, Adenauer so stage-managed the coalition negotiations that the FDP was unable to insist upon a replacement chancellor, so the party 'lost face' and had to serve under Adenauer again (though Adenauer did promise in letters to his own party and to the FDP that he would step down before the next Bundestag election). The SPD, having completed a transformation of image and programme by means of its 1959 Godesberg Programme (see chapter 5), increased its vote-share to 36 per cent, and was to obtain increases of about 3 per cent at each Bundestag election until 1972. From 1961 only three parties had seats in the Bundestag until the breakthrough of the Greens in 1983.

The 1965 election was the first at which Adenauer was no longer the chancellor-candidate of the CDU-CSU. Ludwig Erhard, his respected Economics Minister, had replaced him in 1963. The CDU-CSU increased its vote-share, winning back from the FDP many of the voters lost to it in 1961. The coalition between the Christian Democrats and FDP continued after the election, though it collapsed in 1966 because of differences over economic and financial policy, and because of Erhard's failure to exert strong leadership. A 'grand coalition' under Kurt-Georg Kiesinger (CDU) as chancellor was formed instead.

In 1969, as in 1957, the FDP contested the election without a clear indication of which of the two major parties would be its preferred coalition partner. The fact that the FDP had earlier in 1969 supported the SPD candidate in the election of the federal president was taken as a sign that the FDP would probably give preference to the SPD. The FDP had also used its time in opposition to reorient itself, and had become a more reformist party, emphasising the need for change in numerous areas of policy, including relations with the communist states of central and eastern Europe. The FDP (5.8 per cent) only just surmounted the 5 per cent 'hurdle'. Despite the fact that the Christian Democrats were again the largest single party, the FDP chose to join with the SPD to form a government under Chancellor Willy Brandt, though this coalition had a majority of just twelve seats. This was the first time that the CDU-CSU had been out of power. The radical right-wing NPD had between 1966 and 1968 won seats in several Land legislatures. However, in the Bundestag election it failed to secure the 5 per cent vote-share necessary to win any seats (it obtained 4.3 per cent).

The 1972 election was unusual for two reasons. It was the first time that there had been a 'premature' election, resulting from the dissolution of the Bundestag several months ahead of schedule (after just over three years of the normal four-year term). It was also the first election to be fought primarily on a single theme: the *Ostpolitik* (policy towards eastern Europe) of the Brandt coalition. This controversial policy had already caused several members of the FDP and SPD parliamentary groups to transfer to the opposition; this meant that the government's small majority had disappeared, and it could no longer pass legislation through the Bundestag. Though, unexpectedly, Brandt survived this first ever 'constructive vote of no confidence' (see chapter 7), he was compelled by his lack of a majority to request the federal president to resolve the situation by dissolving the Bundestag ahead of schedule. The popularity of the *Ostpolitik* among the electorate meant that the coalition parties both gained vote-share, while the Christian Democrats' vote-share declined. For the first time, the SPD was the largest single party in the Bundestag. The NPD vote was negligible (under 1 per cent).

The coalition managed to retain its majority in the 1976 election, though both the SPD and FDP vote-shares declined. The CDU-CSU, led by its new, youthful, chancellor-candidate, Helmut Kohl, won its second largest ever vote-share (48.6 per cent), using the slogan 'Freedom instead of Socialism'. Because of a scandal involving the discovery of a GDR spy employed in a position of trust in his office, Brandt had resigned as chancellor in 1974; Helmut Schmidt succeeded him. Also in 1974, Walter Scheel had resigned as FDP leader in order to become federal president. He was replaced by Hans-Dietrich Genscher. Thus all three parties fought the election under new electoral leadership.

Many commentators thought that the FDP would change its coalition partner ahead of the 1980 election. There had been clear signs of conflict between the FDP and the SPD on several areas of policy, and the coalition had lasted eleven years, so, to protect the independence of the FDP, a change of coalition partner might have been tactically advisable. However, the choice by the Christian Democrats of Franz Josef Strauss (an arch-enemy of the FDP) as their chancellor-candidate excluded this possibility. Strauss was undoubtedly a cause of many CDU voters giving their 'list' votes to the FDP (see below), and thus the CDU-CSU vote-share fell to 44.5 per cent, at that time its lowest share since the 1949 election. The coalition once again retained its Bundestag major-ity. The SPD vote-share increased very slightly, and that of the FDP rose to 10.6 per cent, its best result since 1961. For the first time the Greens contested a Bundestag election, but won only 1.5 per cent of the vote.

The FDP did, though, abandon its coalition with the SPD in October 1982, following conflicts in 1981 and 1982 with the SPD over economic policy. In a constructive vote of no confidence, Schmidt was replaced as chancellor by Helmut Kohl (thanks to FDP support). Kohl then sought to legitimise this change of government by an early federal election. Once again, as in 1972, the federal president, controversially, dissolved the Bundestag prematurely (see Appendix 1, 1D), and a new Bundestag election was held in March 1983. This election confirmed the coalition in power: the Christian Democrats just missed securing an absolute majority (48.8 per cent); the FDP survived with 6.9 per cent. The SPD, under a new chancellor-candidate (Hans-Joachim Vogel), only obtained 38.2 per cent of the vote. The Greens this time were successful in meeting the 5 per cent qualification for seats (winning 5.6 per cent of the vote, which gave them twenty-seven seats).

The 1987 election produced the lowest turnout since the 1949 federal elec-tion (84.3 per cent, compared to the range of 86–91 per cent since 1957), partly because it took place in bitterly-cold January weather.[16] The SPD again fought the election with a new chancellor-candidate, Johannes Rau, prime minister of North Rhine-Westphalia. However, the SPD vote-share declined once more, to 37 per cent. The FDP increased its vote-share to 9.1 per cent, which gave it increased influence in the coalition *vis-à-vis* the Christian Democrats, who had obtained only 44.3 per cent. The Greens remained only the fourth largest party, but increased its vote-share (8.3 per cent).

The 1990 election immediately followed the process of German reunification. This issue dominated the campaign, and parties which ques-tioned the desirability of reunification (the Greens in West Germany) or the costs rather than the benefits it was likely to bring (the SPD, under its new chancellor-candidate, the Saarland prime minister Oskar Lafontaine) were punished by the electorate. The Greens in West Germany failed to achieve the 5 per cent needed for seats (4.7 per cent in West Germany), and the SPD, which was anyway weak in East Germany, managed to obtain only 33.5 per cent (and only 24.3 per cent in East Germany). The Christian Democrats benefited from Kohl's association with the reunification process, and obtained 43.8 per cent (though this was down slightly compared to 1987), but the coalition's share of the vote increased thanks to the FDP winning 11 per cent of the vote. The PDS and the East German Alliance '90–Greens electoral alliance obtained seats. They each secured over 5 per cent of the votes in East Germany which, because of the special modification of the electoral system used for this election only, meant that they obtained an allocation of list seats. The Republicans, a radical right-wing party which had had some surprisingly high results in Land elections prior to 1990, obtained only 2.1 per cent. This election campaign was marred by armed attacks on two leading politicians: Lafontaine was stabbed by a deranged women, but recovered; Wolfgang Schäuble, a CDU politician who had played a prominent part in reunification negotiations, was shot, and as a result has since been confined to a wheelchair.

In 1994 the SPD was led by Rudolf Scharping, formerly prime minister of Rhineland-Pfalz, as its chancellor-candidate. Though opinion polls early in the year suggested that a change of coalition was likely, from June 1994 until election day in October Kohl was perceived as the more popular of the rivals for the chancellorship, and it became increasingly likely that the coalition between the Christian Democrats and the FDP would remain in office. However, the unusually large number of other elections in 1994 (Land elections and the European Parliament election among them) added to the uncertainty, especially as they revealed that support for the FDP throughout the Federal Republic and for the Greens in eastern Germany seemed to be declining. There was also some doubt as to whether the PDS would return to the Bundestag, given that the special arrangements which had been created for the 1990 Bundestag election no longer applied. As it turned out, the FDP obtained well over the crucial qualifying 5 per cent (6.9 per cent); so the coalition did receive an overall majority, but one which was boosted from a mere two seats to ten seats by the eight 'surplus seats' that it secured (see above). The SPD managed to win only 36.4 per cent. The Greens (7.3 per cent) overtook the FDP to become the third largest party in the Bundestag. The PDS did return to the Bundestag, despite winning only 4.4 per cent, because it secured four victories in constituency seats in East Berlin, so the 5 per cent rule for distribution of list seats did not apply to it, and it qualified for thirty seats in total.

In the 1998 election campaign it was clear that the Christian Democrats would find it very difficult to retain the chancellorship. Helmut Kohl's popularity was waning, and in opinion polls concerning the preferred chancellor-candidate he always lagged behind Schröder by a large margin. Despite a promise he made during the 1994 election campaign to retire before the 1998 campaign began, Kohl decided to seek another term as chancellor. Some commentators before and after the election suggested that a different chancellor-candidate would have secured a better result for the Christian Democrats. The SPD, having replaced Scharping by Lafontaine as party chairman in 1995, selected Gerhard Schröder rather than Lafontaine as the party's chancellor-candidate, after Schröder had led his party to victory once again in the Lower Saxony Land election in March 1998. The FDP, under its new party leader, Wolfgang Gerhardt, unsurprisingly announced that the party would try to remain part of a coalition with the Christian Democrats. The FDP was again in the position of having to struggle to secure the necessary 5 per cent of votes to retain representation in the Bundestag. The Greens also could not be absolutely certain of obtaining 5 per cent, having lost representation in the Land parliament of Saxony-Anhalt in the 1998 Land election there. The Greens made a decision to seek to join the SPD in a governing coalition, if the election result allowed this. Rather than any particular policy differences deciding the outcome of the election, it seemed that a mood in favour of a change of government was the most significant factor, and Schröder and his party seemed to the voters capable of providing a competent government. The SPD did very well, winning 40.9 per cent (an increase of 4.5 per cent compared to the 1994 election and its best result since 1980). The Christian Democrats declined by 6.4 per cent compared to 1994, obtaining only 35.1 per cent, the worst result since 1949. The FDP (6.2 per cent) and the Greens (6.7 per cent) both lost vote-share compared to 1994, but were quite comfortably over the 5 per cent mark. The PDS, though winning four constituency seats again, was also able to qualify for an allocation of list seats by winning 5.1 per cent of party-list votes. Schröder could, theoretically, have formed a 'grand coalition' with the CDU-CSU, or a coalition with the FDP, though neither of these parties would have been easily persuaded to join such a coalition. However, the SPD and Greens formed a coalition after a period of negotiation, a coalition approved by special party conferences of both parties. This government had a majority of twenty-one seats, thanks to thirteen 'surplus seats' won by the SPD.

Voting behaviour

Three important topics concerning German voting behaviour are:

*   the extent and nature of non-voting;
*   the social composition of electoral support for particular parties; and
*   the effects of reunification on patterns of electoral behaviour in the Federal Republic.

Turnout at German elections before 1990 was relatively high, in comparison to that in other West European democracies.[17] For Bundestag elections, in 1949 turnout was 78.5 per cent. Between 1953 and 1987 it ranged from 84.3 per cent (1987) to peaks of 91.1 per cent (1972) and 90.7 per cent (1976). In 1990 it declined sharply to 77.8 per cent. It has increased in the two Bundestag elections since then: in 1994 it was 79.0 per cent and in 1998 it was 82.2 per cent (see Table 4.1). In contrast, the turnout at the 1997 British general election was 71.3 per cent. However, turnout in reunified Germany is now lower than in some West European countries; for example Sweden had a turnout of 86.8 per cent in its 1994 election; the turnout in the 1995 election in Austria was 86 per cent.

Why has turnout in the Federal Republic been so high and why has it declined over the past decade? Compared to the United Kingdom, turnout has been much higher in the Federal Republic for the following reasons:

- *The electoral system.* In the Federal Republic almost every vote counts towards the election of additional candidates of the voter's preferred party, but in the United Kingdom, additional votes for candidates in safe seats who would win anyway do not help to elect anyone else, and votes for candidates who clearly cannot win a seat also are 'wasted'.
- *Timing of the election.* Elections in Germany must by law be held on a Sunday (or public holiday). In the United Kingdom, they must be held on a working day. So most voters in Germany have more time and opportunity to visit the polling station than in Britain, where shift-working, working away at some distance from the constituency, or delays in workday traffic might prevent voters from going to vote.
- *The registration process.* In Britain electoral registration occurs once a year, and those voters who die or who move out of a constituency are still on the register for the remainder of the year, and thus affect the calculation of turnout. Voters who move cannot register to vote in the new constituency until the new register is constructed, perhaps many months later. In Germany, where changes of residence must be registered with the police, the effective list of electors in an area is always up to date.
- *Political culture* (see chapter 3). Until recently, in the Federal Republic there has been an attitude of moral pressure to use the vote. This has been associated with the idea that democracy is to be valued and protected, especially after the downfall of the Weimar Republic and the experiences of the Third Reich, and, until 1990, because of the contrast with the non-democratic regime in 'the other Germany' – the GDR. In the United Kingdom, this attitude has not been as strong; non-voting is not regarded as in any sense as a significant breach of the obligations of citizenship.

However, over the past decade a decline in traditional forms of political participation generally, and turnout at elections in particular, led commentators to raise the questions: have Germans lost their appetite for democratic politics? If so, is this a threat to the democratic order itself? The term *Politikverdrossenheit* (alienation from politics) was coined to encapsulate this apparent rejection of political participation. A decline in association with, or respect for, party politics, was seen as another part of this syndrome (see chapter 5). Research demonstrated that there had been a decline, especially among the younger generation, in the sense of civic obligation to vote at elections, and the younger generation had the lowest levels of turnout. Those who were socially more isolated (those who lived alone, and those without membership of social organisations, such as churches, clubs or trade unions) also had less likelihood of going to vote than those who lived in families and those who were members of such social organisations.

There was undoubtedly a temporary situational factor involved also. In 1990 and again in 1994 many voters had been called upon to participate in several elections within a few months. East Germans had already had the opportunity in 1990 to vote in the March election for the GDR Volkskammer (and 93.4 per cent of them had used that opportunity), in local elections in May, and in Land elections in October. In four West German Länder, also, Land elections in 1990 had preceded the Bundestag election. In 1994 this situation was even more pronounced. In the so-called '*Superwahljahr*' (super-election year), in addition to the European Parliament election, Land elections took place in five Länder and local elections in eight Länder, prior to the day of the Bundestag election (when three other Länder simultaneously held Land elections and one held local elections). So some voters would have voted three times in 1994, many would have voted twice and all would have had the opportunity of voting once, before the Bundestag election itself. This may well have caused a form of 'election-fatigue'. Certainly in East Germany, where such 'fatigue' might be most prevalent because of this series of other elections, turnout in the 1994 Bundestag election was lower than in West Germany. Only Thuringia – 75.5 per cent – had a turnout rate above 73 per cent, whereas the lowest turnout in West Germany was Bavaria's 77 per cent. Turnout in East Germany actually declined by 1.6 per cent compared to the 1990 election, whereas in West Germany it increased by 2 per cent. However, the more difficult economic situation of East Germans, and their inexperience with competitive democratic elections, might also have contributed to this decline.

Despite the claim of the SPD and Christian Democrats that they are 'catch-all parties', seeking to attract voting support from all sections of the electorate (see chapter 5), in fact electoral support for parties varies according to a variety of demographic, social and geographic factors.[18]

As in many other democracies, younger voters tend to support left-wing parties more than do older voters, who are more conservative in their voting preferences. The Greens in particular benefit from above average levels of support from voters under the age of 45. The FDP, on the other hand, usually receives above average support from those aged over 45, and the Christian Democrats especially from those over 65. Of course, care is required in interpretation of age-related voting data. On the one hand, this could be a reflection of the stage in the life cycle of the voter (i.e. the electoral behaviour of younger voters will come to resemble that of older voters as they themselves become older). There is evidence of this, since the trends mentioned above have been visible in the Federal Republic for over forty years, and they match trends observable in other democratic states. On the other hand, the data also support to some extent an interpretation which identifies a 'generational effect': that voters acquire electoral preferences, perhaps even close identification with a party, at the time of their first election, and many remain faithful to that party as they become older. There is evidence that those young voters who supported the Green party in 1980–87 have retained that preference a decade later, even though they are now in the 35–44-year-old age group.

Gender has not played a great role in terms of differential electoral support in recent years. In the 1950s, the Christian Democrats had a much larger level of support among women than among men but, allowing for the fact that there are anyway more women in the electorate than men, the CDU-CSU now obtains only a slightly above average level of support from women voters. The SPD in 1998 had similar levels of support from men and women, as did the FDP. The Greens had much larger levels of support among women voters than among male voters. Again, care is needed in interpretation. For example, because older voters support the CDU-CSU, and because women supply a much larger share of those voters aged over 65 than they do in the electorate as a whole, these factors of age and gender become intertwined, as does the fact that older women make up a large share of churchgoers, who are also more likely to vote Christian Democrat. Extreme right-wing parties obtain about twice as many votes from men as from women.

Much is made of the 'milieux' which have provided strong support for the two largest parties – the SPD and CDU-CSU. It is unsurprising to observe that support for the SPD from voters who are members of trade unions is very high: 55 per cent of trade union members voted SPD in 1998, but under 40 per cent of non-trade unionists. Similarly, church-attenders, and especially Catholic church-attenders, vote for the Christian Democrats in much larger numbers than do those who rarely, or never, attend church. Seventy per cent of all Catholics who regularly attend church, and half of those who occasionally attend, voted CDU-CSU in 1998. However, those parties no longer benefit from these voting trends to anything like the extent that they did in the 1950s and 1960s, because both trade union membership and regular attendance at church are declining steeply (see chapter 9).

Social class, income, occupation and level of formal education are other social categories which are frequently employed in analysis of the German electorate. They are, of course, related, since completion of university education or securing professional qualifications are often passports to the professions or to high-level managerial positions in industry and commerce, and such opportunities are still linked to social class. In turn, these qualifications are often associated with careers or professions which provide high incomes. Broadly, as one would anticipate, the CDU-CSU has benefited in the past from the support of those with highest income levels and in managerial or white-collar occupations, and who belong to the upper or upper-middle classes. However, in 1998 the Christian Democrats secured slightly higher levels of support among those with low levels of educational qualification, as did the SPD, than among those with university education. The Greens, the FDP and the PDS all had the highest shares of their vote from those with the highest levels of educational qualification. In occupational terms, the Christian Democrats had support especially from farmers, the self-employed and the retired. The SPD had its highest levels of support from blue-collar employees and the unemployed, though since its change of identity arising from the 1959 Godesberg Programme the SPD has made gains among white-collar and managerial sectors of the electorate. The Greens benefited from votes from public sector white-collar employees and those still pursuing educational qualifications. The FDP did well among the self-employed. The PDS had strong support among the unemployed.

Prior to reunification, there were two significant geographic factors which produced differential electoral behaviour. There was, as is so often the case in western democracies, a rural–urban difference. Since this tended to coincide to some extent with occupational and class differences, it was not surprising that many cities and industrial towns were strongholds of the SPD: Hamburg, Bremen, Essen and Frankfurt are examples. Rural areas were mainly Christian Democratic strongholds. These differences have tended to become eroded, with the decline of extractive and manufacturing industries, for instance. The other such difference was a north–south distinction, based largely upon the Catholic predominance in south Germany, the Protestant strength in north Germany. So Bavaria, Baden-Württemberg and, until recently, the Saarland and Rhineland-Pfalz tended to be 'safe' areas for the Christian Democrats; Hamburg, Bremen, and, from the 1960s, North Rhine-Westphalia have been SPD strongholds. Schleswig-Holstein, though northern and Protestant, was a CDU stronghold until the 1980s, Hesse was a stronghold of the SPD until the 1980s but is now 'marginal', and Lower Saxony has swung from one party to the other, though since the 1980s has been governed by the SPD at Land level.

Now reunification has imposed an even more striking geographic division upon Germany's electoral politics – that between the 'new Länder' of eastern Germany and the 'old' Federal Republic. Here a regional difference which would have existed anyway (similar to the north–south difference in the pre-reunification Federal Republic) has been exacerbated by the very different historical experiences prior to reunification of those two areas: West Germany's development under the social-market economic system and pluralist democracy; East Germany's under a collectivised, state-controlled economy and a communist dictatorship. These experiences shaped both the psychological attitudes of the population and the economic and social conditions under which they now live. So it is to be expected that electoral behaviour will be different in these two areas. The differential propensity to turn out to vote in these two parts of Germany has been noted earlier in this section. Another difference concerns levels of support for various parties. The persistent strong support for the PDS in the 'new Länder' is the most obvious feature. The PDS obtained between 16 and 22 per cent in Land elections in eastern Germany in 1994. It obtained 36.3 per cent in East Berlin in the Berlin Land election in 1996, and in the 1998 Land elections won 19.6 per cent in Saxony-Anhalt and 24.4 per cent in Mecklenburg-Vorpommern. It secured 21.6 per cent in the 1998 Bundestag election in eastern Germany (including East Berlin), but only 1.2 per cent in western Germany (including West Berlin). Largely because of that effective competition from the PDS, in eastern Germany all the other main parties in the 1998 Bundestag election attracted lower support there than in western Germany. The gap was 7 per cent for the SPD, nearly 4 per cent for the FDP, over 3 per cent for the Greens and 1 per cent for the CDU-CSU.

The unusual system of giving voters two votes has led to significant developments in electoral behaviour. Since the 1980 Bundestag election, the proportion of voters who have made use of the potential to 'split' these votes (giving the first vote to the candidate of a different party than is selected with the 'list' vote) has increased from a range of between 4 and 9 per cent before 1980, to levels rising from 10 per cent in 1980 to about 15 per cent in the 1990s. The most obvious beneficiary of this trend has been the FDP (Roberts, 1988). Since the 1969 Bundestag election, the FDP has explicitly encouraged voters who might support constituency candidates of other parties, and who even may regard themselves as loyal supporters of other parties, to give their list votes to the FDP. The FDP benefited slightly from split-voting in the elections of 1957, 1961 and 1965. In 1969 the 'bonus' of second votes remained small, but was crucial to the party's survival in the Bundestag: it obtained 5.8 per cent of list votes, but only 4.8 per cent of constituency votes. In 1972 the bonus was 3.6 per cent (with constituency votes – 4.8 per cent – again below the critical 5 per cent level), thanks largely to SPD voters, who, by giving list votes to the FDP, sought to ensure that the SPD's coalition partner would return to the Bundestag. After a decline of the bonus to 1.5 per cent in 1976, an election where the FDP deliberately campaigned for first and second votes, the party had a bonus of between 3 and 4 per cent in all Bundestag elections between 1980 and 1998. In three of those elections (1983, 1994 and 1998) the party's first votes were below 5 per cent. Since the overwhelming share of such 'split votes' come from voters choosing candidates of the FDP's coalition partner, it is likely that many of these voters were supporting the CDU-CSU coalition with the FDP by their voting decision. Most of these may have been voters who identified with the larger party, but some are FDP voters who do not want to 'waste' their constituency vote on their party's candidate who is sure to lose. Other parties have also benefited from such 'split' voting, though to a lesser extent – the Greens in particular (a bonus of over 1 per cent in 1998, for instance). The SPD in 1998 had 2.9 per cent more first votes than second votes and the CDU-CSU had 4.5 per cent more first votes than second votes.

So electoral politics, and the electoral system, matter to the operation of the German political system. The electoral system seems to have contributed to the stability, but also to the flexibility, of democratic politics in Germany. The fact that other countries (such as New Zealand, Scotland and Wales) have imitated the German two-vote system is also a compliment to its democratic qualities. The Commission created by the Ministry of the Interior to examine the electoral system reported in 1955 that 'the continued existence, the consolidation and the reputation of the free and democratic basic order depend to a large degree on a good electoral law' (Schreiber, 1998, p. vii). To that extent, the Federal Republic appears to have been fortunate to have hit upon just such a good electoral law.

Notes

1 This allocation is calculated (since 1987) by the Hare-Niemeyer formula. This formula allocates for each party a quota of seats (Q) by taking the number of votes a party receives (P), multiplied by the total number of seats to be filled (S), and the result of that calculation is divided by the total number of votes for all parties qualifying for seats (V). So, for any party qualifying for seats by having 5 per cent of votes or 3 constituency seats, the formula is:

$$Q = \frac{P \times S}{V}$$

For each whole number of the resulting sum a seat is awarded. Because this leaves remainders (fractional entitlements), remaining seats are allocated to the parties with the highest remainders until all seats are filled. For example, Party A where Q = 56.275 could get fifty-six seats. Party B where Q = 44.665 could get forty-five seats; it qualifies for an extra seat because .665 is, in this case, a 'highest remainder'. Until 1987 the d'Hondt allocation system was used (by which the total number of votes for each party was successively divided by 1, 2, 3, 4 . . . etc., with seats being allocated to the highest numbers resulting from those calculations). This d'Hondt system tended to be of slightly greater advantage to larger parties, compared to the Hare-Niemeyer system.

2 Parties may secure a slightly larger percentage of seats than they do of list votes, although it does not affect proportional representation of parties which obtain an allocation of list seats. This happens where several small parties contest the election but fail to secure an allocation of list seats because they each obtain less than 5 per cent of 'second' votes (and do not win at least three constituency seats). These votes are disregarded for purposes of allocating seats, and the parties which do qualify for an allocation benefit from this. In 1957 7.1 per cent of votes were for parties which failed to qualify for seats, for instance. More recently, in 1990 7.9 per cent of votes were given to non-qualifying parties; in 1994 3.6 per cent and in 1998 6 per cent of second votes were given to parties which received no seats. This meant that the CDU-CSU in 1998, with 35.1 per cent of the vote, received 37.3 per cent of the 656 Bundestag seats (disregarding the thirteen 'surplus seats' which the SPD won).

3 Of course, any party that wins 1 or 2 constituency seats retains these, but unless such a party also has obtained at least 5 per cent of votes for its party lists it will not be allocated any additional seats. Had the PDS won two, rather than four, constituencies in the 1994 Bundestag election, because it obtained only 4.4 per cent of

'second' votes it would have had only those two seats, not the thirty seats which it was allotted. It is not strictly accurate, therefore, to claim that all parties with less than 5 per cent of the vote necessarily fail to qualify for representation.

4 Other than in extremely improbable circumstances, where the vacancy is caused by the departure of an independent (i.e. non-party) constituency MdB. In practice, this is extremely unlikely ever to happen.

5 For example, in North Rhine-Westphalia (in the British zone) in 1947 members of the first Land parliament were elected by means of a 'mixed system': 150 in single-member constituencies, and a further 50 elected from party lists in such a way as to make the overall total for each party proportional. To qualify for list seats, a party had to obtain at least 5 per cent of the total vote in the Land. Voters had only a single vote; so the vote for a candidate was automatically also a vote for that candidate's party list. Hesse (in the American zone) used a similar system in 1946 for its first Land parliament election (25 elected from district lists; 65 from Land party lists). Other Länder in the American zone used variations of list-based proportional representation systems.

6 In 1990, because parties in the former German Democratic Republic had not had time to develop their organisation or publicity in the short period since the fall of the communist regime, and because some of these parties certainly had not had the time or resources to build up support in western Germany, it was agreed that a modified version of the electoral system of the Federal Republic should be adopted for the Bundestag election in December of that year. Following a ruling by the Constitutional Court (see Appendix 2G) it was decided to modify the electoral system so that, to qualify for an allocation of list seats, parties had to win three constituencies, or 5 per cent of 'second' (party list) votes in either western Germany (the former Federal Republic and West Berlin) or in eastern Germany (the former GDR and East Berlin). Qualification in either of these two areas qualified a party for an allocation of seats in the whole of Germany. Thus the PDS won 11.1 per cent in eastern Germany (but only 0.3 per cent in western Germany), and thus qualified for seventeen seats in total, including one seat from western Germany. It won only 2.4 per cent of list votes in the Federal Republic as a whole, so had the 'normal' system been in operation, requiring 5 per cent in the whole of Germany, the PDS would have had only its single constituency seat and no list seats. This modification of the electoral system was used only for the 1990 Bundestag election.

7 In fact, since 1961 only one constituency seat has been won by a party other than the Christian Democrats, the Social Democrats or the PDS – a seat in Halle won by the FDP in 1990. The PDS won one constituency in the 1990 election, and four in the 1994 and 1998 elections.

8 The 'grand coalition' could of course have continued, or a Christian Democrat–FDP coalition could have governed, and would have had a larger majority than the government that was actually formed. Similarly, arithmetically, an SPD–FDP coalition would have had a majority in the Bundestag in 1961 and 1965, or a Christian Democrat–FDP coalition between 1969 and 1980. In 1998 the SPD could, arithmetically, have created an overall majority in coalition with the FDP.

9 The Saarland – an area on the western border of Germany and famed for its coal and steel production – had in 1945 been placed under French administration outside the occupation zone arrangement, pending a peace treaty. Adenauer was prepared to abandon German claims to the return of the Saarland; the FDP opposed such

abandonment. Following a plebiscite, the Saarland became part of the Federal Republic from 1 January 1957.

10 Taking the 1953 result as an example, the FDP then won only 9.5 per cent of party-list votes. This would have meant under this proposed system that the FDP would have obtained only 9.5 per cent of the 234 list seats available: a total of 23 list seats, instead of the forty-eight seats (including fourteen constituency seats) which the FDP actually obtained. The FDP may also have won a few of the fourteen constituencies under this proposed new system, but 6 of them had depended in 1953 on pacts with other parties, who did not contest those constituencies.

11 An Allensbach survey in 1968 found that only 30 per cent of respondents agreed that the Federal Republic should adopt a majority-based, first-past-the-post system for Bundestag elections (*Der Wähler*, 11, February 1968, p. 4).

12 Following a complaint that the allocation of surplus seats contravened the requirements of the Basic Law that elections be 'fair', since parties that received them acquired 'disproportional' representation at the expense of parties that did not receive them, the Constitutional Court ruled in 1997 that allocation of such seats did not breach the Basic Law (see Appendix 1, 1G).

13 In place of this committee, a meeting of all the members of the local party organisation – or organisations, if the constituency contains all or part of more than one district organisation of the party – may undertake the selection; this might occur where membership of a party is low enough to make such a meeting feasible.

14 The relationship between constituency and list seats in any Land can also be affected by other factors. These include discrepancies between population size (the basis of allocation of constituency seats to a Land) and turnout in that Land (affecting total seats for that Land), a tendency for some Länder to have smaller than average electorates for their constituencies, and the way in which seats are allocated to parties. For these reasons, in 1998 Saarland (with the highest turnout of any Land) in fact received only 3 list seats to go with 5 constituency seats, whereas Bavaria, with below-average turnout, received more list seats than constituency seats.

15 Data from Boll (1996) and Roberts (1996). It must be noted that these amounts are only for the Bundestag campaign (in 1994 numerous other elections took place at Land and Local level, as well as the European Parliament election), and are for centrally controlled expenditure. Local candidates and parties would spend considerable additional amounts on their campaigns. At a rate in 1998 of DM2.90 = £1, these sums would covert to £24 million for the CDU and SPD, nearly £5 million for the CSU, nearly £3.5 million for the FDP, £2.75 million for the PDS and about £1.7 million for the Greens.

16 A reason for choosing January, rather than March, was to use the discretionary range of dates available for scheduling Bundestag elections so that the next election could be held in late November or December (the 1990 election was in fact held in early December). This permitted elections after 1990 to be scheduled for late September or early October, allowing electoral campaigning in the late summer and early autumn, after the holiday period but in mild weather.

17 Turnout is, of course, lower in what are called 'second-order' elections in Germany, but is still high compared to some other western European countries. In Land elections in West Germany, for instance, turnout has usually been above 70 per cent, and in some cases exceeded 80 per cent, in the period prior to reunification, though it has declined markedly since 1990. Turnout in local government elections is much

higher than in Britain, for example. In elections to the European Parliament, turnout in the Federal Republic was 62.3 per cent in 1989, and 60.1 per cent in 1994 – among the highest turnout rates other than for countries such as Belgium and Luxembourg, which operate compulsory voting provisions. In 1998 the turnout for the European Parliament elections in Germany was 45 per cent.

18 Data relating to the 1998 election have been drawn largely from Forschungsgruppe Wahlen, (1998) and Veen et al. (1998).

References

Boll, B. (1996) 'Media communication and personality marketing. The 1994 German national election campaign', in G. Roberts (ed.), *Superwahljahr: The German Elections in 1994*, London, Frank Cass.

Forschungsgruppe Wahlen (1998) *Bundestagswahl 1998*, Mannheim, Forschungsgruppe Wahlen.

Roberts, G. (1988) 'The "second-vote" strategy of the West German Free Democratic Party', *European Journal of Political Research*, 16: 317–37.

Roberts, G. (1996) 'The "great escape": the FDP and the Superwahljahr', in R. Dalton (ed.), *Germans Divided. The 1994 Bundestag Elections and the Evolution of the German Party System*, Oxford, Berg.

Schindler, P. (1983) *Datenhandbuch zur Geschichte des Deutschen Bundestages 1949 bis 1982*, Bonn, Presse- und Informationszentrum des Deutschen Bundestages.

Schreiber, W. (1998) *Handbuch des Wahlrechts zum deutschen Bundestages*, Cologne, Karl Heymanns Verlag.

Statistisches Bundesamt (1998a) *Bevölkerung und Erwerbstätigkeit. Wahl zum 14 Deutschen Bundestag am 27 September 1998. Fachserie 1. Sonderheft: Die Wahlbewerber für die Wahl zum 14 Deutschen Bundestag*, Stuttgart, Metzler-Poeschel.

Statistisches Bundesamt (1998b) *Bevölkerung und Erwerbstätigkeit. Wahl zum 14 Deutschen Bundestag am 27 September 1998. Fachserie 1. Heft 3: Endgultige Ergebnisse nach Wahlkreisen*, Stuttgart, Metzler-Poeschel.

Veen, H.-J., Brunner, W., Gluchowski, P., Grof, J., Neu, V., Weilemann, P. and von Wilamowitz-Moellendorf (1998) *Analyse der Bundestagswahl vom 27 September 1998*, Sankt Augustin, Konrad-Adenauer Stiftung.

Further readings

Dalton, R. (ed.) (1996) *Germans Divided. The 1994 Bundestag Elections and the Evolution of the German Party System*, Oxford, Berg.

Green, S. (1999) 'The 1998 German Bundestag election. The end of an era', *Parliamentary Affairs*, 2: 306–20.

Roberts, G. (1988) 'The German Federal Republic: the two-lane route to Bonn', in Gallagher, M. and Marsh, M. (eds), *Candidate Selection in Comparative Perspective*, London, Sage.

Roberts, G. (ed.) (1996) *Superwahljahr: the German Elections in 1994*, London, Frank Cass.

5

The party-state

The role of parties and the legal context

Political parties play a highly significant role in the political system of the Federal Republic. Indeed, recently critics have alleged that they play too great a role (see below). The type of democratic system that the Federal Republic enjoys has been called by some experts 'party government', a concept which includes the ideas that parties give coherence and direction to government through their policy programmes, that governments depend upon popular election (and, in many cases, on the inter-party bargaining that goes on prior to the formation of governing coalitions) and that parties take responsibility for the successes or failures of policy.

This responsible role of parties in the political system is relatively new in Germany, and certainly was not found prior to the Second World War. In the Second Empire parties were secondary to powerful interest groups in terms of influencing and shaping policy. In the Weimar Republic parties remained too ideologically confined, each too concerned with the sectional interests of its clientele, to assume government responsibility or the task of policy development in the way in which parties in the Bonn Republic have done. Of course, the provisions of the Weimar constitution, especially the emergency powers of the president of the Republic, acted as a constraint on political parties, inhibiting the development of 'party government'. The Nazi period then provided 'party government' all right, but of a non-democratic type.

So when, after the Second World War, the time came to allow a degree of self-government to re-emerge in occupied West Germany, parties were seen to be a key feature. Because of their potential to contribute to the development of democracy, they were allowed to form very soon after the commencement of the occupation regime. On the other hand, because of their potential to obstruct or pervert democracy – as experience in the inter-war period had so clearly shown – it was decided by the allies that political parties had to be licensed by the occupation authorities (see chapter 1). When it came to the drafting of a temporary constitution for the Federal Republic in 1948–49, the role of parties in the political system was addressed, and this role was given explicit expression in Article

76

21 of the Basic Law, which also imposed responsibilities and restrictions on the parties. This inclusion of the role of political parties in a democratic constitution was extremely novel, largely because many other democratic constitutions pre-dated the modern democratic activity of parties.

Box 5.1
Article 21 of the Basic Law

1 Parties participate in the formation of the political will of the people. The formation of parties is unconstrained. Their internal organisation must be congruent with the basic democratic order. They must publish accounts relating to their sources of income and their expenditures, as well as their property.
2 Parties whose aims, or whose members' behaviour, are detrimental to or seek to abolish the free democratic basic order or to endanger the continued existence of the Federal Republic of Germany, are unconstitutional. The question of unconstitutionality is to be decided by the federal constitutional court.
3 Details are provided in federal legislation.

The section of this Article of the Basic Law which states that non-democratic parties can be condemned as unconstitutional was twice the basis of cases in the Constitutional Court which resulted in bans being imposed on political parties. The extreme right-wing Socialist Reich Party was banned in 1952, and the Communist Party in 1956, on the grounds that they did not conform to the requirements of Article 21 that political parties should not be hostile to the democratic constitutional system (see Appendix 1, 1A).

The production of legislation to fulfil the requirement of paragraph 3 of Article 21 did not occur for several years. In the early years of the Federal Republic, there seemed to be more pressing priorities than designing rules for political parties in order to implement the requirement in Article 21 of the Basic Law that a law should be produced to provide detailed regulation of political parties. However, once the political parties found that their finances were threatened by the absence of such legislation (see below), they quickly drew up a Party Law, which was passed by the Bundestag and Bundesrat in 1967. This law elaborated on the status and role of political parties, in relation to their constitutional responsibility defined in Article 21 of 'participating in the formation of the political will of the people'. It set out the defining characteristics of political parties for purposes of the law, including the requirement of regular contestation of Bundestag and Land elections. It provided a framework for party structures and procedures, and for the protection of the rights of party members, standards with which parties had to comply and implement in their own statutes. It regulated the financial relationship between parties and the state, by making available subsidies to the costs of election campaigning, based on the relative shares of the vote which parties received at the election.[1]

Together, Article 21 and the Party Law of 1967 provide an unusually explicit legal context within which German political parties must act. Few other West European democracies possess either such constitutional or legal regulation of parties. This context conveys privileges.[2] However, it also conveys responsibilities, and, in doing so, reinforces 'party government' in Germany, since parties can point to this legal context and claim that, alongside the Bundestag and Bundesrat, the chancellor, the federal president, the Constitutional Court and the federal system, they are organs of the state and not just a set of extra-constitutional voluntary organisations.

The structure of the party system

The party system of the Federal Republic prior to reunification in 1990 consisted of four parties with representation in the Bundestag: the Christian Democrats;[3] the SPD; the FDP and the Greens. In addition, a variety of smaller parties existed, few of which were ever of any significance at federal level.

The West German party system had, in the early years of the Federal Republic, consisted of a much larger number of parties, but several factors contributed to the swift reduction in that number, so that from 1961 until the entry of the Greens into the Bundestag in 1983, only three parties were represented in the Bundestag (see chapter 4, Table 4.2).

This reduction in the number of parties by 1961 was produced partly by the strictures of the electoral system resulting from revisions in 1953 and 1956 (see chapter 4). The need to obtain 5 per cent of list votes calculated for the whole of the Federal Republic (or three constituency seats) not only made it more difficult for small parties to retain Bundestag representation; it also made it difficult for new parties to break through and win seats, as the NPD experienced in 1969 and as the Greens found in 1980. A second factor was the transformation of the two largest parties, the CDU-CSU and the SPD, into 'catch-all parties', enabling them to appeal to voters beyond the confines of their traditional church-related or working-class milieux. This made it easier for them to attract voters who otherwise might have voted for alternative parties, such as the Catholic Centre party, which had been so strong in the Second Empire and Weimar Republic periods, and which had survived chiefly in parts of North Rhine-Westphalia after the Second World War, but which soon found competition from the CDU-CSU too strong. Third, the rulings of the Constitutional Court in 1952 and 1956 which banned the extreme right-wing SRP and the KPD were important. These verdicts did not so much have an effect by eliminating those two parties themselves; after all, in terms of national politics they had become of negligible importance and neither had seats in the Bundestag when the ban was imposed. Rather they emphasised that the government and the Constitutional Court were prepared to invoke the provisions of the Basic Law which required parties to be democratic, and this may have deterred other extremist parties from forming at all or, if they did form, from contesting elections. Fourth, the success of Adenauer's Christian Democratic government in providing stability, security and prosperity for West Germany meant that more and more voters were prepared to support that government. It also meant that the Christian Democrats were successful in 'taking-over' politicians and supporters of other parties with which it had been allied, such as the DP. Only the Liberal FDP resisted successfully this gravitational pull of the Christian Democrats, despite Adenauer's attempt to debilitate that party in 1956.[4]

Only one new party succeeded in winning seats in the Bundestag between 1961 and the reunification of Germany in 1990. The Greens were successful in the 1983 Bundestag election, having built up strength in several of the Länder, and after having contested the 1980 Bundestag election without success. They managed to overcome the obstacles and constraints of the electoral system by drawing upon what had become a widespread environmentalist movement, and which coincided with an upsurge in support for the peace movement in the Federal Republic. This in turn reflected a new political mood among some sections of the population, concerned with 'new politics' issues (see chapter 11) and rejective of the orthodox parties and their procedures.

From time to time other parties have promised to attain national significance. The Refugees party (*GB/BHE*) won Bundestag seats in the 1953 election. However, as refugees from areas east of the 'iron curtain' which had once been part of Germany became more integrated into West German society and as the likelihood receded that those territories, which were now part of Poland, Czechoslovakia (as it then was) or the USSR, would ever again be part of a German state, so those refugee voters gave their support to other parties, especially to the CDU and CSU. Radical right-wing parties also found support from time to time. The most prominent examples were the NPD in the 1960s, which won seats in several Land parliaments but failed narrowly in 1969 to win Bundestag seats, and the Republicans, a party formed by dissident CSU politicians, which won seats in some Land parliaments (especially in Baden-Württemberg in 1992 and again in 1996) and in the European Parliament in 1989, but which in Bundestag elections has never won more than just over 2 per cent of the vote.

Of course, Bundestag representation is not everything. Despite their failure to win seats at Bundestag elections, some of these parties, by their policies and because of their intermittent ability to win local or regional support, have influenced the agenda of the Bundestag parties, on matters such as political asylum or the European integration projects.

Reunification had a relatively small effect on the party system. A fifth party, the PDS, has entered the Bundestag, and for one legislative period (1990–94) the West German Greens lost their Bundestag representation. Beyond that, and despite very considerable West German–East German differences in levels of party support, the broad framework of the party system so far remains fundamentally unchanged.

   The party systems of the Länder have tended to mirror that of the Federal Republic. In the early post-war years a number of parties developed locally: the Bavarian Party, and conservative Protestant or nationalist parties in northern Germany, for instance, but since the 1960s have tended to disappear or decline into irrelevance. The party representing the Danish cultural minority in Schleswig-Holstein (and which has protected rights of representation in the Schleswig-Holstein Land parliament under the Land constitution) still exists there as a factor in Land politics. Radical right-wing parties have won seats from time to time in Land parliaments: the NPD in the 1960s; the Republicans in south Germany and the German People's Union (Deutsche Volksunion, DVU) in north Germany more recently (see Chapter 11, Table 11.1). The STATT-party, formed by discontented CDU members in Hamburg, sensationally won seats in the Hamburg Land parliament in 1993, but, though drawn into the Land government as the junior partner to the SPD, suffered from internal quarrels and decline in support and failed to win any seats in the 1998 Hamburg Land election.[5] Of course, the relative weight of the parties in each Land varies very considerably. The PDS is strong in all the East German Länder but in none of the West German Länder. The SPD has its strongholds in Bremen, Hamburg and North Rhine-Westphalia, and more recently also in Saarland and Brandenburg, for instance. The Christian Democrats are strong in Bavaria, Saxony and Baden-Württemberg. The FDP has been relatively strong in Baden-Württemberg, but otherwise finds that its support can fluctuate considerably in every Land, though it is extremely weak in East Germany, and since 1994 has not been represented in the parliaments of any of the 'new Länder'. The Greens have built up support especially in Hamburg, Hesse and Baden-Württemberg, but even though they merged with the East German citizen-movement party, Alliance '90, are also, like the FDP, relatively weak in the 'new Länder'.

The political parties: orientation and support

The Christian Democrats

The CDU was formed as a new party after the Second World War. Before Hitler came to power, Catholics had had their own party, the Centre party, but Protestants had never had an equivalent single party which represented their denominational interests. The moral and physical devastation that the Hitler regime had brought upon Germany led many German Christians to look to their religion as the only social force which had not been perverted by Nazism, and which could serve as a guiding principle for political life in post-war Germany. Indeed, Christian Democracy became a popular political creed in many countries of devastated post-war western Europe. Parties formed locally in the western zones of occupation, based on Christian ideals but without denominational distinction. The main centres for the growth of Christian

Democratic parties were Berlin, Bavaria and the Rhineland. The Berlin party
was restricted and influenced by policies pursued by the Soviet occupation
authorities, and so was not regarded in West Germany as possessing the autonomy or legitimacy which would enable it to offer leadership to other regions.
The Bavarian Christian Democratic party, which developed and remained as a
separate party, the Christian Social Union, was very much a Catholic party,
reflecting the predominance of Catholicism among the population, and one
that was jealous of Bavarian particularism, so was also not seen as suited to
providing leadership to other Christian Democratic parties. The Rhineland
party, led by the aged but ambitious former lord mayor of Cologne, Konrad
Adenauer, was able to give such leadership, especially once Adenauer was
elected as chairman of the Parliamentary Council which drafted the Basic Law
and then became the first chancellor of the Federal Republic following the
1949 Bundestag election.

The CDU was structured very much as a federation, leaving considerable
autonomy to Land party organisations. Indeed, the first federal congress of the
party did not take place until 1950. In the Bundestag, the CDU has always
formed a single Fraktion in the Bundestag with the CSU, and by agreement did
not compete in Bavaria; the CSU, though several times tempted to do so, has
never presented candidates outside Bavaria.[6]

The CDU succeeded in the 1950s and 1960s in attracting electoral support
from voters of all social classes, particularly those who attended church regularly. It had a 'social wing' which emphasised policies of social welfare. It continued to be seen as associated more strongly with the Catholic church than
with Protestant churches. This explains why it has been strongest in south
Germany and those western regions of the Federal Republic close to the river
Rhine, the staunchest Catholic areas of Germany. With the decline in church
attendance over the past two decades, the party has become identified by the
electorate less as a party primarily representing Christian ideas and ideals, and
more clearly as a conservative party, associated with anti-socialism and the free
market economy. Its programme, though still paying lip-service to Christian
values, reflects this emphasis on the economy and growth, and the 'social wing'
of the party has less influence now on policy development.

The Christian Social Union developed a dual role: as the Bavarian 'sister-
party' of the CDU, and so engaged in national politics as part of the Christian
Democratic parliamentary group (and, when the CDU-CSU is in government,
always filling a number of influential cabinet posts); and as the party representing Bavaria's special interests within the Federal Republic. By the mid-1960s it
had overcome the challenge of the Bavarian Party, which had seats in the
Bavarian Land parliament until 1966, and since then the CSU has been dominant within the Bavarian party system, securing absolute majorities of seats
and thus governing without the constraints of a coalition. Relations with the
CDU have sometime been tense, especially while Franz Josef Strauss was leader.
Indeed, Strauss was selected as the Christian Democrats' chancellor-candidate

for the 1980 Bundestag election, though he was not very successful. The support of the CSU in 1990–91 for an East German party, the German Social Union (DSU), also tested the CSU's alliance with the CDU, which had to compete against the DSU for votes in East Germany. The electoral failures of the DSU and its political tactics, such as pursuing radical right-wing policies, anyway soon persuaded the CSU to terminate its aid to the DSU.

The Christian Democratic parties (CDU and CSU) won 41 per cent of list votes in 1994, but only 35 per cent in 1998. In 1996 the CDU had 646,000 members; the CSU had 180,000 members (Jesse, 1997, p. 194).

The Social Democratic Party

The SPD traces its roots back to its formation in 1875 as the German Socialist Workers' Party. It became the largest party in the Reichstag just before the First World War, then played a major role in proclaiming a republican form of government in November 1918 as that war terminated, and contributed to the formation of the Weimar Republic in 1919. It remained an important party throughout the lifetime of the Weimar Republic, providing the first president of the Republic (Friedrich Ebert) and two chancellors, and participating in several governments during the period. The party was banned by the Nazis on 22 June 1933. Many of its leading politicians were imprisoned during the Third Reich or else went into exile in Britain, in the USA or in Scandinavian countries, for example. The SPD was able to revive its organisation after the Second World War, under the licensing arrangements operated by the occupation authorities. In East Germany the Soviets acted as patrons of a merger in 1946 in their zone between the SPD and the Communist Party (to form the SED). However, in the western zones the SPD, led by Kurt Schumacher – a former concentration-camp victim who, like many SPD veterans of Weimar politics, deeply distrusted the Communist Party – rejected any idea of such fusion.[7] The SPD had successes in several of the Land elections held in the period 1946–47, and was for many years the largest party in Hesse, Bremen, Hamburg, and Lower Saxony. However, in Bundestag elections, though it increased its vote share steadily from 1957–72, only in the 1972 election did it emerge as the largest party. It was a member of the 'grand coalition' from 1966–1969, then provided the chancellor from 1969 to 1982, when it was in coalition with the FDP. After it was forced into opposition in 1982, the SPD failed to secure more than 40 per cent of the vote at any Bundestag election until its victory in the 1998 election (40.9 per cent) when, for only the second time since 1949, it became the largest party in the Bundestag. Competition from the Greens for younger, more radical, members and voters has cost the party some of its former support, and the rivalry of the PDS in eastern Germany has restricted the strength of the SPD in the 'new Länder'.

The party has been reliant on the support of working-class voters, especially those who are trade union members, and usually those who are not church-going Catholics. Since the adoption of its Bad Godesberg programme in 1959, which abandoned Marxist ideas and allowed the party to appeal to a more heterogeneous range of voters, it has won electoral support also from 'white-collar' voters. The SPD has centres of support in urban areas, particularly those associated with heavy industry or extractive industries: the Ruhr, the Saarland, Bremen, Hamburg and Berlin. In 1996 the SPD had 794,000 members (Jesse, 1997, p. 194).

The Free Democratic Party

The FDP, like the Christian Democrats, was a newly invented party after the Second World War. In the Second Empire and the Weimar Republic, the liberals had been organised into at least two separate parties, which weakened them politically. The post-war situation provided an impetus to unite the various strands of liberalism into one organisation. This was made easier by the licensing policy of the allies and by the strategy in the western Länder of allowing parties to form locally first, and only then at Land level. This meant that, despite the very wide range of ideas and perspectives included in various local and regional liberal parties, a single liberal party, the FDP, was able to be formed at a conference of delegates of the Länder liberal parties held at Heppenheim in 1948.

However, organisational unity was one thing; ideological agreement was another. The FDP was plagued by internal conflicts throughout its history, especially between a more nationalist and free-market economy-oriented right wing, associated in its early years with the Hesse and North Rhine-Westphalia parties in particular, and the more 'liberal democratic' outlook associated with the Hamburg, Bremen and Baden-Württemberg parties. In broad terms, the 'national liberal' wing dominated until 1966, then (after a period of adjustment of the party's ideas and leaders whilst in opposition to the 'grand coalition') the liberal-democratic wing took the party into coalition with the SPD in 1969. The reassertion of the perspectives of the free-market wing in the 1980s was linked with the change by the party in 1982 from support of the SPD to coalition with the CDU-CSU. This dominance in the party of free-market policies, such as reductions in the tax burden for companies, has remained throughout the period of the Kohl government, with only occasional and not very significant rebellions by those more concerned with civil rights and social policies. The party provided the Foreign Minister in all governments from 1969 until 1998, and so has been influential in shaping the foreign policies of the Federal Republic. These policies have included *Ostpolitik* in the Brandt era and, during the period when Hans-Dietrich Genscher was Foreign Minister, policies promoting *détente* under the chancellorships of Schmidt and Kohl, and of course German reunification.

Not only has the party never overcome its minority status (its vote in Bundestag elections has fluctuated between just under 6 per cent and 12 per cent), it also lacks any significant base of loyal voters. Many of its voters support the party only for one or two elections, then give their support to a different party. It has no 'milieu', such as the churches for the CDU-CSU or the trade unions for the SPD, upon which it can rely for long-term support. It draws many of its votes from those in self-employment, and members of the professions, such as accountants, pharmacists or dentists, but this is not enough to provide a 'cushion' of electoral support. It is therefore not really possible to identify regions where the party is especially strong, though traditionally it has been most successful in Baden-Württemberg, and has recently been relatively strong in Hesse and Rhineland-Pfalz. Paradoxically, despite being a weak party electorally, constantly having to be anxious about retaining its representation in the Bundestag, it has been a member of federal coalitions for more years than either the Christian Democrats or the SPD. However, its pivotal role in the party system has been weakened by its relegation to fourth place behind the Greens in 1994 and 1998, and the presence of the PDS in the Bundestag also reduces the possibility of the FDP again being able to determine which of the two large parties will lead the government. In 1996 the FDP had 76,000 members (Jesse, 1997, p. 194).

The Greens

The Greens (since 1993 officially named Alliance '90/the Greens) formed as a party in the Federal Republic in 1980. Local citizen initiative groups concerned about environmental issues had, in some Länder, contested Land elections and had won significant electoral support, though not enough to win seats. These groups co-ordinated a campaign for the 1979 European Parliament elections, winning 3.2 per cent of the vote: enough to encourage them to create a national organisation. Though the Greens failed to win seats in the 1980 Bundestag election, with only 1.5 per cent of the vote, they did enter the Bundestag in 1983 and 1987. They also won seats in most of the Länder parliaments, and participated in governing coalitions in several Länder. Partly because of the party's hostile attitude to German reunification, partly because it was internally riven by conflicts between its more radical 'fundamentalist' wing ('Fundis') and its more pragmatic 'realist' wing ('Realos') concerning policy and strategy, the Greens narrowly failed to secure the required 5 per cent in the 1990 Bundestag election, and so did not win seats.[8] In the 1994 Bundestag election, the Greens not only easily overcame the 5 per cent hurdle, they also managed for the first time to win more votes than the FDP, and in 1998 they won 6.7 per cent of list votes.

After reunification, the Greens of West and East Germany joined together in one organisation in December 1990, and then in May 1993 this party linked up with the party of the East German citizen movement, Alliance '90 (Bündnis '90). However, in terms both of membership strength and electoral support, the Greens are very much a West German party. They are represented in none of the legislatures of the 'new Länder' of the former GDR, but in all of the West German Länder parliaments. Since 1991, when many of the 'Fundis' left the party, a more pragmatic approach to both party organisation and policy has allowed the Greens to become a coalition partner for the SPD in several Land governments and, since the 1998 Bundestag election, in the federal government also. Their policies, while strongly focused on environmental and ecological issues, also place emphasis on gender equality,[9] anti-militarism, internationalism, and participatory democracy. Whilst still most obviously a potential coalition partner for the SPD, the Greens have co-operated in local government with Christian Democrats, and there have been suggestions that some time in the future coalitions at Land or even federal level with the Christian Democrats would not be impossible. The Greens had 49,000 members in 1997, of which just under 3,000 were in the 'new Länder'. Only 35.5 per cent of members were female (Hoffmann, 1998, p. 264).

The Party of Democratic Socialism

When the Berlin Wall was opened in November 1989, the ruling party, the SED, was in deep crisis. The pressure for reform of the political system meant that the SED could no longer rely on its ideologically and constitutionally anchored role of being the 'leading party' in the state. In December 1989, it decided to undergo a thorough and radical reform of its structures and of some aspects of its ideology and programme. The result was the transformation, in stages, of the SED into the PDS, which sees itself as a left-wing and socialist party (though it contains within it groups who defend communism, such as the 'Communist Platform'). Deliberately, the PDS remained legally the heir to the SED rather than re-forming itself as a completely new party, so that it could retain the offices, the staff, the financial and other resources and of course the membership of the SED. However, this left it open to charges that it was still a party that was ambivalent about multi-party democracy, defensive concerning the misdeeds, corruption and inefficiency of the SED regime, and hostile to reunification, at least to reunification on the terms by which the old GDR was merged into the Federal Republic.

Many observers thought that, precisely because it was so obviously linked to the old regime, the PDS would be unsuccessful in elections, would lose members, and would have to cede most of its financial resources to the state (on the grounds that these resources had been improperly acquired in the days of the GDR). It would thus soon decline into political irrelevance. However, the party managed to do fairly well in the elections of 1990, including successes in the Bundestag election that year (thanks to a special dispensation of the electoral system for the 1990 election: see chapter 4). The party survived various crises, especially associated with its finances, in the period 1991–94, and in '*Superwahljahr*' in 1994 the PDS benefited from the discontent and economic insecurity of many East German voters, who found that reunification did not immediately and universally bring the prosperity and security that they had anticipated. The PDS managed to win four East Berlin constituencies in the 1994 Bundestag election (thus bypassing the 5 per cent provision of the Electoral Law) and, with an increased vote compared to the 1990 Bundestag election, secured a total of thirty Bundestag seats. In 1998 it obtained 5 per cent of list votes, so did not need the alternative route of winning at least three constituencies (though it did in fact win four constituencies, as in 1994). In eastern Germany in the 1998 Bundestag election the PDS won 21.6 per cent of the vote. It has seats in all five of the East German Land parliaments, as well as in the Berlin Land legislature and, since the 1999 election, in the European Parliament. In 1997 the PDS had 100,000 members, of which only 2,600 resided in West Germany (Moreau, 1998, p. 97).

The party has an ageing membership, many of whom are unemployed or already pensioners, and this means that, apart from other reasons, its membership will decline over the next few years. However, many of these members retain the commitment and discipline of the old SED, and are far more active than members of other parties in the new Länder. They are thus able to mobilise voters for elections effectively. In East Germany, the PDS has the largest membership of any party. The PDS electorate includes above average shares of voters under forty-five years of age, but also includes some older voters, fearful that they are the losers from reunification, perhaps unable to find employment, or unable to retain their former employment because of their political activity in the GDR.

The programme of the party focuses on protection of East German interests in the enlarged Federal Republic, is critical of the social market economy and especially the emphasis of the social market economy on economic competition, is opposed to militarism and participation in military alliances, and demands an early end to criminal proceedings against GDR politicians or others accused of 'regime crimes' – proceedings which it views as a kind of 'victor's justice', as 'revenge' by the capitalist West Germans on defeated Communists. The party considers itself the victim of what it sees as almost a conspiracy of the other parties, who seem to wish to deny that the PDS is a legitimate democratic party, and these other parties certainly have regarded the PDS as one with which other parties could not co-operate. However, in the second half of the 1990s, many SPD activists in eastern Germany tried to persuade their party to adopt a more co-operative attitude to the PDS, and a Land coalition government of the SPD and PDS was formed in Mecklenburg-Vorpommern in 1998, following the Land election there.

Parties of the far right

The Federal Republic has always been very sensitive to the possibility of the re-emergence of Nazism in any form. The Basic Law, provisions of the criminal law and the operations of the Federal and Länder Offices for the Protection of the Constitution are evidence of this (see also chapter 11). The policies of the

western occupation powers, including the licensing of parties, also were shaped
by this anxiety about Nazism. Consequently, there is a built in prejudice in the
political system and in the political culture of the Federal Republic against
parties of the far right. Nevertheless, there have been phases in the history of
the Federal Republic when such parties have emerged, sometimes on a regional
basis, and when they have gathered significant electoral support. The Socialist
Reich Party developed in the early years of the Federal Republic, securing substantial electoral support in Land elections in Lower Saxony and Bremen in
1951, but was so blatantly nationalist and anti-democratic that it became the
first party to be banned by the Constitutional Court under the provisions of
Article 21. Several radical right-wing groups merged to form the National
Democratic Party in the 1960s, and that party then secured seats in several
Land parliaments prior to the 1969 Bundestag election. However, it failed –
narrowly – to overcome the 5 per cent 'barrier' for entry to the Bundestag
(winning 4.3 per cent of the vote), and then declined into insignificance,
though in the 1990s has had some successes in local elections.

The German People's Union won seats in the Bremen Land election (in
1987, 1991 and 1999) and in the Schleswig-Holstein Land legislature in
1992, and came extremely close to winning seats in the Hamburg Land election in 1997 (4.9 per cent). It secured a surprisingly high share of the vote in
the Saxony-Anhalt Land election in 1998 – 12.9 per cent. In 1999 it obtained
seats in the Brandenburg Land parliament (5.2 per cent), and won over 3 per
cent in the Thuringia Land election. It is, though, a negligible political force in
Bundestag elections (in 1998, 1.2 per cent).

The Republican party has had greater success. It was formed in 1983 by renegade politicans from the CSU, dissatisfied with the policies and leadership of
Franz Josef Strauss. It surprisingly won seats in the West Berlin city election in
1989, and then in the same year won seats in the European Parliament, in both
elections securing over 7 per cent of the vote. It won over 10 per cent of the vote
in the 1992 Baden-Württemberg Land election, and again won seats in that
Land legislature in the 1996 election. In 1990 it won 4.9 per cent in the
Bavarian Land election, and in 1993 it won 4.8 per cent of the vote in the
Hamburg city election, just missing out on qualification for seats in both elections. However, having support mainly concentrated in south Germany, the
party has had little success in other Land elections, and failed to retain its representation in the European Parliament in the 1994 election, nor did it win
seats in the 1999 European Parliament election. In Bundestag elections, it won
only about 2 per cent in 1990, 1994 and 1998. Crises in the party concerning
the style and decisions of its former leader, Franz Schönhuber, have damaged
the party and it is now no longer considered as a significant party outside the
southern Länder.

In addition, several other organisations have existed, or still exist, which
embrace racist, ultra-nationalist or other extremist ideas. Some of these organisations use the word 'party' in their titles, but few, if any, of them ever compete

in elections or otherwise meet the criteria of the Party Law which would qualify them as political parties. Consequently, they can be – and sometimes are – subject to the imposition of bans by the Minister of the Interior under Article 9 of the Basic Law (see chapter 11).

Why have such parties and organisations, some of them extremist in their policies and political style, had any degree of success in the Federal Republic? After all, denazification and re-education policies of the occupying powers, coupled with the revulsion that the Germans themselves have come to possess against Nazism, surely made Germany the last place in western Europe where racist or xenophobic political ideas could ever again find support? Various theories have been suggested.

One of the least convincing is that the followers of such parties represent a continuation of Nazism. Certainly in terms of the individuals themselves today, very few of them are old enough to have qualified for membership even of the childrens' or youth organisations of the Nazi party, let alone for full membership of that party. In any case, research demonstrates that these right-wing extremist parties appeal mainly to young people. It is true that some radical right-wing movements have defended the policies and actions of Hitler and his associates, and use Nazi symbols to shock as much as for any other purpose. But it is difficult to imagine that the members, let alone the voters or sympathisers, of such parties really know much about the ideology of national socialism; their proclaimed goals do not differ that much from those of extremist organisations and parties in other European countries.

Another theory is that such groups attract support when the economic situation deteriorates. The NPD seemed to benefit from the economic recession in the early 1960s, for example, and the success of the DVU in Saxony-Anhalt was attributed by analysts to the economic problems in eastern Germany. But there seems little evidence that the rise of electoral support for these groups is linked closely to deterioration either in the objective economic situation or the subjective views of respondents about their own economic prospects.

Third, it can be proposed that particular circumstances or situations can lead to increases in support for radical right-wing parties. Certainly the growth of the protest movements of the 1960s in Germany seemed to encourage support for the NPD from those most offended by the activities of protestors. In the 1980s and early 1990s, the influx of migrants and asylum-seekers certainly had much to do with increased electoral support for the Republicans, DVU and, locally, the NPD; and once the provision in the Basic Law and related legislation concerning asylum applications were revised and made more rigorous, such support declined sharply. The changes associated with reunification also led to support for xenophobic groups in East Germany, though their support was not translated into significant electoral support for exteme right-wing political parties, other than in the Saxony-Anhalt Land election in 1998.

This analysis might be a particular case of a fourth type of explanation: that voters support such parties as a protest against the non-responsiveness of the established, orthodox parties, particularly non-responsiveness associated with disturbing social change. When responsiveness improves, this support melts away. This implies that the phenomenon of support for 'populist' or extreme right-wing parties in Germany is not a peculiarly 'German' problem, but that it is a problem shared by several other democracies, including France, Italy, Belgium and Austria.

The political parties: organisation and finances

The organisation of political parties in Germany is based on the way in which parties have developed since the nineteenth century, modified by the demands of the present-day situation (such as modern election campaigning techniques, demands for increased membership participation and the desire to promote greater gender equality within the party). However, since the introduction of the Party Law of 1967, parties have to ensure that their organisational structures and procedures comply with the standards set out in that legislation. Each party has a set of statutes (*Satzung*) which codify the structures and procedures of its organisation.

The sovereign organ of each party is its party congress, which is the kind of 'parliament' of the party. This usually meets annually, and is composed of delegates from the Länder parties (or their equivalent). The congress, among other things, elects the principal officers of the party, including the party leader and the members of the party Executive, discusses and decides on matters relating to the organisation of the party and the policy programme of the party and, when appropriate, issues of electoral strategy (such as coalition options). A smaller version of the party congress, consisting of around 100 delegates, meets occasionally to take decisions in the intervals between party congresses. The party usually has an Executive committee to discuss and take decisions on matters on a day-to-day basis. The party head office – much more generously staffed than those of equivalent British political parties – is controlled on behalf of the Executive committee by a Business Manager (*Geschäftsführer*), who in many parties operates under the political guidance of a General Secretary, elected by the party congress and who co-ordinates the political work of the various organs of the party. The General Secretary may be a Member of the Bundestag, and in practice the post is often a step towards ministerial office.

Because Germany is a federal state, this pattern of organisation – on a much smaller scale, naturally – is repeated at the Land level (or the region – often though not always corresponding to a Land – in the case of the SPD). Here, too, can be found a party congress, an Executive committee, a leader and a head office under the control of a Business Manager (in some ways equivalent to the British constituency agent). Within the Land party there are district party organisations, equivalent to the British constituency party or city party, and each district contains smaller local party organisations. The party statutes describe the ways in which individual members can attend meetings and vote, including voting to elect representatives to higher-level organs of the party.

The party organisation in the Bundestag (known as the Fraktion) also has its structure. Its members will elect its officers (including a Fraktion leader, who sometimes is also the leader of the party), decide on who gets committee assignments and responsibility for particular policy areas, and allocate responsibilities to its paid staff. The complexity of this level of organisation will, of course, vary with the size of the party: the FDP, the PDS and the Greens do not need the same complex structure in the Bundestag as the Christian Democrats or the SPD. Similar forms of organisation, though on an appropriately smaller scale, are to be found in Land parliaments.

All this organisation costs money to maintain. Fortunately for the German parties, they are relatively wealthy, in terms of income. This is not to say that they do not have financial anxieties; having grown used to relatively large incomes, they have become used to equivalently high levels of expenditure. Party financing has long been a matter of controversy in the Federal Republic. Indeed, it was the problem of regulating the financing of parties which led to the passage of the Party Law in 1967 (see Appendix 1, 1C). While the SPD has relied upon contributions from its millions of members, the parties of the right looked to business for donations. All parties expected generous subsidies from the state itself. The Party Law changed this system, instituting restrictions on sources of finance, and formalising the system of state subsidies so that parties received shares according to their electoral strength. Modifications in 1983 and 1988 changed the system again, in a number of ways, with the aim of encouraging more self-financing of parties and providing assistance to smaller parties less able to benefit from membership subscriptions and individual donations. However, many thought the system to be still unsatisfactory. A decision of the Constitutional Court in 1992 on a complaint brought by the Greens, and the report of a presidentially appointed committee of independent experts based on that Court decision, led to radical reform of the system of state financing. Legislation introduced in 1994 provided for the payment to parties of DM1.30 for each vote received in Bundestag elections (and elections to the European Parliament) to a maximum of 5 million votes, then DM1 for each additional vote, together with matching funds related to the subscriptions and donations which a party receives from individuals (up to a limit of DM6,000 per donor).

Following reunification, there was a problem concerning the accumulated wealth of the former 'block parties' of the GDR, but especially the SED, which had enriched themselves through their unconstrained control of the state and the economy. An Independent Committee on Party Property tried to make an accounting of the wealth of each party, identify what funds, offices and buildings and other forms of property each party could justifiably claim as having been acquired legitimately in relation to its activities as a political party, and confiscate the rest. After much travail and controversy, settlements were reached with all the parties involved.

Each party must, by law, publish annual accounts of the sources of its income and – since this was added to Article 21 of the Basic Law in 1983 – also of the forms of expenditure. Such accounts reveal that the smaller parties in particular have, in recent years, relied heavily on state subsidies for a significant portion of their income. Other important sources of income are: membership subscriptions (the level of subscription usually varying according to the income of each member); donations from individuals and groups; a proportion of the salaries received by those elected from the party to the Bundestag, Land parliaments or the European Parliament; and commercial income (such as publishing or the rent of premises owned by the party). The principal forms of expenditure are: salaries of employees; election campaign expenses; and running costs for the offices and meetings of organs of the party.

The political parties: functions

The range of functions of political parties in Germany is not very different from that of parties in other western democratic states. First, by their participation the political parties structure elections and present candidates for election. This function of participating regularly in elections is recognised in the Party Law, which declared it to be one of the defining characteristics of a political party. For Bundestag and Land elections, it is very exceptional for constituency candidates who are not nominated by a political party to stand for election, though in some Land elections non-party groups occasionally present candidates. The electoral campaigns of the parties offer the voter choices; not quite the choice between alternative single-party governments which is the case in the United Kingdom and the USA, but nowadays something approaching the choice between party 'blocks' similar to that on offer in French national elections, since it has been more or less clear at every election since that of 1969 which coalitions were likely to form after every Bundestag election. In the Bundestag elections of 1994 and 1998, for example, it was clear that the existing coalition of the Christian Democrats and FDP would continue in office if it secured an overall majority; it was also clear that a coalition between the SPD and the Greens would very probably come into office if that pairing of parties obtained a majority of seats (despite the avoidance of any explicit declaration to that effect by the SPD). There was a slight degree of uncertainty concerning options should the FDP fail to overcome the 5 per cent qualification requirement and if the size of the PDS contingent prevented the SPD and Greens from having an overall majority (a 'grand coalition' may well have resulted), but these were the only uncertain factors.

So a second function of political parties is to form governments. At federal level, that usually means coalition governments. Only once, in 1957, could one party have governed alone with a majority of Bundestag seats (and even then Adenauer rejected that option). (The constraints on coalition formation and coalition maintenance are analysed in chapter 7.) Thus, government in Germany is 'party government', with parties shaping the policy programmes pursued by governments, providing nominees for cabinet posts and for many other ministerial and administrative positions, and securing support for such policies through their local, regional and national organisations. Parties develop policy in a variety of ways, including through a range of permanent commissions or *ad hoc* working groups, which can utilise expertise from within the party and can link elected representatives with party members, but which also can draw upon experts who are not linked to the party.

A third function is representation of interests particularly associated with the party, and of the supporters upon whom the party relies at elections. In some cases the link between interests and party are obvious: the churches and the CDU-CSU, the trade unions and the SPD, the environmental movement and the Greens, East Germans resentful of the outcome of the reunification process and the PDS, higher-rate taxpayers and the FDP. But the link can be more subtle. Since every vote given to a party counts, each party can benefit from demonstrating that it has the interests of all sections of the public at heart. It does this by means of campaign publicity (and communications directed at members of particular groups, such as lawyers, trade unionists, pensioners or owners of small business companies are an increasingly common form of campaigning now). A party can also show its concern by placing interest group representatives high on its party lists in certain Länder; trade union officials or members of commercial interest group organisations, for example. However, there has been increasing criticism that parties are failing in this function of representation, with consequences for public support for the parties as an institution (see below).

Fourth, parties have a constitutionally recognised function to 'participate in the formation of the political will of the people' (Article 21): in other words, to engage in political education. Indeed, they have relied upon this obligation to make their claim for funding from the state, claiming that it is as much a constitutionally imposed obligation as is legislation for the Bundestag or government leadership for the chancellor. Parties claim that their electoral campaigning in particular is one way in which they perform this function, but other activities, ranging from giving constituents a guided tour of the Bundestag to making speeches in the constituency, can also be part of this function. However, political education in its most explicit form has been 'contracted-out' by the parties, to their associated 'political Foundations' (Stiftungen).[10] These Foundations are, in theory, organisationally separate from the parties. They receive their own subsidies from the state. They undertake a range of activities: holding conferences; providing courses on political or other topics for adults, for party officers, for young people, for trade unionists and other specialised groups; undertaking and publishing research; maintaining archives relating to the party; doing 'political missionary' work in other countries (several were very active in Spain and Portugal when those countries became democracies in the 1970s, and in eastern Europe after the fall of communism); and producing books and pamphlets, for example.

The 'party-state' in Germany

Many commentators have described the political system of the Federal Republic as a 'party-state'. By this they do not mean that it resembles the 'one-party state' systems of Nazi Germany, the USSR or (in effect, if not in form) the GDR. They use the term to highlight the unusually close links between political parties and the state.

These links derive originally from two sources: the tendency of the Germans to look to legal provisions for the structuring and control of social institutions of all kinds – banks, sports clubs, open-air markets, churches, and so on. So the legal framework within which political parties operate in Germany is not seen as inappropriate or remarkable, even though only a very few other European democracies, such as Austria, Portugal and Spain, have imitated Germany in producing such legal regulation of parties. The second source was the desire of the occupying powers after the Second World War to ensure that the perversion of political parties which led to Hitler's dictatorship should never again occur. So the system of licensing led to the inclusion of parties in the Basic Law and that, in turn, led to the Party Law of 1967 and its later amendments.

However, the parties themselves have exploited this legal framework in order to increase their own role in the state. The system of state financing of political parties has been outlined above. In addition to overt financial assistance from the state to political parties, there are other ways in which financial benefits accrue to the parties: the payment of state subsidies to party Foundations and the provision of staff to the party groups (Fraktionen) in the federal and Land legislatures are examples. The parties have also combined to increase levels of salaries and allowances for ministers and elected legislators, and for generous pension payments, both in the Bundestag and in Land parliaments. Parties also operate patronage systems. The appointment of judges to the Constitutional Court (see above, chapter 3), the nomination of members of supervisory boards of the public broadcasting networks, appointments to the top positions in Land banks and many other public or semi-public institutions, and many key administrative positions in the federal and Länder governments are all in the gift of the parties (who often operate a system of proportionality among the parties when making such appointments).

This situation has led to criticism from experts, and to a more generalised feeling among the general public of rejection of, or alienation from, parties (a phenomonenon known in German as *Parteiverdrossenheit*). Such criticism was most dramatically expressed by the then federal president, Richard von Weizsäcker, in 1992. He expressed the opinion that parties had become a 'sixth unwritten organ of the constitution, which exercises a continually-extending, in part totally dominant, influence over the other five' (*Die Zeit*, 19 June 1992). Other critics emphasised how parties were concerned more with their own successes and finances than with representing the views of the electorate, how unrestrained they were in 'helping themselves' to state benefits and high salaries and pensions, how unready they were to reform themselves or become responsive to grass-roots influence. Evidence of public rejection of parties could be found in declining turnout rates at elections, and sometimes steep declines in membership of political parties. Young people especially seemed reluctant to join parties or be active in party politics; some local parties consisted almost entirely of the over-fifties. Especially in eastern Germany, where 'the party' had dominated all aspects of public life so unremittingly for so long, people were unwilling to devote time to working with political parties. Parties were the least trusted of all political institutions, according to surveys.[11] Such mistrust of the 'established' parties found expression also in electoral support for parties of the far right, and for new parties such as the STATT party in Hamburg (see chapter 4), as well as for the Greens and – in eastern Germany – for the PDS.

Parties have had their defenders, though. These champions pointed to the widespread change in levels of commitment to parties in many western European countries, not just in Germany. They blamed the mass media for focusing on the scandals and failures of parties, and never on their successes and the devoted, unpaid work of the many activists whom the parties still possessed. They pointed out that criticism of parties for not doing enough did not seem congruent with complaints that parties tried to do too much. One prominent CDU politician, Norbert Blum, commented that it had always been fashionable in Germany, especially on the part of intellectuals, to denigrate political parties (*Frankfurter Allgemeine Zeitung*, 20 August 1992).

Certainly criticism of German parties must be kept in proportion. Electoral turnout rates in Bundestag elections, which had been declining, stabilised in the 1994 Bundestag election (turnout then was over 1 per cent higher than in 1990, for instance) and in 1998 increased by over 3 per cent compared to 1994 (82.2 per cent).[12] Turnout in Land elections is often very low, however, relative to earlier periods in the history of the Federal Republic, and declined in 1999 in the election to the European Parliament to 45 per cent, having been 60 per cent in the 1994 election. Party membership is still high compared to many other western democracies. Parties are introducing some reforms (membership referenda on policy issues in the FDP, quotas for women in the CDU, more 'openness' to inputs from non-members in most parties, for instance). Support for extremist right-wing parties and the STATT party seems to have ebbed. Germany is still a party-state, but it is one where the rights of party members are – at least formally – better safeguarded than in other democracies, and where the Constitutional Court and the 'court of public opinion' are still effective obstacles to any misuse of power by parties.

Notes

1 In order to receive a share of the electoral subsidy parties had to receive at least 0.5 per cent of all valid list votes (one vote in every 200, not to be confused with the 5 per cent qualification for list seats, described in chapter 4). This subsidy was originally DM2.50 per elector, but increased in stages over time to DM5.00. The subsidy was based on the total electorate, not just those who turned out to vote, so (with a subsidy of DM5 per elector) on a turnout of 80 per cent, each vote would be worth about DM6.25 to the party receiving it. Similar systems of subsidy have operated in Germany for elections for the European Parliament and Land elections.

2 For example, political parties can only be prohibited by the Constitutional Court. Other associations can be banned by the Interior Minister under Article 9 of the Basic Law, a much more rapid and less cumbersome procedure. More obviously, only political parties can present lists of candidates for Bundestag elections.

3 Unless otherwise stated, in this chapter the CDU and the CSU will be regarded as one party.

4 In 1956 when the FDP left the Adenauer coalition, the four FDP ministers remained in post, supported by sixteen other FDP MdBs, thus preserving Adenauer's majority. After their attempt to form a separate party (the Free People's Party, FVP) had met with no real success, this 'renegade' group linked itself to the DP, which was then in turn absorbed by the Christian Democrats.

5 'STATT' means 'instead of', indicating that the party was offering itself as an alternative to the established parties. However, it never really developed a programme of concrete policy proposals, and the decision to extend to other Länder caused rifts within the Hamburg party organisation. The party had no success outside Hamburg.

6 Some Saarland Christian Democrats were elected to the Bundestag in 1957 under the CSU label, because they were displeased by Adenauer's less than enthusiastic attitude to the return of the Saarland to Germany. However, by the time of the 1961 election, the Saarland Christian Democrats were all elected as candidates of the CDU.

7 In Berlin, a membership referendum was held by the SPD on the issue of fusion with the KPD. The vote decisively rejected the idea (19,529 against, only 2,937 in favour). The Soviet authorities prohibited such a referendum in their zone of occupation outside Berlin.

8 A small number of East German Green candidates were elected, on a joint list with candidates from Alliance '90, under the special electoral rules operative for that election only (see chapter 4).

9 The Greens were the first German party to institute gender quotas for party and public elective office, inserting quota requirements into their statutes in 1985. Their party lists for elections, for instance, allocate odd-numbered places to female candidates, even-numbered places to male candidates. At the Hamburg election in 1986 the Greens presented an all-female list, to compensate for the numerical dominance of male candidates elected by the other parties.

10 The principal examples of such Foundations are the Friedrich Ebert Foundation, associated with the SPD; the Konrad Adenauer Foundation, associated with the CDU; the Friedrich Naumann Foundation, associated with the FDP; the Hanns Seidel Foundation associated with the CSU, and the Heinrich Boll Foundation

associated with the Greens. A number of other political Foundations operate at the level of the Land.

11 For example, an EMNID survey in 1992 found that only 21 per cent of respondents trusted political parties; in 1983 50 per cent of respondents had trusted them (Wiesendahl, 1992, p. 3).

12 Paradoxically, this increased turnout was aided by 6,827 voters in the Cologne area who voted for the list of the 'Party of Non-Voters'!

References

Hoffmann, J. (1998) *Die doppelte Vereinigung*, Opladen, Leske and Budrich.

Jesse, E. (1997) *Die Demokratie der Bundesrepublik Deutschland*, Berlin, Landeszentrale für politische Bildungsarbeit.

Moreau, P. (1998) *Die PDS: Profil einer antidemokratischen Partei*, München, Hanns-Seidel-Stiftung.

Wiesendahl, E. (1992) 'Volksparteien im Abstieg', *Das Parlament. Beilage: Aus Politik und Zeitgeschichte*, 34–5: 3–14.

Further reading

Betz, H-G and Welsh, H. (1995) 'The PDS in the new German party system', *German Politics*, 3: 95–111.

Frankland, E. and Schoonmaker, D. (1992) *Between Protest and Power. The Green Party in Germany*, Boulder, CO, Westview Press.

Gunlicks, A. (1995) 'The new German party finance law', *German Politics*, 1: 101–21.

Jesse, E. (1997) 'SPD and PDS relationships', *German Politics*, 3: 89–102.

Kvistad, G. (1999) 'Parteiverdrossenheit? whither the German party-state in the 1990s', in Merkl, P. (ed.), *The Federal Republic of Germany at Fifty. The End of a Century of Turmoil*, Basingstoke, Macmillan.

Niedermeyer, O. (1995) 'Party system change in East Germany', *German Politics*, 4: 75–91.

Padgett, S. (ed.) (1993) *Parties and Party Systems in the New Germany*, Aldershot, Dartmouth, for the Association for the Study of German Politics.

Poguntke, T. (1993) *Alternative Politics. The German Green Party*, Edinburgh, Edinburgh University Press.

Roberts, G. (1994) 'Extremism in Germany: sparrows or avalanche?', *European Journal of Political Research*, 4: 461–82.

Roberts, G. (1997) *Party Politics in the New Germany*, London, Pinter.

Roberts, G. (1999) 'Developments in the German Green party: 1995–99', *Environmental Politics*, 3: 145–51.

Smith, G. (1996) 'The party system at the crossroads', in Smith, G., Paterson, W. and Padgett, S. (eds), *Developments in German Politics 2*, Basingstoke, Macmillan.

Wiesendahl, E. (1998) 'The present state and future prospects of the German Volksparteien', *German Politics*, 2: 151–75.

6

The federal structure

The development of the federal system

The name of the German state – the Federal Republic of Germany – indicates and emphasises one of its fundamental characteristics: its federal structure. This means that sovereign authority is shared between the federation itself and the component Länder, as described in the Basic Law. Unlike the United States, Canada, Australia, India or Brazil – all federal states which cover very extensive territory – the Federal Republic is not particularly large in area – smaller than France or Spain, and not much larger than Italy – so why should it be organised as a federation, when France, for example, is not? There are two principal reasons.

First, when the political arrangements for the Federal Republic were being debated in 1948–49, the members of the Parliamentary Council had to accept that the Länder were already in existence as political structures (and, indeed, the members of the Parliamentary Council had themselves been selected by those Länder). Even had there been any pressure to create a unitary state for other reasons, the existence of Land parliaments, Land governments, Land constitutions and Land party systems would have made such a step unthinkable; the politicians and the public would not have consented to the abolition of the already functioning Länder political systems. The force of tradition also had influence. Even before the unification of Germany in 1871, a number of confederal and federal associations of German states had existed, ranging from Napoleon's Confederation of the Rhine, formed in 1806, to the Customs Union (*Zollverein*) in 1833, to the North German Confederation (formed in 1867) which preceded the unification of Germany. The Second Empire, the regime of the newly unified Germany that was created in 1871, was organised as a federal state, in which the formerly independent states such as Bavaria, Saxony, Württemberg and of course Prussia itself, with their heterogeneous cultures, political and legal arrangements, could be accommodated. The Weimar Republic, Germany's first democratic regime, had been created as a federal state, even though the role of the Länder was always very secondary, and the state structure became increasingly centralised over the lifetime of the regime.

The zonal post-war occupation regimes had been organised on the basis of Länder in 1945–46. Indeed, this tradition of federalism also left its impact on the institutions of the Federal Republic, such as the structure and powers of the Bundesrat (see below and chapter 8) and the important role of the Länder in the administration of policies made by the federal government (see below). So a federal system was an inevitable product of the work of the Parliamentary Council for these reasons, and was emphasised by the requirement that the Basic Law be ratified in 1949 not by a plebiscite of the people, but by decisions of the legislatures of the Länder.

Second, though, a federal system also suited the plans of the western allied occupation powers, who were overseeing the work of the Parliamentary Council, which they themselves had called into being. The occupation authorities had already acknowledged the status of the Länder in their institutional arrangements for, first, the Bizone and then the Trizone (see chapter 1). The United States, itself a federal state, was naturally predisposed to view federalism as a desirable feature of a democratic state. The United Kingdom and France saw many advantages to federalism as a principle of decentralisation for a West German state, which would work against centralisation of power such as had facilitated the rise to power of Adolf Hitler. Above all, a federally structured state would act as an additional bulwark against any possible attempt by a dictator to seize power: it would be little use attempting a *coup d'état* in Bonn, when the federal bank was situated in Frankfurt, the Constitutional Court located (as it came to be) in Karlsruhe, the national press and broadcasting networks scattered from Hamburg to Munich, and powerful Land governments existed in Stuttgart and Düsseldorf, Hanover and Munich. Any attempt to pervert the democratic quality of the Basic Law would also be prevented by the entrenched status and powers of the Länder in the political system. So there was significant allied pressure on the Parliamentary Council to adopt a federal form of state organisation and, indeed, one that gave real powers to the Länder (for example control of education, policing and local government). This was made explicit in the 'Frankfurt Documents' which the western allies issued to the ministers-president of the Länder on 1 July 1948 to guide their discussions which preceded the work of the Parliamentary Council.

Though tradition was a factor in the decision to constitute the West German state as a federal system, in fact the Länder which existed in 1949 had in only a few cases any obvious links to pre-war Länder. Bavaria, Hamburg and Bremen certainly did, but otherwise the dissolution of Prussia after 1945[1] and the importance of zonal boundaries and other occupational requirements meant that other Länder were either completely new structures, or else were parts of, or amalgamations of segments of, pre-existing Länder. Examples were Lower Saxony, formed by amalgamation in 1946 of the previous Länder of Braunschweig, Oldenburg, Schaumburg-Lippe and the Hanoverian province of Prussia; North Rhine-Westphalia, formed from parts of Prussia; and the three south-west Länder (Württemberg-Baden, Württemberg-Hohenzollern and

Baden) which later formed Baden-Württemberg, comprising the pre-war Länder of Württemberg and Baden.

Because the Länder already existed at the time of promulgation of the Basic Law, the new Federal Republic was burdened with a very heterogeneous set of constituent Länder in terms of their size, wealth, population, degree of industrialisation and social composition. Bremen was a tiny Land, separated by a strip of Lower Saxony's territory into its two mainly urban areas, Bremen and the port of Bremerhaven. Bavaria was a large, substantially rural, very Catholic Land, with strong particularist traditions deriving from its uneasy incorporation into the Prussian-dominated Second Empire. North Rhine-Westphalia was also large in terms of area, very large in terms of population, and heavily industrialised in parts, especially the coal- and steel-producing Ruhr area. It was recognised at the time that the new Basic Law would put a strain on some Länder because of the areas of responsibility which were to be given to all Länder, ranging from provision of schools and universities to local government services, from policing and a system of courts to responsibility for highways and the fostering of local economic development. The possibility of territorial rearrangement of the existing structure of the Länder was recognised by the inclusion of Article 29 in the Basic Law, which provides for restructuring in order to enable Länder to fulfil effectively the tasks provided for them in the Basic Law. Prior to German reunification in 1990, the only territorial change which was made was the fusion of the three south-western Länder to form the Land of

Table 6.1 *The area and population of the Länder, December 1996*

	Area (sq km)	Population (million)	Land capital
Baden-Württemberg	35,752	10.4	Stuttgart
Bavaria	70,550	12.0	Munich
Berlin	890	3.5	Berlin
Brandenburg	29,476	2.6	Potsdam
Bremen	404	0.7	Bremen
Hamburg	755	1.7	Hamburg
Hesse	21,114	6.0	Wiesbaden
Lower Saxony	47,612	7.8	Hanover
Mecklenburg-Vorpommern	23,170	1.8	Schwerin
North Rhine-Westphalia	34,077	18.0	Düsseldorf
Rhineland-Pfalz	19,846	4.0	Mainz
Saarland	2,570	1.1	Saarbrücken
Saxony	18,412	4.6	Dresden
Saxony-Anhalt	20,457	2.7	Magdeburg
Schleswig-Holstein	15,770	2.7	Kiel
Thuringia	16,171	2.5	Erfurt
Federal Republic	357,021	82.0	Berlin

Source: Statistisches Jahrbuch für das Bundesrepublik Deutschland, 1998, pp. 32–3.

Baden-Württemberg in 1952 (and this was undertaken on the basis of a special provision of the Basic Law: Article 118, not under Article 29).[2] The issue of restructuring did not disappear, though, and at several times in the future was placed on the political agenda (see below).

The constitutional basis of federalism

The Basic Law makes reference to the federal organisation of the political system in numerous Articles.

The nature of the state: a 'democratic and social federal state', is defined in Article 20 (1), and Article 79 (3) ensures that provisions of the Basic Law affecting the federal nature of the state and the participation of the Länder in the federal legislative process are unamendable. These Articles provide the constitutional basis for federalism.

Article 30 provides for state tasks to be undertaken by the Länder, unless the Basic Law specifically provides otherwise, and Article 70 (1) allocates legislative powers to the Länder, unless the Basic Law explicitly provides otherwise. This means (theoretically, if not in practice) that the Länder have responsibility for all policy sectors other than those explicitly granted to the federal level of government. This provision is modified by the existence of joint and concurrent areas of responsibility. Article 72 regulates concurrent powers, where both the federal and Land governments may legislate (supplemented by Article 74, which lists the areas of concurrent legislation ranging from criminal law and laws on weapons and explosives, to employment law and areas of environmental protection, and Articles 91a and 91b, which are concerned with 'joint responsibilities'). Article 23 now ensures that the Länder participate in the process of European Union (EU) policy-making, in areas which fall within their constitutional competence (see chapter 10). As stated above, Article 29 provides for the revision of the territorial structure of the Länder.

The involvement of the Länder in federal politics is guaranteed by several Articles of the Basic Law. Articles 50–53 are concerned with the status, composition and functions of the Bundesrat as the legislative chamber representative of the Länder (see below and chapter 8). Article 54 (3) requires representation from Land parliaments in the electoral college which chooses the federal president (see chapter 7). Articles 83–5 require the Länder to administer federal laws, except where the Basic Law makes other provision. Article 36 requires that staffing of the principal agencies of the federal government should take account of Länder proportionality (and that implementation of military recruitment should recognise regional loyalties).

Articles 104a, 106 and 107 deal with the financing of the Länder, including those taxes which flow exclusively to, and the provisions for financial equalization among, the Länder (see below). Article 106 (3) includes the requirement that living standards in all parts of the Federal Republic shall be kept in balance, a requirement also mentioned in Article 72, concerning concurrent legislation, and which provides justification for that system of financial equalisation.

So the political status of the Länder can be summarised as follows. The Länder have the right, in principle, to legislate in a number of policy areas, and possess, under the Basic Law, residual powers (i.e. the right to legislate on any matter not explicitly allocated to the federal level of government).[3] However, the Basic Law now contains a very full enumeration of the exclusive responsibilities of the federal government, of concurrent areas of responsibility (areas where the federal government often has 'captured' a policy area so that the Länder now have little or no autonomy), of federal framework laws and of joint tasks where the federal government lays down authoritative policy guidelines. This has meant that, in practice, the rights of the Länder parliaments to make legislation have become extremely restricted. The Länder do, though, participate in the process of federal legislation through their representation in the Bundesrat. They have the obligation to implement and administer federal policy in all areas where such implementation and administration is not reserved for federal agencies (such as foreign and defence policy), often with some large degree of discretion concerning the detail of implementation. The Länder are financed by appropriate allocations of public funds under the terms laid down in the Basic Law, allocations which are, in part at least, independent of federal government control. They have protected rights with regard to participation in the development of policy at the level of the European Union where issues affect Länder responsibilities, such as education, the environment, regional aid and media policy. Where any of these rights and duties are called into question, and especially where there is a conflict of interpretation concerning federal and Länder rights, the Constitutional Court has the responsibility to make an adjudication (see chapter 3).

The Länder have their own political structures to enable them to carry out their responsibilities, structures which are described in the Länder constitutions. While these political structures can vary in detail, the Basic Law (Article 28) requires that the constitutions of the Länder conform to democratic principles based on the rule of law, and gives the federal government the responsibility of ensuring that this is the case. The provision that federal law overrides Land law where there is a conflict of laws (Article 31) is another aspect of the Basic Law which ensures a degree of homogeneity among the Länder. Each Land has its own parliament, elected by a system of proportional representation for a term of either four or five years (see below). A government is formed on the basis of the need to secure a majority in the Land parliament. Civil, criminal and constitutional courts are provided at Land level.[4]

The Länder have legislative responsibility for a range of policy areas. These include:

* education (including university education);
* policing;
* a system of courts;

- aspects of broadcasting;
- transport and highways (except where the Basic Law makes specific exceptions, such as the motorway system and air safety);
- the regional economy;
- aspects of environmental protection;
- cultural matters;
- provision of social services;
- the system of local government.

In some cases, the Länder legislate within the parameters laid down by federal framework laws (under Article 75 of the Basic Law), such as aspects of education policy. In other cases, the Länder share authority with the federal government under so-called 'joint tasks' (as provided by Articles 91a and 91b of the Basic Law). The list of such 'joint tasks' is very limited, because of the reluctance of the Länder to have the scope of their exclusive competences restricted; so construction of universities, measures concerning the improvement of the structure of agriculture, coastal protection and regional economic structure, together with educational planning and the promotion of scientific research, are so far the only examples of such joint responsibilities.

The most distinctive feature of the structure of German federalism, though, is the functional division which exists between the federal government and the Länder. With the exception of foreign affairs and a small number of other responsibilities, administration of all policy, whether made by federal or Land authority, lies with the Länder. They have the obligation to execute these laws within their Land. It is this interdependence between the federal legislative authority and Land administrative responsibility, and the need for co-ordination between them, which have been mainly responsible for the term 'co-operative federalism' being applied to the German federal model. So, in Germany, instead of civil servants employed by the federal government dealing locally with the administration of unemployment benefit, the collection of income tax, safety regulations in factories or federal environmental standards, these responsibilities will be carried out by Land civil servants. Where they carry out tasks (such as the repair of motorways) as agents of the federal government, they are recompensed directly for this; where they administer federal laws under Article 83 of the Basic Law 'as their own responsibility' they receive no special funding.

The Länder derive their financial resources from a range of taxes and grants (as provided in Article 106 of the Basic Law). Certain taxes (such as motor vehicle taxes, some property taxes, inheritance tax, betting tax and beer tax) flow entirely to the Länder. Other taxes, primarily related to property and commerce, contribute to the income of local government organisations. Other taxes are divided between the Länder and the federal government: each receiving equal shares of the product of income taxes, for instance, and a share of value-added tax which is recalculated approximately every two years (in 1999 the

federal government received 50.5 per cent, the Länder shared 49.5 per cent).
In 1996 the total tax product was allocated as follows: the federal government
received 47 per cent; the Länder received 37 per cent; local government
received 16 per cent (Grüske, 1998, p. 23).

Because of the great differences among the Länder in terms of their income
from the product of taxation, their industrial development, their needs in terms
of social service and other provisions, their population size, and so on, a system
of financial equalisation is provided (Article 107 of the Basic Law). This means
that those Länder which benefit most from the shared taxation arrangements
laid down in the Basic Law pay over a portion of their tax income to Länder
which benefit less from the system. This system worked reasonably well –
though not without controversy – prior to reunification. The addition in 1990
of five new, and relatively very poor, Länder to the Federal Republic threatened
to put too large a strain on the system of financial equalisation, because the gap
between western and eastern Länder would have been too great. This might
have meant that the poorest western Länder such as Bremen and the Saarland
would have been contributors, rather than beneficiaries, of the system. It was
therefore not applied to the new Länder until 1995, and instead special subsidies from federal funds were paid to the new Länder. On the basis of a law passed
in 1993, it was decided that, from 1995, the system of equalisation – after
certain modifications which benefited the Länder relative to the federal government – would embrace all sixteen Länder.[5] In 1997, North Rhine-Westphalia,
Baden-Württemberg, Bavaria, Hessen, Hamburg and Schleswig-Holstein paid
money out to the poorer Länder; all the other Länder (including all the 'new'
East German Länder and Berlin) were recipients from the equalisation payments (Kig, 1999, p. 31). In addition, the federal government pays grants to
poorer Länder (so-called 'vertical equalisation', in contrast to the system of
'horizontal equalisation' – the payments from wealthier to poorer Länder). The
equalisation payments from wealthier to poorer Länder, though a substantial
sum (*c.* DM12 billion in 1996, equal to about £4 billion), in fact are only a relatively minor contribution. They are exceeded by part of the Länder share of
value-added tax distributed to aid the poorer Länder together with federal
government payments directly to poorer Länder. No legal constraints on the
utilisation of equalisation payments exist. Länder are not obliged, for example,
to use such payments to support investment which would improve their relative economic position. However, these payments are seen as an expression of
co-operative federalism; they mean that the requirements of the Basic Law in
Article 107 (2) – that differential financial strengths of the Länder should be
appropriately modified – and Article 106 (3) – which requires some attempt at
producing equality in the standard of living of the whole federal territory – are
to some extent complied with. These constitutional requirements of course
took on new significance following reunification.

The system of financial equalisation is often criticised, especially by Länder
which find themselves annually contributing to poorer Länder. Indeed, in 1999

Bavaria, Baden-Württemberg and Hesse were challenging the details of the system of payments which they were compelled to make in a case before the Constitutional Court (*Suddeutsche Zeitung*, 15 January 1999). Critics claim that the methods of calculation used are biased in favour of the small highly urbanised 'city-Länder' such as Berlin and Bremen, which benefit from high density of population in terms of receipts of value-added tax, yet then have that density of population regarded as a reason for special treatment when it comes to financial equalisation. The wealthier Länder claim that poorer Länder do not utilise the equalisation payments for investment, and that these Länder have no incentive to become more efficient economically since their budget deficits tend to be met by subsidies from other Länder or from the federal government.

Local government arrangements vary from Land to Land, though there is a broad distinction between northern Länder (where the creation of local government after the war was influenced by British occupation policy) and the south, where American and – in the south-west – French influence was strong. So the system of directly elected mayors, for instance, is found most generally in the southern Länder and – since reunification – also in the 'new Länder' of the former GDR. The number of local government units varies from Land to Land, without necessarily correlating closely to the population. In 1996, for instance, Rhineland-Pfalz, a relatively small Land, had more local government districts (*Gemeinde*) than Bavaria, more than twice as many as Baden-Württemberg, and nearly six times the number which existed in North Rhine-Westphalia. One reason for this is that, in some Länder, a radical process of fusion of local government districts has taken place. Lower Saxony reduced its districts to one-quarter the number it had had in the 1960s, for instance, Baden-Württemberg and Bavaria to one-third the number, and North Rhine-Westphalia from over seven thousand to just under 400. A similar process of reduction has taken place in some Länder in the numbers of counties (*Landkreise*) and metropolitan authorities (*Kreisfreie Städte*).[6]

Relations between the Länder and the federation

In order to allow the political system to operate effectively in a federal state such as that of Germany, a network of institutions which foster co-ordination and co-operation is necessary. In some cases, the Basic Law explicitly demands such co-operation (such as dealing with natural catastrophes – Article 35 (3)). However, co-operation and co-ordination (the Germans use the term *Politikverflechtung*, political interlinkage) are necessary for effective implementation of all types of policies. Such institutions fall into four main categories: the Bundesrat; the Länder 'embassies' in the capital; the system of committees linking the Länder to the federal government or linking the Länder with each other; and party and electoral politics (the subject of the next section of this chapter).

The most obvious institution of co-ordination is the Bundesrat, the second chamber of the federal legislature, which consists of delegates from the Länder, and which participates fully and often influentially in the legislative process at the federal level. The Bundesrat has the right to give a preliminary opinion on government legislative proposals before they commence their legislative passage through the Bundestag and Bundesrat. The right of the Bundesrat to veto absolutely legislation which affects Länder powers or finances, and its right to a suspensive veto on other matters, gives it more power than most second chambers, certainly those within western Europe. This right of veto is especially potent when the parties which form the governing coalition with a majority in the Bundestag find they are in a minority in the Bundesrat. The Bundesrat has parity of membership with the Bundestag on the powerful Mediation Committee, an institution which seeks to resolve conflicts over legislation that arise between the two chambers of the federal legislature. Because the Bundesrat is so powerful, the federal government tries to ensure in advance of plenary sessions of the Bundesrat that agreement can be reached with the representatives of the Länder whenever possible, even at the price of compromises. (The structure and operation of the Bundesrat are described in more detail in chapter 8.)

In some respects, it can be helpful to regard the Länder as sovereign states, operating within a common overall framework. The existence and activities of the Land 'missions' (somewhat like embassies) in Bonn – and now Berlin – call to mind such a parallel. These missions continue a practice which developed in the Second Empire, and which was continued under the Weimar Republic until 1933. The missions, headed usually by a minister of the Land government, operate closely with the Bundesrat delegations from their Land, and the minister in charge of the 'mission' may act as deputy to the Land prime minister in the Bundesrat and the Mediation Committee. They provide channels of contact for important visitors from Hamburg or Bavaria, Thuringia or Saxony, who wish to put a case to a federal ministry or lobby Members of the Bundestag about a particular policy. They scrutinise legislation, to ensure that the interests of their Land are protected and promoted. They foster links with federal politicians and with the members of such missions from other Länder. They act as a source of information and advice on political developments in the federal capital for their governments. They promote the economic interests and the image of their Land, by exhibitions and seminars, by hosting meetings and providing other forms of hospitality in the Land mission.

Various committees have developed over the years, which link the federal and Land levels of government and politics. These include regular meetings between the federal chancellor and the ministers-president (prime ministers) of the Länder, and meetings between departmental ministers (such as Finance Ministers or Justice Ministers) of the federal and Land governments to discuss matters of mutual concern – somewhat akin to the Council of Ministers of the European Union. Some of these meetings occur within a formalised structure, and treaty-like agreements are sometimes produced to co-ordinate aspects of education policy, for instance, or financial policy. Also to be included within this category of co-ordination mechanism are the numerous committees consisting only of Land representatives, which either meet preparatory to federal-Länder committees or which discuss issues solely within the competence of the Länder, and where co-operation among the Länder is required. The meetings of Länder prime ministers (which commenced in 1946, before the Federal Republic was founded) are perhaps the most important of these Länder meetings. One estimate in 1989 was that, even then, some 330 federal-Länder committees existed, and well over a hundred committees for Länder co-ordination (Männle, 1997, p. 6). Leaders of parliamentary party groups in the Bundestag meet with their counterparts in Land parliaments and meetings of the presidents of the federal and Land parliaments (positions equivalent to the Speaker of the House of Commons) also occur regularly.

Also important as co-ordination mechanisms are the arrangements for allocation of finances to the Länder (see above); the role of the Constitutional Court, which adjudicates on federal-Land disputes, and whose membership is partly selected by the Länder through the Bundesrat (see chapter 3); and the relatively recent formal provisions for participation by the Länder in the development of policies relating to the EU (see chapter 10).

Politics in the Länder

The significance of the federal system for Germany cannot be appreciated or understood by an analysis of constitutional provisions and institutional arrangements alone. Each Land has its own political system, and that means that the political parties may have to play different roles in each Land, and in each Land a somewhat different role from that which they fulfil in federal politics. This has meant that the organisations of political parties reflect the federal structure of the state. The parties have their own Land organisations. They contest Land elections, and form coalitions at Land level which may not correspond to coalitions formed at the federal level of government. For example, in June 1999 the SPD was in coalition with the Greens in North Rhine-Westphalia, Hamburg and Schleswig-Holstein; with the FDP in Rhineland-Pfalz; with the PDS in Mecklenburg-Vorpommern; and with the CDU in Bremen, in Thurinigia and in Berlin. The CDU and FDP were in coalition in Baden-Württemberg and Hesse. Such coalitions may sometimes be experiments to see if a similar coalition could succeed at federal level (Kropp and Sturm, 1999, pp. 41–3).

The Länder organisations of the parties may play a significant role within the national party organisation. The allocations of delegates to the annual conferences of the federal parties are calculated according to Länder strength within the party. There may be explicit arrangements for Land representation on the federal party executive committee. Some degree of Länder proportionality will be looked for in allocation of party and government posts at federal level. Länder party conferences select the candidates for the Land party lists for Bundestag elections. Above all, Land-level ministerial experience or a successful term of office in the party leadership at Land level may be a gateway to a career within the party at federal level, just as the office of governor of a state in the USA may be a pathway to candidacy for the presidency, as it was for Reagan and Clinton, for instance. Gerhard Schröder, his predecessor as chancellor, Helmut Kohl and, before them, Kurt-Georg Kiesinger and Willy Brandt used their Land-level careers as springboards for becoming federal chancellor. Three FDP leaders (Theodor Heuss and Reinhold Maier from Baden-Württemberg, and Wolfgang Gerhardt, from Hesse) have been elected while holding Land party office, rather than a federal-level position. Every SPD challenger to Helmut Kohl as chancellor-candidate since he took office in 1982 came from a position as minister-president (or governing lord mayor) of a Land: Hans-Joachim Vogel (West Berlin, 1983); Johannes Rau (North Rhine-Westphalia, 1987); Oskar Lafontaine (Saarland, 1990); Rudolf Scharping (Rhineland-Pfalz, 1994); and Gerhard Schröder (Lower Saxony, 1998).[7] Of course, the opposite also holds: a successful career in federal politics has sometimes meant a transfer to high office – in the party or in Land government – at Land level. Franz Josef Strauss (CSU), who left Bonn to become minister-president of Bavaria and Gerhard Stoltenberg (CDU), a former minister who became minister-president of Schleswig-Holstein, are two prominent examples.

Land elections are not only significant for their own sake, determining which party or coalition then governs in that Land. They affect the composition and balance of power in the Bundesrat, and are especially significant if they might bring about a two-thirds majority for the parties in opposition in the Bundestag, since that would effectively prevent the governing coalition from passing legislation (see chapter 8). They may also be seen as 'signals' for the parties and the government at federal level, signals that are especially important since there are no by-elections for the Bundestag that could act as mid-term tests of popularity. If a party does unexpectedly well or badly in a Land election, especially one that is close in time to the next Bundestag election, that can have an effect on the whole federal election campaign. The weakness of the Greens and the extremely poor results of the FDP in Land elections prior to the 1994 Bundestag elections were important signals of this type, and the strong performance of Gerhard Schröder in the Lower Saxony Land election in March 1998, as well as the weakness of the CDU and the astonishing electoral support of the extremist right-wing DVU in the Saxony-Anhalt Land election in May 1998, were discussed and evaluated in terms of their implications for the Bundestag election of September 1998.

So it can be seen that party politics and electoral politics at Land level may have significant consequences at federal level, and provide a means for the co-ordination of policy between the two levels of government.

Reform of the federal system?

Throughout the history of the Federal Republic, there have been criticisms of the structure of the federal system, and of the division of responsibilities and authority between the federal and Länder levels of government.

Because of the way in which the Federal Republic was created in 1949, using existing Länder as the constituent units, and because at the time it was expected that the West German state would anyway only be provisional and temporary prior to reunification in the near future, little attention was given to the great variations in size, population, economic structure and wealth of the different Länder. The fact that Bremen (a city smaller than many others that were not given the status of separate Länder, such as Munich, Cologne and Frankfurt), along with Hamburg, Schleswig-Holstein and Rhineland-Pfalz, were expected to carry out the same functions within the federal system as North Rhine-Westphalia, Bavaria, Baden-Württemberg (as it was to become in 1952), Hesse and Lower Saxony did not, at the time, seem to be a great problem. In any case, the Basic Law did provide for the possibility of the amalgamation of Länder, by the process of referenda, under Article 29. However, the issue of the number of Länder and their relative strength led in the 1950s to the creation of two commissions (the Euler Committee and the Luther Commission) both of which recommended revision of the number of Länder by amalgamations in the north and the central area of the Federal Republic. No action followed either of these reports, nor that of the Ernst Commission, created by the Brandt government, which set out specific schemes for amalgamation of the Länder in those two regions. Despite arguments that a minimum population of 5 million was necessary to provide a proper basis for the administrative, economic and political structures of a Land, a basis required by the terms of Article 29 of the Basic Law,[8] the resistance of politicians and the public in the Länder which would lose their independent status (especially the 'Hansa cities' of Hamburg and Bremen) led to these proposals being rejected.

The reunification of Germany in 1990 offered a new opportunity to rationalise the federal structure. Since 'new Länder' were going to have to be created in the GDR so that East Germany could become part of the Federal Republic, this seemed to present a chance to restructure the West German Länder also. One scheme even suggested forming a new Land from Lower Saxony and Saxony-Anhalt, which would cross the old east–west border. However, the pressure of time and the large number of other political and economic aspects of reunification needing resolution meant that this opportunity, too, was missed. Five East German Länder were created, very much corresponding to the Länder which had existed in the GDR prior to their abolition in 1952. The two parts of Berlin became a single Land. The only concession to restructuring of the federal system was a clause in the Reunification Treaty which encouraged a possible merger of the two Länder of Berlin and Brandenburg (which surrounded Berlin).[9] After much discussion in the parliaments of these two Länder, and among and within the political parties, referenda were held on the issue of fusion. Despite both Land parliaments and most of the political parties being in favour of the merger, the referendum produced a large majority in Brandenburg against fusion (and, in Berlin, though there was an overall majority in favour of fusion, a majority in East Berlin voted against the merger).[10]

So structural reform of the federal system seems, for the foreseeable future, to be out of the question. Similarly, proposals of various kinds, ranging from radical revision of the allocation of taxation receipts between the federal government and the Länder, to changes in the Basic Law concerning concurrent powers of legislation (which presently strongly favour the federal government), have not found much support. True, the reform of the Basic Law on the basis of the report of the Joint Commission on the Constitution (1994) did make some changes to the benefit of the Länder in relation to concurrent legislation, but these changes may serve more to defend the *status quo* against further centralising tendencies rather than provide much of a 'roll-back' of already existing federal government powers. The process of reunification itself has led to increased centralisation within the federal system, largely because the 'new Länder' would not have been viable had they had to exist only on the same resources available through the tax allocation system as applied to the western Länder, so subsidisation has been necessary. Such subsidisation has inevitably been accompanied by greater influence on the part of the federal government not only *vis-à-vis* the 'new Länder', but also by extension of such influence to all the Länder as a whole. However, it would be a mistake to perceive the relationship between the federal and Land levels of government in too simplistic a fashion. Politics in Germany is not – only – a struggle between central and Land interests. The Länder are governed by different parties or coalitions of parties, and they can have different interests one from another because of their economic structure, for example, or, now, depending on whether they are located east or west of the former German–German border. Such different patterns of interests find expression, for instance, in the way the Länder vote in the Bundesrat.

Nevertheless the system works, and, in many respects, works well. The existence of a Land level of politics and government may be a complicating and at times frustrating factor in the German political system, but it is undoubtedly also a reinforcement of democracy.

Notes

1 Prussia was not revived as an administrative unit after the war (and anyway its former territory was then divided between the British zone and the USSR zone of occupation). The decision to dissolve Prussia was promulgated as a decree by the Allied Control Council on 25 February 1947, giving as their reason that Prussia had always been a source of militarism and reaction in Germany.

2 An agreement on fusion, as required in Article 118, was not reached by the three south-west Länder, so a law was passed in 1951 to allow referenda on the issue of amalgamating the three Länder. In those referenda, a majority (62.2 per cent) in South Baden voted against the proposal to form the new Land. However, a substantial majority in other areas, and indeed a substantial majority overall (69.7 per cent), voted in favour. In 1970, voters in Baden confirmed in a referendum that they wished to remain part of Baden-Württemberg.

3 It is usual for the constituent units in a federal state to retain residual powers (e.g. the USA, Switzerland and Canada), though the most recent West European state to adopt a federal form of state, Belgium, unusually retains residual powers at the national level.

4 Schleswig-Holstein does not have its own constitutional court. It allows the federal Constitutional Court to adjudicate on matters affecting its Land constitution.

5 The procedure for 'horizontal' financial equalisation using the Länder share of value-added tax is as follows: of the share allocated to the Länder, 75 per cent is distributed according to population in each Land. The remaining 25 per cent is used to ensure that the per head funding of all Länder is at least 92 per cent of the average. Then payments are made from Länder with above average per head tax income to those with below average per head tax income, so that no Land has below 95 per cent of the average per head tax income. Federal grants then are awarded to those Länder still below average, to bring them to 99 per cent of the average.

6 Data from Jesse (1997) citing Hübner E. and Rohlfs H. (1985) *Jahrbuch der Bundesrepublik Deutschland 1985/86*, München, dtv, 138 and H. Rohlfs and U. Schäfer, (1997) *Jahrbuch der Bundesrepublik Deutschland 1997*, München, dtv, 62.

7 Had it not been for revelations about his evidence to an investigation committee which led to his resignation from government and party office, the then minister-president of Schleswig-Holstein, Björn Engholm, would have been the SPD chancellor-candidate in 1994 – yet another example of the importance of Land party office for chancellor-candidates.

8 Article 29 (1) states that the federal structure can be revised, to guarantee that the Länder, by their size and capabilities, are able to carry out the functions which the Basic Law requires of them, though it also states that factors such as regional identity, history, culture and economic rationality are considerations when such changes are proposed.

9 This was later incorporated in the Basic Law as Article 188a, repeating the special provision made for the south-west Länder which later became Baden-Württemberg.

10 The referendum was held in 1996; 53 per cent voted in favour in Berlin, but 63 per cent voted against in Brandenburg.

References

Grüske, K.-D. (1998) 'Föderalismus und Finanzausgleich', in M. Vollkommer (ed.), *Föderalismus – Prinzip und Wirklichkeit*, Erlangen, Universitätsbund Erlangen-Nürnberg.

Jesse, E. (1997) *Die Demokratie der Bundesrepublik Deutschland*, 8th edn, Berlin, Landeszentrale für politische Bildungsarbeit.

Kig, T. (1999) 'Regieren im deutschen Föderalismus', *Das Parlament. Beilage: Aus Politik und Zeitgeschichte*, 13: 24–36.
Kropp, S. and Sturm, R. (1999) 'Politische Willensbildung im Föderalismus', *Das Parlament. Beilage: Aus Politik und Zeitgeschichte*, 13: 37–46.
Männle, U. (1997) 'Grundlagen und Gestaltungsmöglichkeiten des Föderalismus in Deutschland', *Das Parlament. Beilage: Aus Politik und Zeitgeschichte*, 24: 3–11.
Statistisches Jahrbuch für das Bundesrepublik Deutschland, 1998, (1998) Wiesbaden, Statistisches Bundesamt.

Further Reading

Gunlicks, A. (1999) 'Fifty years of German federalism: an overview and some current developments', in Merkl, P. (ed.), *The Federal Republic of Germany at Fifty. The End of a Century of Turmoil*, Basingstoke, Macmillan.
Jeffery, C. and Savigear, P. (1991) *German Federalism Today*, Leicester and London, Leicester University Press.
Jeffery, C. and Sturm, R. (eds) (1992) *Federalism, Unification and German Integration*, special issue of *German Politics*, 3.
Jeffery, C. (1996) 'The Territorial Dimension', in Smith, G., Paterson, W. and Padgett, S. eds., *Developments in German Politics 2*, Basingstoke, Macmillan.
McKay, J. (1996) 'Berlin-Brandenburg ? Nein danke ! The referendum on the proposed Länderfusion', *German Politics*, 3: 485–502.

7

Chancellor democracy

The political system of the Federal Republic is sometimes described as 'chancellor democracy', because of the dominant role in that political system which is occupied by the chancellor.[1] This chapter surveys the way in which the Basic Law provides the political instruments which permit the chancellor to play such a dominant role. It is important, though, to concede that the chancellor's powers in actuality will also depend on the political circumstances of the time, the personality of the chancellor and the party system. The constraints on the chancellor's political authority, such as those associated with the need to form governing coalitions, will also be examined. The roles of the cabinet and civil service, and other agencies within government, also need to be considered.

Compared to the chancellor, and in contrast to the situation in the Weimar Republic, the status of the federal president is very limited. This arises in part from the dominance of the chancellor in the political system, a dominance resulting from deliberate decisions taken by the drafters of the Basic Law. A review of the office of federal president is thus a useful prelude to closer examination of the office of federal chancellor.

The federal president

In analysing after the Second World War what had contributed to the fragility of the political institutions of the Weimar Republic, many experts identified the 'dual executive' arrangements incorporated in the Weimar constitution as one of the key factors which led to the downfall of the democratic regime and its replacement by a one-party dictatorship under Adolf Hitler. The Weimar constitution had instituted the office of chancellor, but had allowed the chancellor to be at the mercy of the Reichstag, which could too easily create majorities to dismiss the chancellor. It also made chancellors too dependent on the president, who could dismiss the chancellor and appoint a replacement. Replacement chancellors could, if necessary, govern by use of the president's emergency

112

powers (Article 48 of the Weimar constitution). The more crisis-stricken the republic was, the more shaky the position of the chancellor became, so that in the period between the dismissal of the last 'democratically chosen' chancellor, Müller, in 1930, to the appointment of Adolf Hitler as chancellor in 1933, no fewer than three chancellors (Brüning, von Papen and Schleicher) were appointed, each ruling by use of presidential emergency powers. In all, a total of sixteen chancellors (including Hitler) were appointed in the fifteen years from 1918 to 1933; a period briefer than the term in office as chancellor of Helmut Kohl (sixteen years), and only one year longer than the chancellorship of Konrad Adenauer (14 years).

Because of this fatal flaw in the constitutional arrangements of the Weimar Republic, the Basic Law therefore instituted the office of federal president as one which had more in common with the position of a constitutional monarch than with that of a politically active president, such as existed in the USA or was introduced in 1958 by the constitution of the French Fifth Republic.

One indication of the diminished political status of the presidency in the Federal Republic is the method of election. Unlike the president of the Weimar Republic, who was directly elected by the people, the federal president is indirectly elected by a special electoral college (the Bundesversammlung) (Article 54 of the Basic Law). This electoral college consists of all the members of the Bundestag, together with an equal number of members drawn from the parliaments of the Länder. It is thus an institution which represents the elected legislatures of both the Federal Republic and the Länder, and one which thus incorporates the federal element. To be elected, a candidate requires to obtain either: (1) the votes of an absolute majority of the members of the electoral college or, if that absolute majority is not obtained in either a first or a second round of voting, (2) a simple majority of votes in the third round of balloting. Voting is by secret ballot. Of the eleven elections between 1949 and 1999, only two (those of Gustav Heinemann in 1969 and Roman Herzog in 1994) went to a third round; three others required two ballots (Theodor Heuss in 1949, Heinrich Lübke in 1959 and Johannes Rau in 1999). All the other elections were settled on the first ballot. A president may serve no more than two terms.[2] In contrast to the arrangements in the constitution of the United States, in the Federal Republic there is no office of vice-president. Instead, Article 57 of the Basic Law provides that the president of the Bundesrat (see chapter 8) fulfils the responsibilities of the presidency in the event of the death or incapacity of the federal president, prior to the election of a new president.

Though the president, once in office, is meant to be non-partisan, and certainly has to divest himself of all overt forms of affiliation to his party, in almost every case the nomination of candidates and the electoral process itself have been intertwined with party politics. The first president, Heuss, who at the time of his nomination was the leader of the FDP (the liberal party which had agreed to be in coalition with Adenauer's Christian Democrats as the Federal Republic's first government in 1949), was put forward by Adenauer as part of

---

Box 7.1
The election of the federal president: May 1999

Party composition of the Federal Assembly

SPD	565
CDU-CSU	548
Greens	96
PDS	63
FDP	57
Others	9
Total membership	1338

Outcome of the election[3]

1st round	Rau	657		Schipanski	588	Ranke-Heinemann 69
2nd round	Rau	690 (elected)		Schipanski	572	Ranke-Heinemann 62

---

the bargaining process with the FDP in the discussions about allocation of cabinet posts. Lübke, Adenauer's Minister of Agriculture, was only nominated in 1959 after Adenauer himself had controversially withdrawn his name from consideration. This followed a long period of contemplation by Adenauer about whether he could use the office of federal president to remain politically active alongside a successor as chancellor, on the lines of the new Fifth Republic presidency in France, and after several other possible candidates (with more prominent political reputations than Lübke) had declined to allow themselves to be nominated. Heinemann was elected in 1969 only because the FDP, undergoing a change of political orientation whilst in opposition to the 'grand coalition', decided to throw its support behind Heinemann (the candidate of the SPD) rather than Gerhard Schröder, the candidate of the Christian Democrats. This decision was seen at the time as indicating that the FDP was prepared to consider entering a coalition with the SPD following the Bundestag election later that same year. The refusal of Scheel (the former leader of the FDP) to stand for a second term in 1979 arose because the CDU-CSU, which had a controlling majority in the electoral college, would not support his candidacy unless the FDP promised to switch coalition partners. Scheel decided it would be harmful to the dignity of the office of president for him to seek re-election unless he was certain to be successful. Roman Herzog was the second choice of the Christian Democrats (or, at least, of Helmut Kohl, the CDU leader and chancellor) in 1994. In autumn 1993 Kohl had put forward the name of the Minister of Justice in the Saxony Land government, Steffen Heitmann, in part because Heitmann's election would have meant that a politician from East Germany would become the head of state, symbolising the integration of the two parts of Germany. However, Heitmann's candidacy was not popular, even within the

CDU, because of some of his expressed political opinions. Kohl was forced to withdraw his support and Heitmann declined to be nominated. The support of the FDP for Herzog (in preference to Rau, the SPD candidate) in the 1994 presidential election was a signal confirming that the FDP would again seek to remain in coalition with the Christian Democrats after the 1994 Bundestag election.

Though denied any significant political discretion, the president does have a number of important functions to fulfil. These include responsibility under Article 63 of the Basic Law of nominating to the Bundestag a candidate for the office of chancellor. It is the responsibility of the Bundestag to vote for or against that candidate. Normally, this presidential duty will be a simple one: following nearly every Bundestag election since 1949 it has been clear which chancellor-candidate can command a majority, since it will have been obvious which coalition is likely to be formed after the election. Only in 1969 was there any doubt, since the FDP had not indicated unambiguously prior to the election which of the two major parties it would choose as its coalition partner after the election. However, talks following the election soon revealed that the FDP was intent upon forming a coalition with the SPD, so President Heinemann nominated Brandt to the Bundestag. Even were it not to be clear after an election which combination of parties might form a coalition, it would be the task of the president, through advisers, to discover which possible chancellor-candidate would be most likely to command a majority. The president also appoints ministers (on the nomination of the chancellor: Article 64 of the Basic Law), and accepts their resignations. The president formally appoints judges, civil servants and military officers, and it is to the president that foreign ambassadors present their credentials. The president possesses the power of pardon (Article 60 of the Basic Law). Potentially of great importance is the power of the president to dissolve the Bundestag on the request of the chancellor, if special circumstances occur following an unsuccessful vote of confidence in which no majority is available for a chancellor (Article 68 of the Basic Law). This situation occurred in 1972 and in 1982, cases where the president played a very significant political role. State treaties are countersigned by the president. Federal legislation requires the signature of the president before promulgation. This signature can only be refused if the president states that the bill contains unconstitutional aspects (which would then have to be tested by the Constitutional Court).

These specific functions (very similar, for instance, to those possessed by the monarch in the United Kingdom) are almost entirely such as to leave no discretion to the president [4] The president must act according to the advice of the chancellor or the relevant minister (e.g. the Justice Minister in respect of judicial appointments). Refusal to appoint a minister nominated by the chancellor, or to sign a bill which had passed properly through the various stages of the legislative process, would provoke a constitutional crisis, just as it would if a constitutional monarch in Britain or the Netherlands, for example, refused to do either of these things. However, informal and unofficial influence is available to the federal president, as it is to a constitutional monarch. President Heuss, for example, under pressure from the then president of the Constitutional Court, Höpker-Aschoff, indicated to Adenauer in 1953 that he could not accept the reappointment of Thomas Dehler (FDP) as Minister of Justice, as Dehler had repeatedly made immoderate criticisms of members of the Constitutional Court. Adenauer therefore persuaded the FDP to nominate an alternative Minister of Justice.[5] President Lübke also made known his objections to certain ministerial appointments, but without succeeding in compelling the chancellor to alter his nominations in these cases.

Where a president can exercise personal influence is through the representational function. Having taken the oath of office prescribed in the Basic Law which refers to devoting him or herself to the 'welfare of the whole people' and 'defending the Basic Law' (Article 56 of the Basic Law), a president can interpret these responsibilities in various ways. These include attendance at official ceremonies (such as state funerals), acting as patron to a range of causes and activities (such as school essay competitions on subjects relating to politics and democracy), confirming by visits to scenes of arson attacks and by public expressions of sympathy the revulsion of the state from acts of terror against immigrants and asylum-seekers, and representing the Federal Republic on state visits abroad. The president can also – usually through speeches or interviews – express views on a variety of topics, especially those concerned with moral or ethical issues or with the constitution and the political system as a whole (as opposed to issues of political partisanship, which of course must be avoided).[6] All presidents have done this, but Heinemann and von Weizsäcker were the two incumbents who are best remembered for such public statements. The speeches of von Weizsäcker (who was perhaps even more highly respected outside the Federal Republic than he was by his own fellow-citizens) on occasions such as the reunification of Germany, and anniversaries of the end of the war, or of the July Plot against Hitler, and his controversial interview with journalists from *Die Zeit* concerning the failure of political parties to behave in accordance with their constitutional position, are examples of such presidential influence. It is this function which led one commentator to call the president 'the most important opinion-former in the country'.[7]

Each incumbent has brought his own special style to the office, of course. Heuss, a former professor and liberal politician in the Weimar period, possessed a dignified, authoritative style. He had good relations with Adenauer, and together they steered the new Federal Republic through the crises that beset the first decade of its existence. Like Adenauer with the office of chancellor, Heuss had considerable influence as first incumbent on shaping the office of federal president. Lübke was very sensitive about the dignity of the office and his own person (knowing that Adenauer and other senior Christian Democrat politicians had turned down the opportunity to be president). He tried – eventually with success – to engineer the creation of a 'grand coalition' of the two major parties. He was unfairly attacked when in office by left-wing journalists and by the GDR for his wartime work on various forms of military construction, attacks based on rumours or half-truths and which ignored the context of the times. Lübke became the butt of radical journalists because of a series of verbal *faux pas* (some of which were perhaps caused by illness). Heinemann brought a puritanical attitude to the presidency, seeing himself as a 'citizen president' and abolishing some of the ceremonial aspects that had accumulated during his two predecessors' terms of office. Heinemann had a personal political career which commenced in the CDU, from which he resigned on the rearmament issue, then, after the failure of his own newly formed small party (the All-German People's Party), he joined the SPD. Thus he was well placed to have contacts with politicians across the party spectrum. He refused a second term. He was succeeded by Scheel, a more jovial, extrovert president. Carstens, Scheel's successor, administered the office with dignity and emphasised approachability. As a way of meeting the people, he set out to walk, in stages and accompanied by local residents, from the northern border of the Federal Republic to Lake Constance on its southern border. After three one term presidents, von Weizsäcker served two terms. He used his incumbency to set a high moral and ethical tone for the Federal Republic, and very competently fulfilled the responsibility of being head of state at the time of the downfall of the communist regime in the GDR and the reunification of Germany. He used his office to express concerns about the need to integrate western and eastern Germans after reunification. Herzog, a former president of the Constitutional Court, earned a reputation as a skilled and authoritative president. Rau, for many years minister-president of North Rhine-Westphalia, is respected by politicians from all parties, and brings political experience and a very approachable style to the presidency.

Box 7.2
Presidents of the Federal Republic of Germany

1949–59	Theodor Heuss (FDP)
1959–69	Heinrich Lübke (CDU)
1969–74	Gustav Heinemann (SPD)
1974–79	Walter Scheel (FDP)
1979–84	Karl Carstens (CDU)
1984–94	Richard von Weizsäcker (CDU)
1994–99	Roman Herzog (CDU)
1999–	Johannes Rau (SPD)

The federal chancellor

In contrast to the federal president, the federal chancellor is given considerable political authority by the Basic Law. Indeed, Article 65 states that the chancellor 'determines the guidelines of policy' within which the government operates:

the so-called *Richtlinienkompetenz*. Ministers have to run their departments within these guidelines. Chancellors may be tempted to try to extend the scope of the *Richtlinienkompetenz* by playing an active role in various policy sectors, where responsibility should lie with the minister concerned. This was certainly the case with Adenauer in various policy fields. Brandt, in pursuit of his *Ostpolitik*, took close personal interest in matters which were the responsibility of his Foreign Minister and his Minister for Inner-German Relations. Kohl has also played an active role in foreign affairs (especially concerning the European Union) and, prior to reunification, in policies affecting relations between the two German states. The fact that, especially in the cases of Adenauer and Kohl, chancellors have had longer periods in office than most of their ministers gives them authority when they are persuaded to take a detailed interest in the policies of particular ministries. For example, Adenauer was his own Foreign Minister from 1951 to 1955, then handed over to von Brentano and, from 1961, Schröder, but Adenauer of course retained considerable personal authority in foreign policy. The chancellor also has the responsibility of selecting his or her own cabinet (the nominated ministers are then formally appointed by the federal president). This allows also for the dismissal or transfer of ministers.

Though formally elected by the Bundestag after nomination by the federal president, the chancellor is, in effect, elected by the people. Bundestag elections have always been contests between two identifiable potential chancellors, representing the two main parties – CDU-CSU and the SPD; since the 1953 election one chancellor-candidate at every election has always been the incumbent. Given that the parties' preferred coalition partnerships are normally known at the time of the election campaign, it has thus usually been clear from the election result which of the two chancellor-candidates the federal president will nominate to the Bundestag. Only in 1969 was there any possible doubt following the election as to which name the president would send to the Bundestag (and that doubt soon disappeared as talks among the parties proceeded). Election by the Bundestag gives the chancellor an explicit expression of support by a majority in the lower chamber.

The chancellor's position is reinforced by the requirement set out in Article 67 of the Basic Law, that a chancellor can only be removed by the Bundestag if that chamber passes a *constructive* vote of no confidence in him or her, that is, a vote on a motion stating that the Bundestag has no confidence in the incumbent *and* simultaneously nominating a named successor. This prevents the situation which so often occurred in the Weimar Republic, whereby majorities of opponents (including Nazis and Communists) could – and did – frequently combine to vote against an incumbent chancellor, but could not have found a majority which would support any successor. This led to governmental instability. So far, the constructive vote of no confidence has only been utilised twice by the Bundestag. It was attempted in April 1972 against Brandt, after he had lost his small majority through individual members of the FDP and SPD parliamentary parties switching to the opposition benches. That motion failed by two votes.[8] The other occasion was in October 1982, after the FDP had left the coalition with the SPD. The FDP indicated that they would be ready to join a coalition with the CDU-CSU, and supported the constructive vote of no confidence which replaced Helmut Schmidt as chancellor by Helmut Kohl. Except in most unusual circumstances, it is likely that this method of changing chancellors will only be used when the junior partner in a coalition wishes to switch partners, or if a form of political emergency requires the creation of a 'grand coalition' of some sort.

The exceptional degree of stability that the Basic Law provides to the chancellor, together with relatively stable electoral behaviour and a party system which has also been fairly stable over long periods, has meant that of the six changes of chancellor since 1949, only one (Schmidt to Kohl in 1982) has been the result of a constructive vote of no confidence, and only two followed a Bundestag election (Kohl to Schröder in 1998 and, before that, Kiesinger to Brandt in 1969; but even this was not a necessary consequence of the election, as the FDP in 1969 could have decided to provide Kiesinger with a majority instead). The other three have all been changes within the same party during legislative periods: Adenauer to Erhard in 1963; Erhard to Kiesinger in 1966; and Brandt to Schmidt in 1974, caused by age and political pressure in the first case, coalition difficulties in the second case, and a security scandal – the Guillaume affair – in the third case. So far, no chancellor has had to leave office because of ill health, and none has died in office.

Box 7.3
Chancellors of the Federal Republic of Germany

1949–63	Konrad Adenauer (CDU)
1963–66	Ludwig Erhard (CDU)
1966–69	Kurt-Georg Kiesinger (CDU)
1969–74	Willy Brandt (SPD)
1974–82	Helmut Schmidt (SPD)
1982–98	Helmut Kohl (CDU)
1998–	Gerhard Schröder (SPD)

As well as the authority to set guidelines for the government and the stability provided by the constructive vote of no confidence, several other factors have contributed to the authority which the chancellor possesses. One of the most important of these factors is the chancellor's relationship with his or her party. Usually the chancellor is also the elected leader of the party, which buttresses his or her authority in the government and gives him or her considerable control over the party organisation. However, there are several instances when this has not been the case. Adenauer remained as CDU party chairman until 1966, after resigning from the chancellorship, which weakened Erhard's position as chancellor. Erhard then became CDU chairman, and retained the post until 1967, even though Kiesinger had replaced him as chancellor on 1 December 1966. Brandt remained as party chairman for thirteen years after resigning as chancellor, giving up the party leadership only in 1987. Schröder, when he became chancellor in 1998, was not the party chairman; Lafontaine (Schröder's Minister of Finance) held that position. However, when Lafontaine resigned from the government in 1999, he also resigned as party chairman, and Schröder was elected in his place. In each of these cases of separation of the office of chancellor from that of party leader, there have been problems concerning the chancellor's control over his party. Adenauer, Brandt and Kohl, on the other hand, holding the dual offices of chancellor and party chairman, were able to reinforce their authority within the government by being seen to be in – usually undisputed – control of their party organisation. Indeed, Kohl's domination of his party and his strategy of preventing potent rivals to his party leadership from emerging can be regarded as major contributory causes of his power as chancellor. Similarly, the links between the chancellor and the parliamentary leadership of his party group in the Bundestag (the Fraktion) are also of great importance (see chapter 8).

The personalisation of government and of Bundestag election campaigns commenced under Adenauer, but has continued since then, so that several elections have been fought by the governing party with slogans such as: 'It all depends on the chancellor!' In 1994, the CDU even used a poster campaign which showed Helmut Kohl surrounded by a crowd of people, but without any slogan or even the name of Kohl appearing on the poster, on the assumption that he was too well known to need such identification. Survey evidence indicates that a considerable number of voters make their choice on election day because of their opinion about the chancellor (and about the chancellor-candidate of the main opposition party), rather than on the basis of policy issues or long-term identification with a particular party. The extension in importance of the Office of the Federal Chancellor (the Bundeskanzleramt), very approximately comparable to the White House staff in the USA or the Office of the Prime Minister in Blair's government in Britain, has also supplemented the authority of the chancellor. This Office assists the chancellor by co-ordinating the work of the various ministries, providing the chancellor with information and contributing to forward planning of government business. It is now usually headed by a minister, though at times in the past it has been directed by a senior civil servant.

The powers of the chancellor also owe much to the incumbency of Konrad Adenauer, the first chancellor. He set precedents for the scope of the authority of the chancellor, particularly in relation to the president and the cabinet. The fact that he had to negotiate with the occupation authorities in the first years of the Federal Republic, and then acted as his own Foreign Minister from 1951 to 1955 after the Federal Republic was granted the right to conduct its own foreign policy, necessarily added to the importance of the office of chancellor. However, Adenauer's attempts to exert authority over his coalition partners failed in the case of the FDP, leading to coalition crises (especially in 1956 and over the 'Spiegel Affair' in 1962), and subsequent chancellors have been more sensitive to the autonomy and interests of the FDP.

Indeed, the first of the constraints on the powers of the chancellor which requires consideration is the need to govern in coalition with other parties. Only Adenauer in 1957 secured an absolute majority of votes and seats in a Bundestag election, and even then he decided to entice the small DP into his cabinet, to enlarge his majority. Since 1961 (with the exception of the 'grand coalition' between the CDU-CSU and SPD 1966–69) coalitions have consisted of the Christian Democrats governing with the FDP or else the Social Democrats governing either with the FDP or, since 1998, with the Greens. In addition, CDU chancellors have had to respect the autonomy and importance of their Bavarian counterpart, the CSU, in terms of allocation of cabinet posts and of policy development. The rivalry between the CSU and FDP, though milder since the death of Strauss, the CSU leader and long-time adversary of the FDP, has been a source both of strength and weakness for CDU chancellors. On the one hand, the chancellor can 'play off' the demands of one of these parties against the other, claiming that coalition necessity requires him to take a particular course of action. Kohl's refusal to offer Strauss the post of Foreign Minister in 1982–83, on the grounds that the FDP insisted that Genscher must remain in that office, is an example. In this way, the chancellor's personal political capital is not eroded. On the other hand, the desire of both these partner-parties to profile themselves within the coalition, and the difficulty of getting them to agree on policy in some cases, makes the task of finding compromises and developing a proactive policy programme that much more difficult. (A more detailed consideration of the process of forming coalition governments is provided later in this chapter.)

The federal structure of the state, and the powers given to the Bundesrat by the Basic Law, provide another set of constraints on the powers of the chancellor. Since some areas of policy are the responsibility of the Länder, or else are joint or concurrent responsibilities, shared by the federal government and the Länder (see chapter 6), the chancellor and his government have to take this federal element into account, and often must negotiate with the Länder to persuade them to harmonise policy with that of the federal government, for example in terms of public expenditure, higher education policies or environmental protection. Even if the chancellor is successful in this, there is still the need to pass legislation through the Bundesrat, which can veto any legislation affecting the areas of competence of the Länder, federal-Länder relations and certain other matters (see chapter 8). When the Bundesrat votes by a two-thirds majority against legislation not requiring its consent, then the government needs to obtain a two-thirds majority to override that veto, so when the opposition is especially successful in Land elections, the federal government could be placed in a position where it cannot pass legislation (including a budget) unless the opposition agrees – virtually a 'grand coalition' situation.

Constraints arise from the autonomy of other institutions in the Federal Republic. The powerful role of the constitutional court (see chapter 3), the control function of the Bundestag (see chapter 8), the autonomous status of the Bundesbank in relation to monetary policy and the constitutional responsibility for the operation of their own departments granted to ministers by Article 65 of the Basic Law have all acted as constraints on policy choices and freedom of action of even the most powerful of chancellors. The 'Five Wise Men' (Sachverständigenrat), have the obligation to present an annual report on the state of the economy to the Bundestag, and the government must respond to this report. This requirement makes the economic policy-making assumptions of the government more transparent, and compels the government to respond to criticisms from the committee concerning, for example, fiscal or monetary policy measures.[9] Another constraint on government action is the 'military ombudsman' (Wehrbeauftragter), appointed by the Bundestag to protect the rights of members of the armed forces and to report to the Bundestag on the state of the military. This official has unrestricted access to information from the Minister of Defence (except where such information is protected as a state secret). Externally, international agreements and especially obligations arising from Germany's membership of the European Union (see chapter 10), may constrain the freedom of action of the chancellor. Obligations stemming from the Federal Republic's membership of NATO complicated Schmidt's relations with his own party and his coalition partner, the FDP, and Kohl's freedom of action in dealing with the aftermath of reunification had to take into consideration regulations deriving from EC membership, to state but two examples.

Cabinet and government

In forming a government after a Bundestag election, a chancellor will necessarily have to take several factors into account. The first and foremost of these will be the coalition negotiations procedure, which will deal with both the policy programme of the new government and the allocation of ministerial posts that each party will receive. Such negotiations vary in terms of the time they take: in 1961, for instance, 58 days elapsed between the Bundestag election and the appointment of the cabinet; in 1969 only 24 days elapsed – an indication of the relative degree of difficulty involved in those two cases.[10] Since the 1960s, the outcomes of coalition negotiations have been embodied in a formal coalition agreement, to serve as a record and reference guide for the parties in government. In 1998, this agreement between the SPD and the Greens was signed on 20 October, just over three weeks after the Bundestag election.

Unusually, the agreement was then subjected to the approval a few days later of separate party conferences of the two coalition partners, where overwhelming majorities voted in favour of its acceptance.

In the Federal Republic, it has almost always been the case that the composition of potential coalition governments has been made known to the electorate in advance of Bundestag elections. Only in 1957 and 1969 did the FDP deliberately opt for an 'open to both sides' coalition strategy. In 1957, the FDP was not needed by the Christian Democrats as a coalition partner, because the CDU-CSU had obtained an absolute majority of votes and Bundestag seats, and in 1969 the FDP had given strong indications (not least by its support for the SPD candidate for the federal presidency, Heinemann) that it would probably prefer a coalition with the SPD rather than with the CDU-CSU, if such a choice were available. On other occasions, the FDP has always made its coalition preference clear to the electorate in advance, and in every case that has been a preference for its existing partner in government. In 1998 it was fairly certain that, if the arithmetic permitted, the SPD would form a coalition with the Greens, even though, unlike the Greens, the SPD had not made that coalition choice explicit in its campaign. Coalition negotiations tend to proceed fairly smoothly, if only because only two parties now are usually involved, and the FDP has realised that it generally has no alternative to supporting its senior partner. In 1961, negotiations were complicated because the leader of the FDP, Mende, insisted in the late stages of the election campaign that his party would not accept Adenauer as chancellor, though he confirmed that the FDP would seek to enter a coalition with the CDU-CSU. Adenauer outmanoeuvred the FDP by obtaining the support of his own party for a further term as chancellor in advance of coalition negotiations, and by insisting that policy issues be negotiated first, and the personal composition of the government later. This put pressure on the FDP not to break off negotiations after several weeks of talks, over the issue of Adenauer's nomination as chancellor.[11] The negotiations following the Bundestag election of 1983 were complicated by demands from the CSU that its leader, Strauss, should be given the post of Foreign Minister in place of Genscher, the incumbent Foreign Minister and FDP leader. Kohl used the insistence of the FDP that Genscher should be retained as Foreign Minister as an excuse not to award such an influential post to Strauss. As Strauss then refused offers of other posts, he did not become a member of the Kohl government.

The FDP (the SPD in the case of the 1966–69 'grand coalition'), the Greens, and – for CDU chancellors – the CSU will have demands to make concerning not just the number of ministries they wish to receive, but also their prominence. Junior partners have usually received a disproportionately large number of cabinet posts. They have been successful in obtaining some of the more important ministries also. The FDP provided the Minister of Justice from 1949 to 1956, 1961 to 1965 and 1982 to 1998; the Minister of the Interior from 1969 to 1982; the Minister of Finance from 1961 to 1966 and the Minister of

Economics from 1972 to 1998; and it provided the Foreign Minister from 1969 to 1998.[12] In governments led by Adenauer, Erhard, Brandt, Schmidt and Kohl an FDP minister has almost always been given the position of deputy chancellor. In 1998, the Greens obtained the post of Foreign Minister (as well as two other cabinet posts) in the SPD–Greens coalition government, and that Foreign Minister, Joschka Fischer, became deputy chancellor. With few exceptions, the choice of nominee to these ministerial positions has been left to the party concerned. There have been a very small number of cases where a veto has been exercised by the chancellor (in the case of Dehler, for instance – see above), but otherwise the coalition partner has complete freedom. This applies also to nomination of a replacement where a ministry held by a junior coalition partner becomes vacant.[13]

For ministers from the chancellor's own party, other considerations will be taken into account. At least in the early years of the Federal Republic, for CDU chancellors a mix of Catholics and Protestants was essential, to prevent the CDU being perceived as exclusively a Catholic party, on the lines of the Centre party in the Second Empire and Weimar Republic. A regional mix is important: neglect of, say, south Germany by a north German chancellor or, since 1990, of the 'new Länder', would be politically unwise. Attention today is given to ensuring representation of women in the cabinet,[14] and to providing a range of age-groups. There may be trends towards the appointment of politicians who support the particular political tendency of the chancellor within the party, but, for the sake of party unity, a need also for one or two ministers who represent other political tendencies. The selection of Ertl by the FDP as Minister for Agriculture in 1969, for instance, was a 'consolation prize' to the right wing of the FDP, a grouping not easily reconciled to the novelty of the FDP now supporting a Social Democratic chancellor. The CDU usually has a representative of the left wing of the party (the 'social wing') as its Minister for Labour (e.g., Hans Katzer 1965–69 or Norbert Blum 1982–98). The SPD will tend to select a leading trade unionist for the post of Minster for Labour, as has been the case with Walter Arendt in 1969 or Walter Riester, deputy leader of the Metal Workers Union, in 1998. The Greens ensured that one minister from the more pragmatic 'Realo' wing (Fischer) and one from the more ideological 'Fundi' wing (Jürgen Trittin, Minister for the Environment) were included in its ministerial team in 1998. Political ability and special expertise are other factors which will be taken into account: clearly Ludwig Erhard in Adenauer's governments, Gerhard Schröder in Adenauer's last cabinet and in Erhard's government, Helmut Schmidt in Brandt's government and Wolfgang Schäuble in Kohl's government (until his transfer to the position of chairman of the parliamentary party group) were included above all because of their outstanding abilities. Ministers are not always drawn from politicians who have come to prominence in the Bundestag, and there have been several examples of ministers who have not held a Bundestag seat on appointment to office. Successful experience as minister (perhaps as minister-president) in a Land government

---

Box 7.4
Governments of the Federal Republic⁽ᵃ⁾

1949–53	CDU-CSU; FDP; DP
1953–56	CDU-CSU; FDP; DP; GB/BHE⁽ᵇ⁾
1956–57	CDU-CSU; DP; FVP⁽ᶜ⁾
1957–61	CDU-CSU; DP⁽ᵈ⁾
1961–66	CDU-CSU; FDP
1966–69	CDU-CSU; SPD
1969–82	SPD-FDP
1982–98	CDU-CSU; FDP
1998–	SPD; Greens

[a] Temporary and unimportant changes to the composition of governments (such as the brief period of SPD minority government in 1982) have been ignored.
[b] GB/BHE (the Refugee party) left the coalition in 1955.
[c] FVP: the Free People's Party was the short-lived party formed by the former FDP ministers and their supporters, who broke with the FDP when the FDP decided to leave the Adenauer coalition in 1956.
[d] The DP Fraktion split in 1960; some left the coalition, others (including the two DP ministers) joined the CDU.

---

has always been a potential path to cabinet office in the federal government: Willy Brandt (from Berlin), Helmut Schmidt (Hamburg), Rita Süssmuth (Lower Saxony) and Walter Wallmann and Hans Eichel (Hesse) are examples. Since 1967, a number of parliamentary state secretaries have also been appointed and, like ministries, these posts are shared out among the coalition partners.[15]

The cabinet has varied in size from fourteen in 1949 – when the federal government had lacked responsibility for foreign affairs and defence – to just over twenty under Erhard's chancellorship, and consisted of sixteen ministers, including the chancellor, after the 1998 Bundestag election. It usually meets once a week, under the chairmanship of the chancellor (in his absence, the deputy chancellor). The procedural aspects of cabinet meetings are the responsibility of the staff of the Office of the Federal Chancellor. The work of the cabinet has become less significant, because of the importance of cabinet committees (as in the United Kingdom also, for instance), the work of various inter-ministerial committees and, above all, the growth in significance of the 'coalition committee', at which leading representatives of the coalition partners meet. This coalition committee has come to usurp some of the decision-making functions of the cabinet, and has acquired increased formality of procedure over the past decade, with a formal agenda and, prior to the entry into office of the Schröder government in 1998, regular weekly meetings.[16]

The federal government is supported in its work by the civil service. Each ministry has its own state secretary (the chief civil servant of the ministry). The status of the civil service is protected by the Basic Law and various judicial decisions in cases arising out of the Basic Law. An agreement in 1972 between the federal government and the governments of the Länder provides for the exclusion from the public service (including the civil service) of anyone whose political behaviour has given grounds for supposing that they would not reliably and at all times protect the basic democratic order. This 'Radicals Decree' gave rise to considerable controversy concerning its appropriateness within a democratic political system, and to legal challenges. However, it remains an important part of the regulations governing the civil service (Braunthal, 1990). Unlike the case in the United Kingdom, where few civil servants seek elected office, and have to resign from the civil service if they wish to stand for election, it is quite usual for civil servants to seek election to the Bundestag or to Land parliaments, and to put their careers on 'hold' if elected. They can then return to their civil service careers if later defeated at an election, or if they wish to terminate their activities as elected politicians.

The policy process

There are various sources of policy initiation in the Federal Republic. Some policy-making will derive from routine obligations, such as the annual budget. Indeed, the annual debate on the budget tends to be a more wide-ranging affair in Germany than in Britain. It is an opportunity for the opposition to seize upon any policy area they wish, to compel the government to defend its policies. The 'government declaration' (*Regierungserklärung*, the equivalent of the 'Queen's Speech' in the case of the United Kingdom) will set out the programme of agreed policies for the coalition. The coalition partners will have their own electoral programmes, the manifestos upon which they will have campaigned in the previous Bundestag election, and will each desire to implement as many of their election promises as possible.[17] Some policy-making will be a response to external pressures: policies of the European Union concerning monetary union, environmental protection measures, immigration policy and asylum law, or subsidies for industry, for example. Other policies may be reactions to crises: the erection of the Berlin Wall in 1961, the oil crisis in 1974, or the downfall of communist regimes (and especially the end of the SED-regime in the German Democratic Republic) from 1989 onwards were such cases. Policy may originate in demands from interest groups (see chapter 9): examples include tax concessions for particular groups (flying clubs, farmers, West German civil servants seconded to the 'new Länder', for instance); protection measures for members of a profession (such as pharmacists, lawyers, engineers); or policy changes demanded by 'new social movements' such as ecologists or feminists.

Policies will be developed by either a single ministry, or by a committee representing two or more ministries. Where the interests of the coalition partners are likely to be divergent, the coalition committee may become involved. The cabinet will discuss and ratify the policy before the policy is presented to the Bundestag and Bundesrat for discussion and approval assuming legislation is required (the legislative process is outlined in chapter 8). At all stages, the effect of the policy on the Länder will be an important consideration (see chapter 6), and its constitutionality will also be scrutinised, to avoid having the policy challenged before the Constitutional Court (see chapter 3). Interest group concerns will be anticipated, if possible, and their objections taken into account. If a policy requires an amendment to the constitution, or if a potential veto on a matter which requires the assent of the Bundesrat is to be avoided (where the opposition, as was the case in 1998, holds a majority of votes in the Bundesrat), then consultation with the opposition will be essential. Chancellor Kohl had to abandon in 1998 his cherished plan for tax reform because agreement could not be reached with the SPD, which had a majority in the Bundesrat.

These various constraints – the Länder, the Constitutional Court, the coalition parties, the opposition, interest groups – mean that policy-making in the Federal Republic tends, generally, to be a more 'consensual' process than is the case in the United Kingdom or France, where single-party or single-bloc government and a more adversarial policy-making procedure is the rule. However, some contentious policies are implemented: several of Adenauer's policies, such as rearmament and West German participation in institutions of European integration; Brandt's *Ostpolitik* treaties; Helmut Schmidt's acceptance of NATO's 'twin-track' military strategy; Kohl's crusade for a single European currency, or his government's willingness to use German military forces 'out of area' are some examples. Just occasionally, policies will be controversial even within the coalition. Not all such policies will result in parliamentary defeat just because one of the coalition partners fails to support it unanimously, as happened in 1998 with legislation to permit 'bugging' of residences of suspected criminals, where many FDP MdBs refused to vote for that legislation. But the knowledge that one coalition party (or even a minority of that party's Bundestag group) will not support a particular policy, or at least not support all its provisions, may mean that a proposal is withdrawn or substantially modified.

So policy-making in Germany tends to be 'conservative', to involve much consultation, little radical content and a relatively long procedure prior to implementation. In the past, this has been seen as a strength, as a reason for other countries to look to the Federal Republic as a 'model'. In post-reunification Germany, some critics claim that it is a weakness, a hindrance to the kind of 'flexible response' which is required by policy-makers to demographic, economic, social and international forces of change, if Germany is to be adaptable, peaceful and prosperous.

Notes

1 The term originated as a description of the dominance of Konrad Adenauer as chancellor in the 1950s, and was used as early as 1953 (Niclauss, 1999, p. 36). There has been debate concerning whether, or to what extent, it could be applied to later chancellors. Certainly several of the features of the political system which permitted Adenauer to exert such dominance in government continued to allow other chancellors (especially Helmut Kohl) to take such a prominent role within government as to warrant the continued use of the term 'chancellor democracy'. Niclauss claims that all chancellors, at least some of the time, have focused on co-ordination of other actors in the policy-making process – such as the chancellor's own party, the Bundesrat, other ministers, interest groups – but that each chancellor has had the opportunity to dominate the policy-making process, by use of the media, by personalisation of the political process by assertion of the chancellor's role in foreign policy and so on (Niclauss, 1999, p. 37).

2 The wording of the Basic Law is slightly ambiguous: Article 54 of the Basic Law simply states that *successive* re-election is only possible once (author's italics). This leaves open the possibility of someone serving a third term after an interval during which some other incumbent has served. However, it is very improbable that such a circumstance would arise.

3 Rau was the candidate of the SPD and Greens; Schipanski was nominated by the CDU-CSU; Ranke-Heinemann was a candidate representing the pacifist movement, supported by the PDS. With 1,338 members, the absolute majority required for election on the first or second round was thus 670.

4 In the event of the Bundestag failing to elect a chancellor with the required absolute majority of its membership on either the first or a second ballot, it is at the discretion of the federal president either to accept a minority chancellor (i.e. one elected by a simple majority vote on a third ballot) or to dissolve the Bundestag and hold new elections. So far, this extreme case has not been necessary.

5 This – reluctantly – the FDP did (Fritz Neumayer was selected as Dehler's replacement). The FDP MdBs demonstrated their support for Dehler by electing him the leader of their Bundestag Fraktion, and in 1954 the party congress elected him as party leader.

6 An example of expression of concern for a constitutional type of issue was the letter of reprimand to the Bundestag which President Herzog sent to the President of the Bundestag, Thierse, in February 1999. This criticised the Bundestag for increasing the level of public subsidy for political parties by DM15 million, after an independent commission had proposed an increase of only DM14.49 million. Herzog regarded this amount of 'rounding-up' in favour of the parties as excessively generous. However, he indicated that it was not a sufficiently severe deviation from the report of the independent commission to warrant a complaint to the Constitutional Court (*Der Spiegel*, 1 March 1999, p. 17).

7 Baring, A. (1982) *Machtwechsel. Die Ära Brandt-Scheel*, Stuttgart, Deutsche Verlags-Anstalt, p. 28, cited in Schwarz (1999, p. 3).

8 This surprised most observers, since the CDU-CSU fully anticipated that the secret ballot used for the constructive vote of no confidence would encourage other FDP MdBs to vote for Barzel, the chancellor replacement nominated by the CDU-CSU in the motion of no confidence. It appeared that this did not happen, but that some

members of the opposition were 'persuaded' to vote for Brandt (one at least as a result of a bribe). The failure of this motion of no confidence did not, of course, alter the fact that the government lacked a majority, and a premature Bundestag election was held in November 1972 to resolve the situation. In that election Brandt obtained a comfortable, and reliable, majority for his coalition.

9 This committee was created under a law passed in 1963. The experts are generally professors drawn from the major university economic research institutes. An informal convention exists whereby the trade union federation and the employers' organisation are consulted about two of the nominees.

10 Information from Schindler (1983, pp. 367–8). Of course, in some cases talks continue even after a cabinet has been appointed, but such talks occur within the context of the already agreed composition of the government, and are usually on matters of detail rather than cross-party controversy.

11 Adenauer was, however, persuaded to provide a written promise to his own party and to the FDP that he would resign as chancellor before the next Bundestag election. The political crisis in 1962 over the 'Spiegel Affair' (see chapter 4) eroded Adenauer's authority, and he resigned the following year.

12 These dates omit the brief interruption when the SPD governed alone in 1982, after the FDP had withdrawn from the coalition.

13 However, embarrassment has occurred on several occasions in recent years where a nominee for a vacancy to be filled by the FDP has been agreed between the leadership of the FDP and the chancellor, and then announced to the press, only for the FDP Fraktion to assert its independence and to hold an election, in which the original choice of the FDP leadership has then been defeated by an alternative candidate (e.g. Kinkel's election as nominee for Foreign Minister in 1992, following Genscher's resignation). Though this right of nomination is not stated in so many words in the 1998 coalition agreement between the SPD and the Greens, this 'ownership' of ministerial portfolios is indicated at the end of the document.

14 In the cabinets of Adenauer and Erhard, there was no female minister until 1961. Only one woman was then appointed – Elizabeth Schwarzhaupt, Minister for Health from 1961 to 1966. Only two women served in the cabinet of the 'grand coalition' (one from 1966, the other only from 1968). In the cabinets of Brandt and Schmidt, there was only a single female minister until 1976, then two until 1978 and only one from 1978 to 1982. Kohl included only one female minister in his first cabinet in 1982, and in 1998 immediately prior to the Bundestag election there were still only two. In the Schröder cabinet, formed after the 1998 Bundestag election, five women were appointed as ministers (four from the SPD and one from the Greens).

15 Unlike ministers, who do not need to be elected members of the Bundestag – though most are, of course – parliamentary state secretaries (since 1974 termed 'Ministers of State' in the case of the Chancellor's Office and the Foreign Ministry) must by law be drawn from elected members of the Bundestag, though an exception was made in 1998 to allow Michael Naumann to be appointed as Minister of State in the Chancellor's Office. Several ministries now have two such parliamentary state secretaries, and the mammoth Ministry for Construction, Town Planning and Transport now has three. In the government formed after the 1994 Bundestag election, there were eighteen ministers – including Helmut Kohl – but twenty-seven parliamentary state secretaries. The Schröder government had twenty-four such parliamentary state secretaries in 1998.

16 This committee was especially important at times when, as was the case when Lambsdorff was leader of the FDP (1988–93), and then under the leadership of Wolfgang Gerhardt (from 1995), the leader of the FDP is not a member of the cabinet. The Schröder government formed in 1998 decided to use the coalition committee only for issues of an exceptional nature, to be summoned by either coalition partner, but soon found more frequent meetings of the coalition committee both useful and necessary.

17 Research has shown that, interestingly, the manifesto of the FDP has been a better guide to the policy programme implemented by the government than either the manifesto of its senior governing partner (the CDU-CSU or the SPD) or the agreed 'government declaration' at the commencement of a legislative period. See, for example, the findings of Hofferbert and Klingemann (1990).

References

Braunthal, G. (1990) *Political Loyalty and Public Service in West Germany*, Amherst, University of Massachusetts Press.

Hofferbert, R. and Klingemann, H.-D. (1990) 'The policy impact of party programmes and government declarations in the Federal Republic of Germany', *European Journal of Political Research*, 3: 277–304.

Niclauss, K. (1999) 'Bestätigung der Kanzlerdemokratie?', *Das Parlament. Beilage: Aus Politik und Zeitgeschichte*, 20: 27–38.

Schindler, P. (ed.) (1983) *Datenhandbuch zur Geschichte des Deutschen Bundestages: 1949–82*, Bonn, Presse- und Informationszentrum des Deutschen Bundestages.

Schwarz, H.-P. (1999) 'Von Heuss bis Herzog. Die Entwicklung des Amtes im Vergleich der Amtsinhaber', *Das Parlament. Beilage: Aus Politik und Zeitgeschichte*, 20: 3–13.

Further reading

Clemens, C. (1994) 'The Chancellor as Manager', *West European Politics*, 4: 28–51.

Clemens, C. (1998) 'Party management as a leadership resource: Kohl and the CDU/CSU', in Clemens, C. and Paterson, W. (eds), *The Kohl Chancellorship*, special issue of *German Politics*, 1: 91–119.

Marshall, B. (1997) *Willy Brandt: a Political Biography*, Basingstoke, Macmillan.

Padgett, S. (ed.) (1994) *Adenauer to Kohl. The development of the German Chancellorship*. London, Hurst.

Smith, G. (1991) 'The Resources of the German Chancellor', *West European Politics*, 2: 48–61.

8

Parliamentary politics

Historical background

Parliamentary assemblies have a long history in Germany. A form of parliament can be traced in the states of Germany to the Middle Ages. In the modern period, parliaments were founded even before 'Germany' was created as a modern state; several of the southern states which later became part of the Second Empire had parliaments in the early nineteenth century: Baden, Bavaria and Württemberg, for example. The 'Frankfurt Parliament' which sought to design a scheme for unification of the German states was convened in the St Paul's church in Frankfurt in 1848–49, even though for different purposes than those which 'legislative' parliaments have. The North German Confederation had its parliamentary assembly from 1867 to 1871. When Germany was unified in 1871, the Second Empire and its successor regime, the Weimar Republic, of course possessed legislative assemblies, each with two chambers, and the component Länder of these two regimes also had their own parliaments. Once the Second World War came to an end in 1945, the allied occupation authorities, in line with provisions in the Potsdam Agreement, soon came to encourage the Länder in their zones of occupation to hold elections for Land parliaments, a chief function of those parliaments being to draft democratic constitutions for the Länder. Some of these Land legislatures were elected in late 1946 (such as in Bremen, Hamburg, Hesse, Württemberg-Baden and Bavaria), others in 1947. This creation of Land legislatures did mean two things of great relevance for the design of parliamentary structures for the new Federal Republic in 1949. First, there were both historical and contemporary models to use as patterns when planning such parliamentary structures for the new Federal Republic and, second, there was already in existence in the Länder a group of politicians with parliamentary experience, to guide the drafters of the Basic Law. As with other institutions of the political system of the Federal Republic, the legislature was designed with the lessons of the Weimar Republic very much in mind. In particular, the authority of the Bundestag to elect the chancellor directly, and the constraint on its power to dismiss the chancellor (and thus the government) imposed by the 'constructive vote of no confidence'

131

provision, reflect this desire to avoid the weaknesses of the Weimar constitution.

This chapter will describe the structures of the two chambers of the legislature of the Federal Republic: the Bundestag and the Bundesrat, analyse the ways in which the functions of the legislature are carried out, and examine the social composition of the Bundestag in relation to its representative function.

The Bundestag

The Bundestag is the lower chamber of the legislature of the Federal Republic of Germany, which in 1999 relocated from Bonn to the refurbished Reichstag building in Berlin. It has currently a *basic* membership of 656, though because of the possibility of the existence of 'surplus seats' following an election, *actual* membership may be larger (see Chapter 4). In the years since reunification, because of such 'surplus seats', there have been 662 MdBs in 1990, 672 in 1994 and 669 in 1998. As from the election scheduled for the year 2002, the basic membership will be reduced to 598, following acceptance of recommendations of a select committee which examined the case for reforming the structure of the Bundestag. Members of the Bundestag are elected for a four-year term (though suggestions have been made by prominent members of the SPD, for instance, that the term should be extended to five years, in line with the legislative periods of several of the Land legislatures). Only in very exceptional circumstances can the four-year term be shortened, as happened in 1972 and in 1982–83, following elimination of the government's majority in the first place and a change of chancellor and of coalition in the second case. There is no provision for premature dissolution by decision of either the Bundestag itself or the government. Only the federal president can bring about a premature dissolution, though this has to be at the request of the chancellor (Article 68 of the Basic Law).[1] The mode of election of MdBs, within 328 single-member constituencies and from party lists in each Land for the remainder, is described in Chapter 4.

Besides operating under relevant provisions of the Basic Law, and under legislation such as the Electoral Law and the Party Law, the Bundestag conducts its business and arranges its organisation under the provisions of its own regulations, the *Geschäftsordnung des Bundestages* (Rules of Procedure). Such regulations can be modified from time to time by decision of the Bundestag itself, of course. This obviates the need either to secure a special majority (as is required to amend the Basic Law) or obtain the consent of the Bundesrat, as would be the case with ordinary legislation (see below for a description of the legislative process). The Rules of Procedure are subject to review by a committee of the Bundestag – the 'Rules of Procedure Committee'. These regulations cover matters such as how many MdBs must be present for the Bundestag to be quorate; what percentage or minimum number of MdBs a party requires to qualify as a Fraktion (in 1999, 5 per cent); the composition of the Council of

Elders (see below) which supervises the schedule and other managerial matters of the Bundestag's work and procedures for various forms of parliamentary question. Clearly, many of these regulations can have considerable political significance, such as the rule concerning the minimum number of MdBs to qualify for Fraktion status. The PDS in 1990 and 1994 did not have this minimum number of 5 per cent of the membership of the Bundestag, because it had qualified for seats under provisions which were alternatives to the general requirement that a party needs 5 per cent of list votes to obtain proportional representation in the Bundestag. On both occasions, the PDS was given only the status of a party group, which to an extent limited the parliamentary funding it could receive and restricted its rights in relation to Bundestag procedures, compared to a Fraktion, though from 1994 to 1998 these restrictions were minimal. In 1998 the PDS did obtain sufficient seats to qualify for full status as a Fraktion.

The main supervisory committee of the Bundestag is the praesidium. This consists of the president of the Bundestag (not to be confused with the federal president, of course!) and the five vice-presidents of the Bundestag. The president normally acts as chairperson for plenary sessions of the Bundestag, much as the Speaker of the British House of Commons or the Speaker of the House in the US Congress does for plenary sessions of the House of Representatives. He or she also represents the Bundestag on official occasions, presides over the electoral college which elects the federal president (see Chapter 7), and is responsible for defending the rights and dignities of the Bundestag. The convention has developed that the largest Fraktion nominates the president of the Bundestag, who is then formally elected by the Bundestag, though that party is expected to consult with other parties on the nomination, and certainly should not nominate a controversial personality. The president of the Bundestag elected in 1998, Wolfgang Thierse, is only the second SPD president. The first was Annemarie Renger from 1972 to 1976, the only other period when the SPD enjoyed the status of having the largest Fraktion. Each of the other parties, by convention, nominates a vice-president.[2] These vice-presidents substitute for the president during absences.

The vice-presidents also are available for consultation by the president, though such consultation more usually involves the Ältestenrat (Council of Elders), which consists of the members of the praesidium and 23 other MdBs, chosen in proportion to party strength, and including the important business managers of each party (Fraktionsgeschäftsführer, equivalent to the 'chief whips' in the House of Commons). The head of the staff of the Chancellor's Office or his deputy attends as an observer. This Council of Elders, at its weekly meetings when the Bundestag is in session, helps to arrange the fair distribution of committee chairmanships by consultation with the parties, mediates between party groups on matters affecting the operation of the Bundestag, plans the schedule of the Bundestag (taking into account such events as Land election campaign dates and party congresses) and is responsible for preparing the budget of the Bundestag and for the management of its staff and facilities

---

Box 8.1
The Bundestag praesidium, 1998

President of the Bundestag

Wolfgang Thierse
First Bundestag president to come from East Germany. Only the second president from the SPD. Active in the reform movement in the GDR in 1989–90, first in New Forum, then in the GDR Social Democratic Party, becoming chairman of that party in June 1990. He then became a deputy chairman of the SPD when the West German and East German parties fused. Elected as president with 512 votes in favour, 109 votes against.

Vice-presidents of the Bundestag

(i) Anke Fuchs (SPD)
Formerly federal business manager of the SPD. Received 486 votes in favour, 148 votes against.

(ii) Rudolf Seiters (CDU-CSU)
Interior Minister in the previous government. Served for twelve years as business manager of the CDU-CSU Fraktion. Received 445 votes in favour, 142 votes against.

(iii) Antje Vollmer (Greens)
The only member to have served on the praesidium in the 1994–98 Bundestag. Twice acted as one of the (joint) Fraktion leaders of the Greens. Received 421 votes in favour, 191 votes against.

(iv) Hermann Otto Solms (FDP)
Leader of the FDP Fraktion 1990–98. Received 423 votes in favour, 150 votes against.

(v) Petra Blass (PDS)
Acted as supervisor of the 1990 GDR Volkskammer election before joining the PDS. Received 355 votes in a run-off election against another candidate (Michaela Geiger of the CDU-CSU Fraktion, who received 285 votes).

(with more than 2,000 employees, the Bundestag staff is the size of a small ministry). Since these responsibilities involve consultation and persuasion rather than the exercise of authority, members of the Council of Elders are chosen for their parliamentary expertise, personal skills and reputation within the Bundestag. Though the president and vice-presidents are expected to be impartial in the exercise of their functions, they remain members of their Fraktion and may, for example, speak in debate (when not presiding over the Bundestag) and participate in electoral campaigning. They may return to an active party career after their term of office, and many of them continue to hold high office within their parties even while serving as officers of the Bundestag. Thierse, for example, remained a deputy chairman of the SPD during his period as Bundestag president.

A large part of the legislative activity of the Bundestag takes place in committees. These are of various sizes, with membership in all cases shared out among the parliamentary parties, in such a way that: (1) each Fraktion has at least one seat on each committee and sub-committee, and (2) membership is in proportion to the strength of the parliamentary parties. The positions of committee chairperson are shared out so that each Fraktion receives a proportional number of such positions (see Box 8.2). The committees discuss bills which fall within their field of competence. The allocation of bills is facilitated by the fact that committees tend to parallel the division of responsibilities among ministries in the government.[3] These committees may call expert witnesses to give evidence, as well as ministers, civil servants and representatives of interest groups. They report to the Bundestag on each bill before that bill receives a second reading. In addition to the committees which deal with legislation, there are other committees, such as that which considers petitions from members of the public and the European Union committee (see chapter 10).

Box 8.2
Committees of the Bundestag, 1998

Twenty-three committees were formed in the Bundestag elected in September 1998. Ten committees were allocated to the SPD to chair, nine to the Christian Democrats, two to the Greens and one each to the FDP and PDS. Membership of these committees ranged from fifteen to forty-two MdBs.

Committees chaired by the SPD

Foreign affairs	Defence	Internal affairs
Employment	Cultural affairs	Environment
Health	Family and the aged	Sport
Bundestag rules of procedure		

Committees chaired by the CDU-CSU

Legal affairs	Infrastructure	Economy
European affairs	Agriculture	The budget
Tourism	Development aid	East German reconstruction

Committees chaired by other parties

Finance (Greens)	Human rights (Greens)
Education and research (FDP)	Petitions (PDS)

Special committees are created from time to time to investigate particular matters. One type is the investigatory committee (*Untersuchungsausschuss*), most of which have been instituted at the request of the opposition. These committees have investigated matters such as the Guillaume spying affair (1974–75), improper financial contributions to political parties made by the Flick company (1983–86), and the scandal surrounding a company supplying 'social housing' (the *neue Heimat* affair, 1986–87). Another type of special committee is the expert commission (*Enquete-Kommission*), first founded in 1969, whose membership includes experts from outside the Bundestag as well as MdBs. These expert commissions have analysed problems such as the reform of the Basic Law, women and society, the future of nuclear energy, and, following reunification, the history and consequences of the SED-regime in the GDR. Joint committees with the Bundesrat are sometimes created. As well as the permanent Mediation Committee (see below), the Joint Commission on the Constitution was created in 1991, for instance, to consider possible reforms of the Basic Law as a consequence of reunification.[4]

Another, though rather different, set of committees which play a key role in Bundestag affairs are the Fraktion committees. Each Fraktion has its own organisational structure, with a chairperson (the party group leader) elected by members of the Fraktion at the commencement of each legislative period – though generally the choice of chairperson has been arranged through consultations in advance of that meeting. A number of other officers, depending on the size of the Fraktion, are also elected. The business manager of each Fraktion is also an important post.

The importance of the position of the Fraktion was illustrated after the 1998 Bundestag election by three developments. First, there was a much publicised dispute in the SPD between Scharping, leader of the SPD Fraktion during the previous Bundestag term, and formerly party leader of the SPD, who wanted to retain the leadership of the Fraktion in the new Bundestag, and Lafontaine, who had defeated Scharping for the party leadership in 1995, and who wanted to prevent Scharping from continuing to hold the powerful position of Fraktion leader. Neither Scharping nor Lafontaine would give way on this matter. As a contested vote in the Fraktion would have been embarrassing for the chancellor's party so soon after the Bundestag election, in the end Chancellor Schröder intervened and persuaded Scharping to accept appointment as Minister of Defence. A new Fraktion leader was then elected – Peter Strück, the former business manager of the SPD Fraktion. The second case involved the leadership of the CDU-CSU Fraktion. Schäuble, who had held that position when Kohl was chancellor, retained that post, but also became the CDU leader in November 1998 in succession to Kohl, who decided to give up the chairmanship of his party after his defeat in the 1998 Bundestag election. It is important for the leader of the opposition to hold the post of Fraktion leader. The third case was that of Wolfgang Gerhardt, leader of the FDP. He had been elected as party leader in 1996, though not then an MdB. Having been elected to the Bundestag in 1998, he decided that it would be appropriate that he should also act as Fraktion leader. The previous Fraktion leader, Solms, therefore did not present himself for re-election, and instead became the FDP's nominee as Bundestag vice-president.

Usually the position of Fraktion leader is held for a considerable length of time. In the period 1949–99 there were only eight CDU-CSU Fraktion leaders, nine for the SPD and eight for the FDP. The Greens have always had joint holders of this position: three co-leaders until 1990 (when the West German Greens lost their Bundestag representation) and two from1994. Famous politicians who have held the position of Fraktion leader, even though – at least for part of the time in that office – they were not leaders of their parties include Rainer Barzel (CDU, 1964–73), Helmut Schmidt (SPD, 1967–69); Herbert Wehner (SPD, 1969–83); Erich Mende (FDP, 1957–63); Wolfgang Mischnick (FDP, 1968–90); and Gregor Gysi (PDS, leader of the PDS party group from 1991 and of the Fraktion from 1998).

A Fraktion will also have a number of committees, or 'working groups' (called an *Arbeitsgruppe* in the SPD and CDU-CSU, and an *Arbeitskreis* in the FDP, PDS and Green party), which discuss the line which the party should adopt on pending legislation, decide who should speak on behalf of the party in debate, and consider what amendments should be sought at the committee stage of a bill. Each party will have a designated MdB to take responsibility for a particular policy area (a kind of 'shadow minister'). Even the parties in the governing coalition will designate particular back-benchers to take such policy responsibility.

There may also be other groupings within the Fraktion. Some of these have formal status, such as the Employees' Group (Arbeitnehmergruppe) and the Middle Class Discussion Circle (Diskussionskreis Mittelstand) in the CDU-CSU Fraktion. Others are unofficial groupings within the Fraktion, such as the left-wing 'Parliamentary Left' (Parlamentarische Linke) and the moderate Social Democrat MdBs associated with the 'Seeheimer Kreis' and who can, by their voting strength within the Fraktion, exert considerable influence on matters such as election of the Fraktion leader and deputy leaders, committee assignments and the attitude of the Fraktion to legislation. The 'social liberals' in the FDP associated with Burkhard Hirsch and Gerhard Baum, especially after the party switched coalition partners in 1982, the 'Fundis' in the Green party in the 1980s, and the East German MdBs within the CDU are other example of such informal factions which have existed in the Bundestag parties.

The structure and powers of the Bundesrat

The Bundesrat (Federal Council) is the most powerful second chamber in western Europe. It possesses considerable positive and negative rights in relation to the legislative process (see below), rights which are explicitly described in the Basic Law and which have been confirmed in various judgements of the Constitutional Court. The Bundesrat also has an important role, equal to that of the Bundestag, both in the selection of judges of the Constitutional Court and in the passage of constitutional amendments. Article 50 of the Basic Law also refers to the rights of the Bundesrat in relation to federal administration and affairs of the European Union.

The Bundesrat imports the 'federal' element to the legislative process, alongside the Bundestag's representation of the national 'popular' element. Each Land is allocated a number of seats (and hence votes) in the Bundesrat: a minimum of three, a maximum of six (since German reunification added the five 'new Länder' to the Federal Republic). The number of seats for each Land is increased according to the population of the Land: a fourth seat is added when the population exceeds 2 million, a fifth when it exceeds 6 million; a sixth when it is above 7 million.[5] These seats are filled by representatives of the governments of each Land. Each Land government is required to inform the Bundesrat which ministers are designated as that Land's Bundesrat representatives, and

---

Box 8.3
Allocation of Bundesrat seats and composition of Land governments, May 1999

Länder with an SPD prime minister

Brandenburg	4 votes	SPD single-party government
Bremen	3 votes	SPD-CDU coalition
Hamburg	3 votes	SPD-Greens coalition
Lower Saxony	6 votes	SPD single-party government
Mecklenburg-Vorpommern	3 votes	SPD-PDS coalition
North Rhine-Westphalia	6 votes	SPD-Greens coalition
Rhineland-Pfalz	4 votes	SPD-FDP coalition
Saarland	3 votes	SPD single-party government
Saxony-Anhalt	4 votes	SPD single-party government
Schleswig-Holstein	4 votes	SPD-Greens coalition

Länder with a CDU or CSU prime minister

Baden-Württemberg	6 votes	CDU-FDP coalition
Bavaria	6 votes	CSU single-party government
Berlin	4 votes	CDU-SPD coalition
Hesse	5 votes	CDU-FDP coalition
Saxony	4 votes	CDU single-party government
Thuringia	4 votes	CDU-SPD coalition

Votes controlled by SPD-led Länder = 40
Votes controlled by CDU or CSU-led Länder = 29

of any changes in that membership. Usually, the delegation from a Land will include its minister responsible for representing Land affairs in Bonn, and now Berlin (see chapter 6).

A Land group of Bundesrat members must always cast the votes of that Land *en bloc*. It is not possible to divide the number of votes or for part of the group to abstain. This rule may cause difficulties when a Land government, and therefore its Bundesrat representation, is formed by a coalition of two or more parties, who may disagree on particular issues about the way in which the Land representation should vote in the Bundesrat. Frequently the coalition 'treaty' for that government will provide guidance on this. For example, it may state that on policies concerning the environment, the Land will not vote in opposition to the wishes of the ministers who belong to the Green party, or that on issues of internal security policy a Land with a coalition consisting of the CDU and FDP will not vote against the wishes of the FDP ministers. In other cases, disagreement among coalition partners may involve the Land abstaining on an issue. This situation has to be taken into account in interpreting the voting figures in Box 8.3, particularly with regard to the several 'grand coalition' governments which existed in 1999, as does the fact that in Saxony-Anhalt the SPD depended upon the 'toleration' of the PDS, who, though not in coalition with the SPD, could by their status as a party supporting the SPD influence the way in which that Land government voted on issues in the Bundesrat.

Though originally designed, and in the early years of the Federal Republic generally perceived, as a second chamber to represent Länder interests at the level of federal legislation, the Bundesrat increasingly in recent years has been a chamber in which party-political concerns have assumed ascendancy. Land elections are seen as important because, among other reasons, they may affect the balance of power in the Bundesrat, or even create a 'blocking' two-thirds majority for the opposition (see below). Länder or regional interests may be relegated to a secondary role, compared to party loyalties. A significant exception to this recently has been the tendency, on a small number of issues, for East German Länder – irrespective of which party is in government in those Länder – to vote together when an issue such as taxation reform appears likely to affect the 'new Länder' specifically.

For the federal government, therefore, the situation in the Bundesrat is especially critical when the opposition parties command a majority in the second chamber, as in the period immediately prior to reunification, and then again in the closing years of Kohl's chancellorship or, earlier, at times during the period of the SPD–FDP coalition. When this happens, some legislation may be subject to an absolute veto by the Bundesrat, and other legislation to a temporary veto (see below). Of course, the role of the Mediation Committee then assumed particular significance (see below).

The Bundesrat meets in plenary session about twelve times a year (as it did in 1998), between February and July, then between September and December.[6] In such plenary sessions, ministers from the federal government may address the Bundesrat, but of course cannot take part in votes there. Unlike the House of Lords in the United Kingdom, which is affected by the dissolution of Parliament and does not meet after a general election until the new House of Commons assembles, the Bundesrat is independent of federal elections; it can schedule its meetings at any time. At such plenary sessions, an absolute majority of *votes* (not of Länder) constitutes a quorum.

The organisation of the Bundesrat is relatively simple and straightforward. A president and three vice-presidents, each elected for one year, constitute the praesidium, which manages the operational aspects of the second chamber. By convention, the presidency rotates among the Länder in a sequence determined by the size of population. The 'new Länder' have been inserted into this sequence, so that Mecklenburg-Vorpommern, for example, held the presidency in 1991–92, between Hamburg and Saarland.[7] The praesidium is advised on political, administrative and managerial matters by a permanent Advisory Council (Ständiges Beirat), consisting of the Land plenipotentiaries in Bonn (now Berlin), which meets weekly with the members of the praesidium.

As is the case with the Bundestag, much of the important work on legislation and related matters occurs in committee. The Bundesrat has sixteen committees, on policy areas such as agriculture, defence, finance, transport and postal affairs. Each Land has one member on each committee. That member must be a member of that Land government or else be 'accredited' by that government as its commissioner to that committee. He or she need not, though, be a nominated member of that Land's delegation to the Bundesrat. There is an additional committee, the European Chamber (Europakammer), again with one member from each Land, which acts on behalf of the Bundesrat on all matters relating to the EU.

An important resource enjoyed by the Bundesrat is the administrative and policy expertise of the various Land administrations, upon which members of the Bundesrat, whether from parties in the federal coalition or from the parties in opposition, can draw.

Functions of the legislature

Legislation

Obviously, the legislature in the Federal Republic is there to legislate. Normally between 500 and 900 bills have been introduced in each four-year legislative period, of which 300–550 became law.[8] Bills can be introduced by the federal government, by the Bundesrat or from within the Bundestag itself. Over half, and in some sessions two-thirds, of all bills in a legislative period are introduced by the government, and on average three-quarters of all successful bills originate from the government. In fact, many bills which formally originate from a Fraktion from the governing coalition are really government bills in disguise.

The government may choose this legislative route, rather than introducing the bill itself, because such bills do not have to go to the Bundesrat for preliminary comment (see below). The Bundestag itself initiates the greater proportion of other bills, though in recent years there has been a tendency for more bills to originate from the Bundesrat (7–12 per cent since 1969), in part because the opposition has sometimes had a majority in the Bundesrat. Bills initiated by the Bundestag which pass into law usually, of course, stem from a Fraktion belonging to the governing coalition; opposition initiatives, understandably, rarely make progress. Under the Bundestag Rules of Procedure (and in contrast to the House of Commons), individual MdBs cannot initiate legislation. Only a recognised Fraktion can do so.

A government bill results from a decision in cabinet, after the bill has received formal approval with regard to the legality of its content from the Minister of Justice. It is then sent to the Bundesrat, as the representative chamber of the Länder, for comment. The appropriate Bundesrat committee will identify weaknesses and suggest improvements. The government then sends the bill, together with Bundesrat comments and its own responses to those comments, to the Bundestag, where a 'normal' set of procedures occurs, not unlike those in the legislatures of the United Kingdom, France or the USA. Bills which do not originate from the government do not require this preliminary scrutiny by the Bundesrat, though bills originating from the Bundesrat must first be sent to the government for comment before proceeding to the Bundesrat (Article 76 of the Basic Law).

A bill is given a first reading in the Bundestag, usually with a debate in which the principles affected by the bill, rather than details, are discussed. No vote is taken on the fate of the bill, and no binding amendments are accepted at that stage. The bill is then sent to the appropriate Bundestag committee (or committees), which discuss it, co-ordinating as necessary with the Fraktion 'working groups', and taking evidence from interest groups, experts, civil servants and any other sources which the committee regards as relevant. The committee 'reports' the bill, with its amendments, to the Bundestag, where the second reading of the bill then occurs. This gives an opportunity for the committee's proposals to be discussed, for details of the proposed legislation to be analysed and for a vote on the revised version of the bill to take place. If this vote is against the bill (as might happen with bills originating from the Bundesrat or from an opposition Fraktion in the Bundestag, for instance), a third reading is normally dispensed with. If the vote is in favour of the bill, a third reading, generally without debate, produces a vote which completes the Bundestag procedural stage.

A bill which receives a third reading in the Bundestag then is submitted to the Bundesrat, where it also undergoes committee consideration and plenary debate. It is at this stage that a distinction between two classes of bills becomes important.

Bills which affect the constitutional responsibilities or financing of the

Länder *require* the agreement of the Bundesrat (*Zustimmungsbedürftige Gesetze*). If that agreement is not forthcoming, the bill cannot become law. In other words, the Bundesrat possesses an absolute veto. Such bills include those which seek to change Land boundaries, impose new tasks on the Länder, affect the salaries and conditions of employment of civil servants (except civil servants employed in those areas where the federal government has exclusive competence), or provide general framework conditions for what are otherwise Länder policy responsibilities, such as education or policing.

The second class of bills (*Einspruchsgesetze*) are those which do not *require* the consent of the Bundesrat. In such cases, the Bundesrat has a suspensive veto only. This means that, if the Bundesrat rejects the bill by a simple majority, the Bundestag can overrule that veto by an absolute majority (i.e. 50 per cent plus one of all MdBs must vote in favour). Should the Bundesrat veto such a bill with a two-thirds majority, the Bundestag would have to vote with a two-thirds majority in favour of the bill to override that veto and for the bill to become law. In such a case of a two-thirds Bundesrat veto, this would mean that the government could no longer count on passing any legislation without the consent of the opposition, since otherwise Bundesrat vetoes could never be overridden. The consequence would be either a 'grand coalition' situation, informally or in fact, or else a need for a premature dissolution of the Bundestag and new elections, as occurred in 1972 when the SPD–FDP coalition lost its majority in the Bundestag.

If there is disagreement between the two chambers concerning the classification of a bill as requiring, or not requiring, the approval of the Bundesrat, the federal president in effect adjudicates by agreeing or refusing to sign a bill; that is to say, the Bundestag would submit the bill for signature, on the grounds that the consent of the Bundesrat was not required (and that the Bundestag had overruled a suspensory veto). The decision of the federal president could then be challenged in the Constitutional Court. Generally well over 50 per cent of all bills now fall into the category which requires Bundesrat consent. These include many bills of great significance for domestic policy, as well as, especially since changes to the Basic Law since 1990, matters of policy within the context of the EU. Of course, all constitutional amendments require two-thirds majorities in both chambers of the legislature, as would any further surrender of competence to the institutions of the EU (Articles 23, 79 of the Basic Law).

However, this veto power of the Bundesrat is modified by the existence of a very important institutions of the legislature, the Mediation Committee (Vermittlungsausschuss). This consists of sixteen MdBs, chosen in proportion to party strength in the Bundestag, and sixteen members of the Bundesrat, one from each Land. The task of this Mediation Committee is to attempt to find acceptable compromises where the two chambers are in disagreement on aspects of proposed legislation. The Committee must be convened when the Bundesrat makes amendments to a bill if those amendments are not accepted by the Bundestag, or when the Bundesrat rejects a bill. The utility of the Mediation Committee is demonstrated by the fact that, up to August 1997, 664 bills had been submitted to it; 550 of those bills were then passed into law. This indicates that compromises were reached successfully. Members of the Committee have considerable authority to commit their party or Land to particular compromises reached by discussion and bargaining in the Mediation Committee, which accounts for the success rate of well over 80 per cent.[9] Obviously the Mediation Committee is utilised much more frequently at times when the government does not possess a majority of votes in the Bundesrat.

Bills which have passed successfully through these procedures in the Bundestag and Bundesrat (and the Mediation Committee if necessary) then receive the signature of the federal president and become law.

Control of the government

Legislatures are expected to exert control over governments, though they may have varying degrees of authority to do this, as comparisons between, say, the US Congress and the French National Assembly or the British House of Commons will reveal.

In the Federal Republic, both chambers have procedures and institutions which may be used to exert control or enforce accountability *vis-à-vis* the federal government. Ministers may be required to address the Bundesrat, for instance, and knowledge that the Bundesrat majority is controlled by the party in opposition in the Bundestag acts as a deterrent to the federal government concerning controversial legislation. But it is the Bundestag, as the popularly elected chamber, which possesses the greater arsenal of weapons which can be deployed to challenge, criticise and control the government. The fact that the federal chancellor is required to obtain the assent of the majority of MdBs by means of a secret vote in order to be appointed by the federal president, and the provision that the chancellor can (only) be removed by a constructive vote of no confidence in the Bundestag demonstrate the central role of the Bundestag in the German political system.

On a day-to-day basis, other means are available for the Bundestag to exercise control over the executive branch of government. The particular conditions under which these can be used are generally laid down in the Rules of Procedure.

Various types of 'parliamentary question' are available as a means of controlling the government, ranging from detailed inquiries by individual MdBs or Fraktion, which may receive written replies, to batteries of related questions from parliamentary parties (normally, of course, from those in the opposition), the responses to which may give rise to short debates on aspects of government policy (*Grosse Anfrage*, major questions). Topics for such major questions have included transport policy, the abuse of civil rights in Turkey, right-wing extremism, and the relationship between the environment and the motor car. Brief debates on matters of immediate importance (*Aktuelle Stunden*) can be initiated by the opposition to criticise or embarrass the government, or by supporters of the government to publicise some particular policy success. Where some serious matter has arisen, an investigatory committee can be established, provided that the proposal to do so is supported by at least 25 per cent of the membership of the Bundestag. Those on the 'Flick Affair' and the 'Guillaume scandal' (see above) are examples. One of the – potentially – most important institutions for the control of the government is the budget, since without parliamentary consent to its spending plans the government cannot carry out its functions. The debate on the budget lasts for several days, on a topic-by-topic basis, and allows especially the opposition parties to criticise the general lines of policy development as well as the details of policy. The fact that the budget debate is televised and widely reported in the press adds to its potency as an opportunity for criticising the government. Other procedures are also used from time to time. Some of these are rooted in legislation, which compels the government to note and respond to criticism. The reports to the Bundestag of the Commissioner of the Armed Forces (the Wehrbeauftragter), who is appointed by the Bundestag and responsible to it, and who receives and investigates complaints from members of the armed forces, are one of these control mechanisms. Another is the Council of Economic Experts (Sachverständigenrat), instituted by a law passed in 1963. This council, whose five members are appointed by the federal president for five-year terms, is required to make an annual report to the Bundestag on the state of the economy and its predicted development, with regard to issues such as inflation rates, unemployment and investment. The government is obliged to respond to that report.

Though, as in many other legislatures, ultimately a government which enjoys a parliamentary majority can override criticism and evade effective control by a parliamentary opposition, in fact governments in the Federal Republic are aware of the increasing importance of 'image' and reputation, especially in relation to prospects of re-election and the need to win Land elections in order to obtain or protect a majority in the Bundesrat. Therefore the exercise of the rights associated with opposition in the Bundestag does not entirely deserve dismissal as 'shadow boxing'. The skilful use of the instruments of parliamentary control can embarrass governments, they can be forced into abandonment or modification of policy and they can be compelled to justify their actions.

The government also has to give careful attention to criticism from back-benchers from the coalition parties. Particularly the various policy experts of the government parties from the Bundestag committees and the Fraktion working groups can exercise a potent form of control over government plans and activities. Back-benchers from the FDP, whether in coalition with the CDU-CSU or the SPD, as well as, on occasion, back-benchers from the CSU within the CDU-CSU Fraktion, have used their positions to block or force amendment of proposals from the government. Members of the Bundestag from the SPD Fraktion during the chancellorship of Helmut Schmidt, for example, severely limited the room for manoeuvre which the government possessed, particularly on economic policy, social welfare or defence issues. The Schröder government had to be very sensitive to criticism from back-benchers in the SPD and the Greens concerning the government's support for NATO intervention in Kosovo in 1999.

Other functions

A number of other functions of the Bundestag and Bundesrat have been referred to elsewhere, such as amending the constitution and nominating judges for the Constitutional Court. The Bundestag also makes up half the membership of the electoral college which elects the federal president (see chapter 7). Either chamber could, in an extreme case, institute impeachment proceedings against the federal president, when the case would then be decided by the Constitutional Court.

There are four other significant functions, less explicit than those of legislation and control of the executive, which the German parliament also undertakes.

Parliaments should be representative assemblies, and the Bundestag and Bundesrat meet this criterion. The Bundesrat represents the sixteen Länder; that is the constitutional basis of its composition and underlies its various activities. The Bundestag represents the people more generally. Article 38 of the Basic Law states that MdBs are 'representatives of all the people' (and this obligation has been taken seriously by the Constitutional Court in decisions concerning Bundestag Rules of Procedure or the electoral system, for instance). In addition, MdBs represent their constituents. Not only those MdBs elected in constituencies do this. Many MdBs elected from Land lists (many of whom were unsuccessful candidates in constituencies) undertake constituency representation, perhaps in order to strengthen their claim to be elected from a constituency next time, perhaps to boost the image and electoral prospects of their party locally, for Land or Bundestag elections, but also from a sense of public duty. Members of the Bundestag also represent interests of various types (see chapter 9 and the next section of this chapter): agriculture, a trade union, motorists, single parents, or consumers, for instance. It is for this reason that the social composition of the Bundestag (the subject-matter of the concluding section of this chapter) is so relevant. Of course, MdBs also represent their supporters, especially those closely associated with their party. Since party affiliation is so central to the career of an elected politician, and since party contacts are the most frequent and intensive that an MdB will possess, it is not surprising that she or he will be especially sensitive to the perceived opinions and needs of party members.

The Bundestag, and to a lesser extent the Bundesrat, carry out functions of publicity and political education. Bundestag debates are widely reported in the press, by radio and on television. The Bundestag itself publicises its general functions and organisation and its debates and other activities more directly, in the form of periodic publications such as the periodical *Blickpunkt Bundestag* (Bundestag Outlook) and other leaflets and books, and indirectly by providing public funds to support organisations such as the Federal Centre for Political Education, which publishes, among other things, a weekly newspaper called *Das Parlament* (Parliament). Visitors are encouraged to come to the Bundestag (and Bundesrat), both to attend plenary sessions and, when these are available, public hearings of committees, and to view the chamber when the legislature is not in session. Members of the Bundestag and the parties of course publicise (selectively) aspects of the work of the Bundestag and Bundesrat, both as a public service and as part of their promotional activity with an eye to the next election. Bundestag election campaigns are themselves important agencies of political education. For example, levels of knowledge about the working of the electoral system tend to rise steeply during election campaigns, compared to such knowledge in the intervals between Bundestag elections.

Third, the Bundestag offers a link between the federal and Land levels of government and politics. Many MdBs commence their careers as elected politicians in Land parliaments. Some return later to Land-level politics as Land ministers or leading members of the opposition.[10] Members of the Bundestag, whether elected from local constituencies or from Land lists, appreciate that they must convince their local and Land party associates, as well as their electors, that they have been fostering Land interests in the Bundestag. Contact between MdBs and members of Land legislatures and Land parties also provide such co-ordination and linkage. Of course, the Bundesrat is even more obviously a chamber which links these two levels of government.

Finally, the Bundestag is a platform for political careers. It recruits potential members of the political elite. Not all ministers have seats in the Bundestag (though all parliamentary state secretaries – junior ministers – must have Bundestag seats[11]) or have worked their way towards ministerial office through long years of work as back-benchers and as diligent members of Fraktion and Bundestag committees, but most ministers do have such a background. As in other democratic countries, the legislature serves as a filter mechanism and as a testing-ground so that those politicians with special talents can be identified, promoted and finally recruited as ministers. The Federal Republic also has Land legislatures and Land governments which serve this filtering and testing function, but the Bundestag is the most important arena within which ambitious politicians can develop their careers. Franz Josef Strauss (MdB, 1949–78; leader of the CSU and chancellor-candidate in 1980), Helmut Schmidt (MdB, 1953–62 and 1965–83; SPD chancellor, 1974–82), Hans-Dietrich Genscher (MdB, 1965–94; leader of the FDP, 1974–85; Foreign Minister, 1974–92) and Wolfgang Schäuble (MdB since 1972; leader of the CDU since 1998) are a few examples of prominent personalities whose successes as elected politicians were based mainly, if not exclusively, on their membership of the Bundestag at some important stages in their careers.

Social composition of the Bundestag[12]

Though there is always room for dispute concerning the degree to which a legislature should reflect the social composition of the electorate if it is to claim that it is representative of the people, it is legitimate to investigate the social composition of a legislature and discover to what extent biases in its social structure and recent changes to its social composition may have relevance to its representative function.

In West European democracies, there has long been an accusation that parliaments have been distorted in terms of social structure by the 'three Ms': they have been overwhelmingly male, middle aged and middle class. It has certainly been the case that most MdBs have been male. Until the 1980s, over 90 per cent of successful candidates for the Bundestag were male. In recent years the proportion of female MdBs has increased: in 1987 15.6 per cent; in 1990 20.7 per cent; in 1994 26.3 per cent and in 1998 30.9 per cent (207 women MdBs). To a considerable extent, the recent increase in the proportion of female MdBs has been due, directly and indirectly, to the entry of the Greens to the Bundestag. Due to the quota rules of the Greens, there is a high percentage of female MdBs in that Fraktion (1998, 57.4 per cent). Other parties have been compelled to follow this lead, either by introducing quotas themselves or by taking other measures to encourage an increase in the number of female candidates. The PDS also has a high proportion of women in its Fraktion – 58.3 per cent. The percentages for the other parties in 1998 were: SPD 35.2 per cent; CDU-CSU 18.4 per cent; FDP 20.9 per cent. Most women MdBs are elected from the party lists rather than from constituencies, though the ratios are becoming more equal.[13] In part, this is because no Green MdBs are elected from constituencies, and only four of the PDS Fraktion come from constituencies (though two of these constituency MdBs are women). There is still a reluctance to adopt women as candidates in constituencies that are 'safe' or even in those regarded as marginal for the party concerned. However, quota rules and electoral prudence dictate that women should be considered for 'winnable' list places on more or less equal terms with men.

The Bundestag remains (in line with the House of Commons, the French National Assembly and the US Congress) a 'middle-aged' institution. The average age of MdBs has always been between 45 and 52. The Bundestag elected in 1998 had an average age of just under 50 (49.77 years); male MdBs had an average age of 50.8, and female MdBs an average age of 47.6. The Greens, with an average age of 43.2, had the youngest Fraktion. A factor associated with age is incumbency. It has always been the case that most MdBs who present themselves for reelection succeed in returning to the Bundestag. For example, in 1987 only 21 per cent of MdBs were elected for the first time, and 64 per cent had been MdBs for at least two legislative terms previously. (Ismayr, 1992, p. 69). In 1998 178 MdBs were newcomers, constituting 26.6 per cent of the Bundestag. Seventy-four incumbents sought reelection in vain, of whom fifty-one came from the CDU-CSU (a consequence of the electoral decline of that party in the 1998 election).

In terms of occupation and education, and again in line with legislatures elsewhere, the Bundestag is overwhelmingly middle class and well educated. Between 30 and 40 per cent of MdBs in the 1980s and 1990s have had the status of *Beamte* (established civil servant), though this category includes 15–20 per cent of MdBs who are either university professors or teachers, as well as those who are academically qualified as judges or state prosecutors and those employed by local authorities. About 15 per cent of MdBs now come from employment with political parties or have been on the staff of interest-group organisations, including staff of trade unions. Between one-fifth and one-quarter have been self-employed or have pursued a career in one of the independent professions. Because of the education requirements of many of these occupations, it is not surprising that 65–70 per cent of MdBs possess a university degree. The number of housewives or those describing themselves as 'working class' together amount to under 5 per cent of all MdBs in the 1990s.[14]

How do these MdBs perceive themselves in their role as representatives? One study found that 47 per cent regarded themselves as primarily representatives of their voters, 15 per cent as primarily representatives of their party, 9 per cent as primarily representative of social groups, 17 per cent regarded themselves as independent and 13 per cent gave other answers.[15] In actuality, most MdBs will balance pressures from their voters, their party and social groups, and, at least on certain issues such as abortion reform or the choice between Bonn and Berlin as the post-reunification location of the Bundestag, their own opinions and beliefs. All in all, the Bundestag can be considered to serve the people reasonably well as a representative chamber.

A declining parliament?

That parliaments are 'in decline' is a favourite theme of political commentators. It is difficult to justify this charge when applied to the Bundestag, if only because unlike, say, the House of Commons, there is no 'golden age' of German parliaments to look back upon. Neither the near powerless Reichstag of the Second Empire nor the chaotic and overly-obstructive Reichstag of the Weimar Republic can serve as models for an improved Bundestag.

It is valid to complain that parties exercise too much power within the Bundestag. Almost all the initiatives, all the control and authority, stem from the parliamentary parties. Individual MdBs or even the party group too small to qualify for Fraktion status (as was the PDS before the 1998 election, for instance) have a restricted role within the Bundestag, though individual MdBs who hold leadership positions within the Fraktion, on Bundestag committees or within factions of their party can exercise considerable influence, and more so than back-bench MPs in the House of Commons. Members of the Bundestag tend to follow the party line fairly rigorously in their speeches and votes, to a greater extent than British MPs in the House of Commons. It is also valid to suggest that the function of controlling government could be facilitated by parliamentary reforms, directed at improvements to question-time, greater discipline with regard to the length and content of speeches, better provision of information for the opposition and more opportunities for opposition parties to expound their critiques of the government. But reforms have already taken place which have provided greater opportunities for opposition parties and the size of the Bundestag (and therefore its cost) will be reduced after the Bundestag election in 2002, a change which should also improve its efficiency. Parties are aware that more female MdBs, more MdBs under the age of forty, and more MdBs drawn from a wider range of occupations would all make the Bundestag a more representative institution. Still, accusations that the Bundestag is too much in thrall to established interests (chapter 9), such as the civil service, farmers, the medical profession or the trade unions, and that too many MdBs are 'professional politicians', with little in the way of previous experience in other careers and with no ambitions beyond political advancement, justify suggestions that the reform of the Bundestag will have to be a continual, ongoing process.

Notes

1 Under Article 63 of the Basic Law, the federal president can dissolve a newly elected Bundestag if it fails to elect a chancellor by an absolute majority. Alternatively, the president can accept a chancellor elected by a simple majority.
2 There were disputes concerning this convention in 1994 and 1998. In 1994, the Greens nominated Antje Vollmer, against the opposition of the SPD. With the aid of Christian Democrat votes, Vollmer was elected as a vice-president. In 1998 there were those, especially among Christian Democrat MdBs, who could not accept that the PDS – the successor-party to the SED and still not convincingly supportive of the version of democracy embodied in the Basic Law, in the opinion of some – should have the honour of providing a vice-president. This led to a contest between the PDS candidate and a candidate from the CDU-CSU.
3 In some cases, of course, a bill will affect the responsibilities of more than one committee. In such cases one committee will de designated as responsible for the report to the Bundestag, after consultation with other committees which have considered the bill.
4 The Joint Commission met for the first time in January 1992, and operated until 1993. It held a number of public hearings. It consisted of thirty-two MdBs, chosen in proportion to party strength, and thirty-two members of the Bundesrat (two from each Land). Some of the proposals of the Joint Commission were adopted later as constitutional amendments, but other reforms supported by some members of the Joint Commission either did not find a majority within the Commission, or else were insufficiently-widely supported to command the two-thirds majority in each chamber needed for them to be imposed as constitutional amendments.

5 The only change in allocation of seats since 1990 has been the award to Hesse of a fifth seat in 1995, when its population rose above 6 million.

6 In the early years of the Federal Republic, when a large number of issues had to be dealt with urgently, the Bundesrat met much more frequently: nearly 30 times annually until 1953, then nearly 20 times annually until 1957. Since 1957 it has met only 12–15 times annually as a rule (*Deutsche Bundesrat*, 1998, pp. 7, 283).

7 As this now means that each Land only holds the presidency every sixteen years, the likelihood of one *person* serving more that one term is remote. In the past, Ehard (CSU, Bavaria), Zinn (SPD, Hesse), Altmeier (CDU, Rhineland-Pfalz), Koschnick (SPD, Bremen), Rau (SPD, North Rhine-Westphalia) and Röder (CDU, Saarland) have held the presidency twice.

8 Only in 1976–80 (485 bills) and the abbreviated legislative period of 1980–83 (242 bills) have there been fewer than 500 introduced, and only in 1980–83 (139) were fewer than 300 laws passed (Schindler, 1983, p. 681; 1986, p. 633).

9 Data from Deutsche Bundesrat (1998, pp. 286–7).

10 Few MdBs have simultaneously held seats in Land parliaments and the Bundestag, and then usually only for very brief periods. Most of these cases occurred before 1961: there were eighty-four such cases in 1949–53, fifty-two between 1953 and 1957, and twenty in 1957–61 (Schindler, 1994, pp. 204–5). However, about two-thirds of MdBs hold *party* office in their Land party organisation (Ismayr, 1999, p. 16).

11 The exception, which required passage of a special law, is the case of Michael Naumann in 1998, as junior minister (minister of state) in the Chancellor's Office (see chapter 7).

12 Data in this section comes principally from Schindler (1983; 1994) and Deutsche Bundestag (1998).

13 in 1972 there were 6.5 female MdBs elected from party lists for each one elected from a constituency. In 1983 the ratio was 4.1 list female MdBs to each female constituency MdB. In 1990 2.4 female MdBs were elected for each female constituency MdB (Schindler, 1994, p. 256).

14 Jesse (1997, pp. 101–2), citing H.-H. Rohlfs and U. Schäfer (1997) *Jahrbuch der Bundesrepublik Deutschland 1997*, München, dtv, 175–7.

15 Ismayr (1992, p. 44), citing D. Herzog et al. (1990) *Abgeordnete und Bürger*, Opladen, Westdeutscher Verlag, 61.

References

Deutsche Bundesrat (1998) *Handbuch des Bundesrats, 1997/8*, Bonn, Deutsche Bundesrat.

Deutsche Bundestag (1998) *Blickpunkt Bundestag*, 4, Bonn, Deutsche Bundestag.

Ismayr, W. (1992) *Der Deutsche Bundestag. Funktionen. Willensbildung. Reformansätze*, Opladen, Leske und Budrich.

Ismayr, W. (1999) '50 Jahre Parlamentarismus in der Bundesrepublik Deutschland', *Das Parlament. Beilage: Aus Politik und Zeitgeschichte*, 20: 14–26.

Jesse, E. (1997) *Die Demokratie der Bundesrepublik Deutschland*, 8th edn, Berlin, Landeszentrale für politische Bildungsarbeit.

Schindler P. (ed.) (1983) *Datenhandbuch zur Geschichte des Deutschen Bundestages 1949–82*, Bonn, Deutscher Bundestag.

Schindler, P. (ed.) (1987) *Datenhandbuch zur Geschichte des Deutschen Bundestages 1980–84*, Baden-Baden, Nomos.

Schindler, P. (ed.) (1994) *Datenhandbuch zur Geschichte des Deutschen Bundestages 1983–91*, Baden-Baden, Nomos.

Further reading

von Beyme, K. (1998) *The Legislator: German Parliament as a Centre of Political Decision-Making*, Aldershot, Ashgate.

Jeffery, C. and Greeen, S. (1995) 'Sleaze and the sense of malaise in Germany', *Parliamentary Affairs*, 4: 675–87.

Saalfeld, T. (1997) 'From dictatorship to parliamentary democracy', *Parliamentary Affairs*, 3: 380–95.

9

Interest-group politics

Introduction

Politics in the Federal Republic is influenced by, and in some ways is dependent upon, the activities of interest groups. The political system which developed after the Second World War placed emphasis on pluralism as a desirable characteristic, one that belonged to democratic politics. This meant that social groups (and not only political parties) were seen as having important functions – of representation, of policy initiation, of linkage between government and governed – and that these group therefore should be protected and fostered. It is thus not surprising that freedom of association is one of the constitutional rights protected by the Basic Law (Article 9),[1] or that the rules of procedure of the Bundestag and the federal government permit and encourage interest-group inputs to the policy-making process. Nor is it surprising to find that many reports in the media of political developments, such as new policy proposals, election campaigns, or arguments within or between political parties, refer to interest groups as important participants in the political process.

Of course, interest-group politics in Germany was not an invention of the Federal Republic. In the nineteenth century, even before the unification of Germany in 1871, groups played a role in the politics of the states that later became part of the Second Empire. Groups were formed – both before and after the Frankfurt Parliament of 1848–49 – to press for the creation of a unified German state. Others were founded to protect the interests of various trades or industries or the interests of landowners (for example, when these were threatened by changes to import regulations for agricultural produce). Associations with social or cultural interests, such as feminist groups or campaigns against alcohol, sometimes entered the political arena. Trade unions were formed; the German Federation of Trade Unions was founded in 1868, for example. The churches frequently found it necessary to try to influence political decisions. Associations pressing for a stronger German navy or with interests in the promotion of German colonial activity became involved in politics. Indeed, at least until the creation of the Weimar Republic in 1919, it was possible to claim that

152

interest groups rather than political parties were the principal form of political mediation between government and governed.

In the Weimar Republic, interest groups continued to be politically important. Freedom of association was guaranteed under the Weimar constitution (Article 159). Political parties were usually closely associated with particular interests: the Communist and Social Democratic parties with their trade unions and other working-class organisations; the Centre party with the Catholic church; the right-wing parties, including the German People's Party (DVP, the national liberals), with business and commercial interests or with agrarian interests; the German Democratic Party (DDP, the left-wing liberal party) with trades and professions and with white-collar employees such as teachers or journalists. The Nazi party, until it took power, tried to present itself as a friend to various interests, a kind of pioneer 'catch-all' party, since it regarded cleavages within society as damaging to the nation. Business interests were especially favoured by the party, since businesses supplied much of the party's funding. There were even in the Weimar party system small parties which were little more than electoral manifestations of interest groups, such as the *Wirtschaftspartei* (party of the economy). As well as trade unions and commercial and industrial associations, there were associations concerned with the protection of the new Republic, and others to press for expansion of German military power, to foster the interests of national minorities within Germany or to campaign for or against various referenda proposals (such as those concerned with schemes for reparations payments) that occurred intermittently during the lifetime of the Weimar Republic.

From 1933, the Third Reich ensured that all interest groups were either 'nazified' or eliminated. Though the Nazis before coming to power had attempted to win over various groups in society by speaking out for their interests, ranging from farmers to the military, from employees and owners of small businesses to the large industrial corporations and banks, once the Nazis had successfully imposed a totalitarian dictatorship, that regime could not tolerate any association, and especially any association involved in politics from time to time, other than those firmly under its own control, such as the German Workers' Front (Deutscher Arbeitsfront). Trade unions, industrial associations, cultural groups, professional organisations such as those for doctors, architects or lawyers, were all dissolved, as had happened with political parties other than the Nazi party itself, or were perverted into nazified organisations. Pluralism was anathema to the Nazi regime. Only the churches remained outside the nazification process, and even there the regime attempted, by measures ranging from the formation of a 'nazified' national Protestant church to persecution and disruption, to ensure that the churches did not become a source of opposition to the Third Reich.

The emphasis on pluralism reintroduced to post-war Germany by the occupation authorities in 1945, including the swift formation of trade unions and other associations under similar terms of licensing as were applied to political parties, was in part a reaction to Nazi policy and a strategy to ensure that such a dictatorship could not re-emerge in post-war Germany. Trade unions, for example, formed at Land and zonal level. The German Federation of Trade Unions (DGB, Deutscher Gewerkschaftsbund) was founded in the British zone in 1947, and then extended to become an organisation for the three western zones in October 1949. The Federal Association of German Employers' Organisations (BDA, Bundesvereinigung der Deutschen Arbeitgeberverbände) was founded in 1949 (taking its current name in 1950), as was the Federal Association of German Industry (BDI, Bundesverband der Deutschen Industrie). The churches enjoyed an authority and status in the post-war period that enabled and encouraged them to play a political role (in influencing aspects of the Basic Law, for instance). Refugee associations were formed to protect the interests of the hundreds of thousands of refugees from what used to be the eastern areas of the Third Reich, but which were now administered by Poland or the USSR. As the political system developed in the half-century following the establishment of the Federal Republic, and as the economy and society of West Germany became more complex, so the number of interest groups expanded and the intensity of their political activity increased.

Types of interest groups in Germany

In reviewing the range of interest groups which participate in the political process in Germany, two things must be emphasised. First, as is the case with any pluralist democracy, there are so many interest groups that, in contrast to political parties, for instance, it would be impossible to list them all; and anyway, new groups form, other groups disband, others enter the political arena only briefly, so that the attempt to list them would be pointless. Second, Germany shares many characteristics with other highly developed democracies, in terms of its economic and social structures as well as in the broad dimensions of its political system, so it is not surprising to find that its principal interest groups resemble those found in, say, the United Kingdom, France or the USA. This section will identify the more significant interest groups, in relation to the policy sectors in which they are mainly involved, and will also refer to examples of groups which are less significant, but which illustrate the range and variety of such groups.

In the area of economic policy and industrial relations, of course the trade unions are very important. The main trade union federation, the DGB, is, like many of the most significant interest groups, what is called a 'peak organisation' (*Dachverband*); that is to say, it is an umbrella organisation which consists of other organisations, like the British Trades Union Congress, rather than representing individuals directly. When trade unions were permitted to form after the Second World War, the occupation authorities were keen to ensure that a single federation was created, in order to make employee representation more efficient and less politicised, rather than reintroducing the several, party- or denominational-based, federations which had existed in the Weimar Republic (and which still exist in France today, for example). This federation was to be non-political, in the sense that it would not formally be affiliated to any one party.[2] Of course, the DGB is closely associated with, and sympathetic towards, the Social Democratic party, and its executive board usually consists almost entirely of SPD members, though there are 'token' CDU members also. The DGB represented thirteen member-unions in 1998 (the number having been steadily reduced by a process of fusion since the1980s). These unions, themselves newly formed after the war, are all what are called 'industrial unions': they represent all the employees within a particular industry or occupational sector, so that, for instance, an electrician employed in a textile firm is in the textile and clothing trade union, but if employed by a motor-car manufacturer would be a member of IG Metall (the metalworkers trade union). As in other western European countries, trade union membership has declined. The DGB had 9,354,670 members in 1995, but only 8,623,471 at the end of 1997, for instance. The Basic Law prohibits the 'closed shop'. Employees have the right to join, but also the right not to join, trade unions, and the extractive and manufacturing industries which used to have the most members in trade unions have been marked by sharp declines in employment, which also has had its effect on trade union membership.

The DGB does not have an absolute monopoly on employee representation; other types of trade union exist. These include the white-collar union, the *Deutsche Angestellten-Gewerkschaft*; the civil service assocation, the *Deutscher Beamtenbund*; and a small federation of Christian trade unionists. In terms of membership, though, these cannot rival the size of the DGB.

There are also, of course, interest groups representing 'capital', management and the self-employed. The three most significant of these are also 'peak organisations': the BDA, representing over fifty member-organisations; the BDI, which has over thirty member-organisations; and the German Chambers of Commerce (*Deutscher Industrie und Handelstag*, DIHT). These all have organisations as their component members; organisations representing sectors of production or commerce, such as the chemical industry, retail shops, transport firms or banks, within the BDI, for example. In the case of the DIHT, the regional chambers of commerce are the component organisations. In agriculture, a number of different organisations exist, such as the German Farmers' Association (*Deutscher Bauernverband*, DBV). The professions have their associations which act as interest groups in certain situations. These include the chambers (which have compulsory membership) for doctors, pharmacists, architects, lawyers, accountants and so on, as well as the 'peak' organisation, the Federal Association of Independent Professions (*Bundesverband der Freien Berufe*). Owners of small businesses, such as plumbers, garage-owners and bakers, form their own interest groups. Even the military has its own interest group – the German Soldiers' Association (*Deutscher Bundeswehr-Verband*)

Box 9.1
Trade union membership, 1997

Member unions of the DGB:

Metalworkers	2,660,951
Public services and transport	1,643,692
Mining, chemicals and energy	1,010,555
Construction and agriculture	655,356
Commerce, banking, insurance	488,271
Post	487,814
Railways	367,734
Foodstuffs and catering	294,546
Education and science	289,014
Police	196,536
The media	191,610
Textiles and clothing	183,349
Timber trades and plastics	154,043
Total DGB membership	8,623,471

Other trade union organisations:

German civil service association	1,116,714
German salaried employees union (DAG)	489,266
Christian trade union	302,874

Source: *Statistisches Jahrbuch für das Bundesrepublik Deutschland, 1998* (1998, p. 733).

formed in 1956 shortly after the Bundeswehr itself was called into existence. Temporary interest groups are created in this commercial and economic sector when needed. For example, an 'Action Committee for Pure Beer' tried unavailingly in the 1980s to prevent the importation of foreign beers which did not meet the traditional production standards of German beer, but the EU Court of Justice confirmed the right to import non-German beer in a judgement in 1987.

There are large numbers of interest groups concerned with what might be broadly termed social and welfare issues. Groups represent the interests of a range of persons with special problems or needs, ranging from prisoners to the handicapped, from residents of foreign origin to orphans. The churches, and church-associated groups such as the *Zentralkommitee der deutschen Katholiken* (Central Committee of German Catholics), of course play an important role in matters relating to social policy, education and welfare, as do the trade unions. A number of interest groups concerned themselves with abortion reform from the 1960s onwards, including feminist groups and the churches.[3] A law to reform the financing of health care was passed in 1992, but only after intense opposition from groups representing health care professions (especially doctors, dentists and pharmacists) whose incomes might suffer as a result of the legislation (Blank and Perschke-Nartmann, 1994). In 1998 groups were formed in Schleswig-Holstein and Bremen to obtain referenda in their Länder to try to prevent reform of guidelines for written German (*Rechtsschreibreform*) from becoming law. Though the Greens have now become an established political party involved in government at federal and Land level, a range of environmental interest groups still play a part in politics, at local, regional and national levels, as was evident in the attempts in 1998–99 to prevent the transport of nuclear waste in Germany. Local groups still form to press for environmental improvements or to prevent projects which would harm the local environment, on the lines of the citizen initiative groups (*Bürgerinitiativen*) that were so numerous in the 1970s and were the forerunners of the Green party.

Other groups are primarily concerned with activities which may have both a commercial as well as a cultural or social focus to their activities. Motorists are represented by the German Motor Club (ADAC), which has some 13 million members, and a number of other organisations. The Association of Taxpayers (*Bund der Steuerzahler*) watches out for the taxpayers' interests when changes in taxation are proposed or costly new legislation is introduced, and has also played a part in trying to publicise and control the high levels of salary and other financial privileges that Bundestag and Landtag legislators tend to acquire by means of their own votes. The German Sports Federation (*Deutscher Sportbund*) concerns itself with the interests of the 26 million Germans who engage in all forms of sporting activity, but individual sports, such as football, athletics, handball and bowling, also have their own associations. Shareholders, consumers, property owners and those who rent houses or flats all have their interest groups.

There are organisations which interest themselves directly in issues concerning politics. The German Voters' Association (*Deutsche Wählergemeinschaft*), for example, was involved in campaigns to dilute or remove the proportionality element in the electoral system of the Federal Republic when it was first designed in 1949 and when the system was amended in the 1950s, and pressed strongly for adoption of a majoritarian electoral system at the time of the 'grand coalition' in the late 1960s. Radical right-wing groups exist which seek to impose stricter controls on immigrants and asylum-seekers (sometimes using such extreme methods that they attract the attention of the Federal Office for the Protection of the Constitution, see chapter 11). The Association of those Persecuted by the Nazi Regime attracted 30,000 members in the years following its formation in 1947, and still has a few thousand members. The Alliance of Refugees (*Bund der Vertriebenen*) is a 'peak' organisation of forty-three associations representing over 2 million members. A variety of groups, including trade unions, the ADAC and business interests, as well as a special group formed for the campaign, 'Alliance for Brandenburg', were active in the campaign for merging the two Länder of Berlin and Brandenburg in 1995–96. In 1998 a group called 'Mehr Demokratie' ('more democracy') was formed to campaign for more direct democracy, including federal-level referenda. It had 1,650 members in 1998, organised in ten Länder groups (*Stern*, 8 October 1998, pp. 240–1).

These interest groups exhibit a wide variety of organisational forms, ranging from organisations which have the special status of 'institutions in public law' (*Körperschaften des öffentlichen Rechts*), a status that bestows special privileges in law as well as imposes special obligations, to temporary coalitions of organisations and individuals which may create some kind of structure to co-ordinate activities during some campaign of very limited duration (to oppose German adoption of the European currency, for instance). It is important to remember that, as in the United Kingdom or the USA, thousands of organisations exist which never engage in political activity, and thousands more only do so on rare occasions, when some proposed policy may affect their activities, resources or freedom of action.

Opportunities for interest-group activity

The influence of interest groups in the political process of the Federal Republic depends – as in other pluralist political systems – on the availability of suitable opportunities for the exertion of such influence.

Leaving aside in this chapter the exertion of political influence on the political institutions of the European Union (a theme included in chapter 10), six 'arenas' for interest-group activity can be identified: public opinion (since, according to Article 20 of the Basic Law, 'all state power derives from the people'); the electoral process; the parties; the legislature; the executive; and – though perhaps not strictly to be regarded as part of the political process – the courts. It must be emphasised that, because Germany possesses a federal political system, these 'arenas' can be relevant at local and Land levels of government, as well as at the federal government level.

Public opinion is necessarily a diffuse target for interest groups. True, the public can vote in elections; so, in general terms, the public can make or bring down governments, can reward or punish policy decisions which affect them and affect others who share the concerns of some interest group. But, as in other West European democracies, few voters are 'single-issue' individuals. As well as being a trade unionist, a voter may be a mother, may attend regularly her local Catholic church, be a motorist and a supporter of Greenpeace, and care for a disabled aged parent. As well as being an estate agent, a voter may be a shareholder, the child of a former refugee from Silesia (now part of Poland), a member of the Federation of Taxpayers, support two children at university, and be taking flying lessons. In these cases, a convincing argument from one interest group (the trade union, the Silesian refugee organisation) to vote in a particular way or even to take some action such as participating in a demonstration, may be counterbalanced by arguments from, say, the Catholic church or the Taxpayers' Association to vote in a different way. In any case, cross-pressures or political apathy or shortage of time available to a busy working mother or self-employed professional may deter the individual from undertaking political activity. Even if a particular political campaign does prove relatively successful in mobilising voters, it is rare indeed that sufficient numbers of voters can be persuaded to vote differently to make a difference to the outcome of an election. Public opinion as a target serves either as a backdrop for other, more precisely-directed, activities (a parliamentary lobbying campaign, for instance) or as a long-term effort to change public opinion on an important issue such as attitudes to environmental protection or more liberal citizenship laws and the introduction of dual citizenship for long-term foreign residents.

Election campaigns, though, are utilised by interest groups in Germany to try to produce a Bundestag (or a Land parliament) more favourable to the aims and concerns of the group than might otherwise be the case. A notorious example in the 1950s and 1960s was the Catholic church, which used various tactics (including the reading out in churches of letters from bishops just prior to the election, advising the faithful how to vote) in order to promote the Christian Democratic parties and dissuade Catholics from voting for the SPD. Interest groups present candidates and parties with demands, in the hope that those candidates and parties will look favourably on such demands in order to win votes. The DGB, for example, as guidance for its members, at every Bundestag election publishes a comparison of the policies of the main parties on a range of issues relevant to the trade union movement, in the hope of persuading members and sympathisers to vote for parties friendly to the unions. Some interest groups, such as trade unions, farming organisations, industrial federations, professional associations and – in the first decades of the Federal Republic at least – refugee organisations, try to ensure that their representatives are selected as candidates in winnable constituencies or in safe places on Land lists. The success of this 'influence by selection' becomes apparent when the composition of a newly elected Bundestag is analysed. Many MdBs have links, sometimes as former officers of the interest group, sometimes simply as members or supporters, with occupational associations (civil servants, industrialists, trade union members, farmers, teachers, and so on), as well as with other forms of interest group, such as the churches, charitable concerns, sporting or leisure groups (as becomes apparent when speed limits on motorways are proposed, or when a campaign gets under way to exempt from fuel taxes those who fly aeroplanes for a hobby).

A special form of interest group utilisation of the electoral process for the exertion of influence is for the group to form a party of its own. Since 1945 cases include the refugees (the *Bund der Heimatvertriebenen und Entrechteten*), environmentalists (the Greens and the Ecological Democratic Party, the ÖDP) and, more recently, pensioners (the 'Greys', *Die Grauen*). In the European Parliament elections of 1994, imitating its more successful Swiss counterpart, a motorists' party presented a list – but received only about 20,000 votes. In the 1998 Bundestag election, a group opposed to German acceptance of the Euro, Pro-DM, presented lists but obtained fewer than half a million votes (under 1 per cent), despite extensive advertising during the campaign. Other unsuccessful parties in the 1998 election had names such as Tierschutz (animal protection), which received over 130,000 votes and Familie and Die Frauen (parties promoting the family and women's interests) but these obtained only about 25,000 and 30,000 votes respectively. Clearly, there is little support for such 'single-issue' parties. Even those sympathetic to their aims prefer to use their vote to support one of the larger parties, with more extensive programmes, nor do voters want to waste their votes on parties with no likelihood of securing 5 per cent of the vote and thus of winning seats in the Bundestag.

Since political parties play such an important part in controlling and steering the political process in Germany, they present obvious targets for interest-group influence, between elections as well as during election campaigns. Such influence can be exercised outside the party organisation itself. For example, until 1994 (when it was forced to economise) the DGB provided free offices and other facilities for some politicians elected to national, Land or local legislatures, and paid full salaries to its own employees elected to the Bundestag or Landtag. Clearly, the DGB expected to benefit from its association with parties in these ways. Groups, such as farmers, environmentalists, lorry-drivers or feminists, may 'lobby' at party congresses. Alternatively, they may try to persuade local party officials to put forward proposals supported by the group to decision-making institutions more senior in the party hierarchy: party congresses, the party Executive committee, working groups which include members of the parliamentary party, for instance. Interest-group influence can also be exercised inside the party. Existing party members who are also members of an interest group or sympathetic to some cause (such as more liberal abortion legislation, or subsidies for coal-miners) may be mobilised to persuade the party of the merits of some policy or issue, or even to secure the selection of candidates favoured by the group for Bundestag and Landtag elections. Trade unionists in the SPD, feminists in the Green party, anti-abortionists in the CDU and CSU, former employees of the GDR state bureaucracy in the Party of Democratic Socialism and the self-employed in the FDP are examples of such 'internal' interests. Most parties have institutions within their organisation which cater for some of these groups; committees for local government councillors' and the self-employed in the CDU, for instance or for lawyers in the SPD. These are in addition to groups for young party members and for women, which most parties have. Some parties deliberately invite interest-group participation in policy formulation by including them in groups of expert advisers.

A more extreme form of influence on parties is 'entryism', where the interest group tries to actually 'capture' the party by a strategy of getting its supporters accepted as members of the party, then ensuring that they are active in the party and get elected to positions of power. The group of former Nazis who tried to 'capture' the FDP in North Rhine-Westphalia in the 1950s (the Naumann group[4]), the flood of membership applications from estate agents, dentists, lawyers and other self-employed professionals and business owners in the early 1980s (which played a part in the decision of the FDP to change coalition partners in 1982) and a, seemingly-ineffective, Internet-facilitated campaign by students to win influence in the FDP by mass applications for membership in 1998 (*Der Spiegel*, 26 January 1998, pp. 26–27; 8 June 1998, p. 62), are examples, as was the more generalised threat of the student movement radicals in 1968–69 to 'march through the institutions', including the parties.

The legislature offers a range of opportunities for interest-group influence. Most MdBs have links to various interest groups – as members, as sympathisers or simply by belonging to some particular social group (such as Catholics, motorists or Berliners). The social characteristics of MdBs, discussed in chapter 8, give indications of those links. Thus it is probable, certainly when policies affect the interest group directly, that the segment of the membership of the Bundestag composed of, say, farmers, civil servants, the self-employed or trade union members, will exert influence on behalf of the group's aims. Of course, this does not mean that they will always vote as a consolidated, cross-party association, but it will be likely that they will impose pressure on their own parliamentary parties, perhaps even applying a veto. This is more probable when, as often occurs, MdBs with interest-group ties (e.g. farmers) get appointed to Fraktion and Bundestag committees related to their interests. However, because of loyalty to the party and because of their own career concerns, MdBs will, when it comes to it, almost always support their party even at the cost of abandoning group interests. Nor must it be supposed that MdBs only take a position on an issue on the basis of either party or group affiliation; their mature political judgement, the interests of their local constituents and their ethical or moral sense are other factors which have to be considered in analysing why an MdB votes in a particular way.

The legislature anyway offers formal opportunities to interest groups to present their case to the select committees,[5] when legislation is under consideration. So there is no lack of access for groups affected by policy decisions. In some special cases, such as abortion legislation or liberalisation of shop opening hours, intensive lobbying by affected groups may take place. Less intensive forms of lobbying occur as a matter of course. The Bundestag has, since 1974, issued annually a list of organisations that are registered with it as recognised 'lobbyists' – somewhat similar to the procedures adopted by the US Congress. The list for 1996 contained 1,614 associations. These associations maintain regular informal contacts with MdBs, especially those who are influential on party or Bundestag committees, who transmit such views to those committees, to their colleagues, perhaps even to ministries. In this way, the Bundestag may be regarded as 'a channel rather than the target of interest group influence' (Saalfeld, 1999, p. 44), since it is the preparation of policy rather than the completed bill that groups may seek to affect.

Box 9.2
Examples of interest groups registered with the Bundestag

The Action Committee for Children in Hospital
Amnesty International
The Association of German Engineers
The Association of the German Leather Industry
The Association of German Midwives
The Association of German School Books Publishers
The Association of German Stamp-Collectors
The Central Association of Opticians
The Federal Association of German Newspaper Publishers
The Federal Association of the Producers of Instant Coffee
The Federal Association of Toy Shops
The German Association for Political Education
The German Sports Association
The International Society for Human Rights in Kurdistan
The Non-Smoker Initiative of Germany
The Professional Association of Bavarian Detectives
The Veterinary Association for Animal Protection

Source: *Woche im Bundestag*, 18, 1996 (supplement).

It is the government, though, that is the principal target for most interest groups most of the time. A survey of interest group representatives placed federal ministries ahead both of the Bundestag and its committees and Land ministries as their most important contact (Sebaldt, 1997, p. 30). Almost all legislation originates from the government; the government can decide whether to accept amendments (including those from the Bundesrat: see chapter 8) during the legislative process; the government (at federal or at Land level) then is responsible for administering the legislation once it has completed its passage through the Bundestag and Bundesrat. So it is clear that an interest group wishing to dilute the terms of legislation, or wishing to promote its interests via such legislation, needs to make out its case to the government. Parties and the legislature (e.g. through legislative committees) will be channels for communicating with the government, but such communication can also be more direct, in the form of delegations to ministers or correspondence with the ministry, and through links to civil servants. The rules of procedure of the federal government require that relevant interest groups be consulted during the process of preparation of legislation, so access for some groups is in this way guaranteed. The efforts in early 1999 of the operators of nuclear power facilities to get the

SPD-Green government to modify its legislation concerning the abandonment of nuclear power in Germany and provisions for the treatment of nuclear waste is an example of such interest group pressure on government. The Catholic church and pro- and anti-abortion groups to modify abortion legislation, especially following reunification, and the various groups (including owners of retail shops, trade unions and consumer organisations) involved on both sides in arguments about relaxation of permitted opening hours for shops are other examples from the 1990s of pressure on government. It must be emphasised, though, that much of the most successful pressure by interest groups on government is the result of quiet, unspectacular and ongoing inter-communication between civil servants and the staff of organisations such as the trade unions, the German Chamber of Commerce, the motorists' organisations or the farmers' interest groups, for example, at meetings of advisory committees where both interest groups and civil servants are members.

The propensity of Germans to seek legal, binding solutions to social and political problems, in preference to the less tidy methods of bargaining and compromise which constitute the political process, means that interest groups (as well as political parties) sometimes have recourse to the Constitutional Court when they consider that the Court is likely to rule in their favour against a government decision or parliamentary legislation. Though the operation of the Constitutional Court is the subject-matter of chapter 3, a few illustrations of such interest group activity can be noted here. Organisations representing university staff in 1973 used the Constitutional Court to challenge a new law in Lower Saxony changing the conditions under which universities in that Land were to be governed. Business firms and employers' associations challenged co-determination legislation in the 1970s. Interest groups concerned with civil liberties and data protection have used the courts to delay or amend requirements associated with the national census. Opponents of the extension of European integration (by means of introduction of a common currency, for example) have taken cases to the Constitutional Court to try to prevent Germany from applying such policies.

The Federal Republic: an 'interest-group' state?

Just as some commentators have feared that the parties exercise too much power in the Federal Republic of Germany, so others have expressed concern that the state is the tool of powerful interest groups. Certainly high-profile cases such as the Flick Affair (involving accusations of the illegal supply of funds by a firm to political parties for purposes of improper advantage), the powerful position of banks, farmers, miners, the medical profession, civil servants and the motoring organisations, when it comes to policies which threaten their interests, and the close relationships that seem to exist between the parties and interest groups or ministerial departments and interest groups lend some

credence to the view that interest groups in Germany are powerful organisations which intervene in the political process in ways that could sometimes be
regarded as undemocratic. In the 1970s there were suggestions that an
'Associations Law' to regulate interest groups, similar to the Party Law which
regulates political parties, should perhaps be introduced but, apart from anything else, there are difficult problems of defining interest groups in such a way
as to make them subject to a common set of rules and procedures.

Other commentators are concerned about the trend towards corporatism in
the German political process. This concern focuses upon the close relationships
which exist between government and some – especially the larger – interest
groups; the degree of privileged access to government which such 'insider'
groups enjoy (access which 'outsider' groups are denied); and the bypassing of
the democratic political process by policy-making involving government and
interest groups, rather than parties and the legislature. While such corporatist
relationships are not as advanced as they seem to be in countries such as
Austria, Switzerland and some of the Scandinavian countries, it is true that
ministries tend to have their own lists of groups which are granted access,
whose views are given weight and whose contribution to policy-making is
significant (e.g. the Ministry of Agriculture and the DBV; the Ministry of
Economics and the BDI; the Ministry of Labour and the DGB). The creation of
a tripartite institution to regulate economic policy involving trade unions, the
government and business groups – called 'Concerted Action' (Konzertierte
Aktion) – which met from 1966 to 1977, a similar arrangement in the area of
health policy in the 1970s and 1980s, and the 'Alliance for Jobs' – 'Bündnis für
Arbeit' – operating at national and regional levels created by the SPD-Green
party coalition government elected in 1998 are other indications of a penchant
for corporatist arrangements in certain sectors of policy.

Certainly interest groups play an important part in the political process of
the Federal Republic. West German interest groups swiftly extended their activities to East Germany after reunification, replacing both old, discredited com-
munist-sponsored organisations (such as the Free German Trade Union) and,
in several cases, the fledgling democratic organisations which the East Germans
had themselves created, which can be taken both as an indicator of the importance of interest groups in politics and the importance of organisational and
political integration of the two parts of the new Germany. However, the low
levels of membership of many of these groups in the new Länder is an indicator that, for whatever reason, pluralist political activity is still not regarded with
the same degree of enthusiasm in East Germany as it is in the old Federal
Republic, and the social and economic contexts in East Germany are also not
yet conducive to the development of interest-group activity on the West
German model.[6]

The idea of a pluralist political system which was fostered by the allies and
the West Germans themselves after the Second World War, a system involving
federal and Land levels of political activity, the intermediation of parties and

multiple and varied interest groups, and informed and enthusiastic political participation by the public, has been realised to a considerable extent, and much more so than many pessimists in the early days of the Federal Republic would have imagined. The role of interest groups, like that of parties, or the Bundestag or the federal government, has not been without its critics, but by and large interest groups have played their part in the development of democracy in the Federal Republic.

Notes

1 Article 9, though, prohibits associations which have illegal purposes or undertake illegal activities.
2 In fact organisations of any kind cannot become corporate members of a political party in Germany; only individuals can do so. The Party Law (1967), section 2 (1) refers to membership being restricted to 'natural persons'.
3 The battle over abortion reform is outlined in Prützel-Thomas (1993).
4 Werner Naumann had been a high official in the Nazi government Propaganda Ministry. He and his allies joined the FDP, and soon occupied positions close to the party leader. The British occupying authority arrested Naumann and several others in 1953 on the grounds that he represented a threat to security because of this attempt to 'penetrate' the FDP.
5 Bundestag rules of procedure, s. 70.
6 See Boll (1994); Padgett (1996). This would seem to indicate that Germans in the new Länder are still lacking in the 'social capital' that is so evident in the more established West German system, and which contributes to the development of 'civil society' by encouraging and reinforcing social ties.

References

Blank, B. and Perschke-Nartmann, C. (1994) 'The 1992 health reform: victory over pressure group politics', *German Politics*, 2: 233–48.
Boll, B. (1994) 'Interest organisation and intermediation in the new Länder', *German Politics*, 1: 114–28.
Padgett, S. (1996) 'Interest groups in the five new Länder', in G. Smith, W. Paterson, and S. Padgett (eds), *Developments in German Politics 2*, Basingstoke, Macmillan.
Prützel-Thomas, M. (1993) 'The abortion issue and the Federal Constitutional Court', *German Politics*, 3: 467–84.
Saalfeld, T. (1999) 'Germany: Bundestag and interest groups in a party democracy', in P. Norton (ed.), *Parliaments and Pressure Groups in Western Europe*, London, Frank Cass.
Sebaldt, M. (1997) 'Verbände und Demokratie: Funktionen bundesdeutscher Interessengruppen in Theorie und Praxis', *Das Parlament. Beilage: Aus Politik und Zeitgeschichte*, 36–7: 27–37.
Statistisches Jahrbuch für das Bundesrepublik Deutschland, 1998 (1998) Wiesbaden, Statistisches Bundesamt.

Further Reading

Boll, B. (1994) 'Interest organisation and intermediation in the new Länder', in *German Politics*, 1: 114–28.
Padgett, S. (1996) 'Interest groups in the five new Länder', in G. Smith, W. Paterson, and S. Padgett (eds), *Developments in German Politics 2*, Basingstoke, Macmillan.
Saalfeld, T. (1999) 'Germany: Bundestag and interest groups in a party democracy', in P. Norton (ed.), *Parliaments and Pressure Groups in Western Europe*, London, Frank Cass.

10

Germany and Europe

Germans aren't Europeans because they have to be, but because they want to be
(Gerhard Schröder, *Newsweek*, 7 December 1998, p. 73)

In one way, this chapter title is misleading: Germany is, very obviously, part of Europe, by whatever definition of Europe is applied – a part of Europe in a way that, perhaps, the United Kingdom is not. Geographically, it is very much in the heart of Europe, with borders to the Czech Republic and Poland in the east, Switzerland in the south, Denmark in the north and France to the west. However, the relationship between Germany and Europe requires exploration in a textbook on German politics for three reasons. Post-war Germany was very much affected by its relationship with the rest of Europe, and the Federal Republic was shaped by its European links. Even the reunification of Germany was affected by – and perhaps only came about because of – the reassurance by Chancellor Kohl that an enlarged Germany would be a Europeanized Germany. Second, the German political system includes arrangements that would not exist were Germany not a member of the EU and the political culture of the Federal Republic is coloured by the close linkages between the Federal Republic and European integration. Third, the Federal Republic possesses a central, if still a rather exceptional, status within the EU (and within NATO and other European institutions), which modifies and constrains many of its domestic and foreign policy options, ranging from its agricultural policy to its relations with eastern European states, from its asylum and immigration policies to its military activities. In turn, the EU and its predecessor institutions have often been shaped and influenced by the political initiatives of the Federal Republic.

This chapter will focus especially upon two rather different, though very significant, organisations: NATO and the EU (and its predecessor organisations). Both have been essential to Germany's post-war development: NATO to provide external security, and the EU to develop economic prosperity. Even though NATO is a transatlantic organisation, it has held a central position with regard to the European arena of German politics, and the relationship of the

167

Federal Republic to NATO has been important, though often controversial, as the participation of German military units in the Kosovo crisis has demonstrated.

Creating a European Germany

It had been clear even during the Second World War that western Europe could not prosper without the German economy and could not be secure without the integration of German military potential' (Stirk, 1996, p. 119).

Even before the Federal Republic was brought into existence, the western zones of occupied Germany were very much affected by matters European. Two of the three western occupying authorities were European, and the third, the USA, fostered post-war European co-operation. Even during the war, European integration as an idea had been seen by some as the only conceivable option for the re-establishment eventually of a sovereign German state, since such integration would provide protection for other countries against any possible revival of German militarism. West Germany became a recipient of Marshall Aid under the European Recovery Programme which commenced in 1948 and included West Germany within its scope of operation. The recovery of the West German economy was regarded as essential to the economic recovery of western Europe.[1] In May 1948 a German delegation which included Konrad Adenauer attended the Hague Conference, which paved the way for the creation of the Council of Europe in May 1949. The Federal Republic became an associate member of the Council of Europe in 1950, and a full member in 1951.

However, it was during the chancellorship of Konrad Adenauer (1949–63) that the Federal Republic deliberately and, on the part of the governing Christian Democrats at least, energetically became involved in the process of European integration. In some respects, this was part of a wider process of tying the Federal Republic to the west, under the security umbrella of the USA, as the 'cold war' intensified and hence the division of Germany became more and more a *fait accompli*. Adenauer himself, as a Catholic from the Rhineland, was personally more comfortable with the notion of close association with France, Italy and the Benelux states, than might have been some other political leaders, from different backgrounds. Kurt Schumacher, the leader of the SPD, brought up in a part of Prussia that was now behind the 'iron curtain', and who had studied in Leipzig and Berlin, was personally unsympathetic as well as politically opposed to Adenauer's policy of integration of the Federal Republic with western Europe, a policy which he perceived as obstructing progress towards eventual German reunification. Adenauer's policy of western integration was not only undertaken because it promoted the security of the Federal Republic and enabled it to participate in the control of the Ruhr, for instance (see below); it was also a means of reassuring its West European neighbours that Germany would never again be a threat to European peace, and of slowly earning for the Federal Republic the status of an equal partner in international relations: it was 'a basis for international rehabilitation' (Bulmer and Paterson, 1987, p. 5).

The first major step towards the institutional linkage of the Federal Republic to western Europe was the creation of the European Coal and Steel Community on 18 April 1951 (and which took effect from July 1952). This was based on the Schuman Plan, named for the French Foreign Minister, who, with his adviser, Jean Monnet, designed the arrangements. This new organisation was intended to replace the unsatisfactory International Ruhr Authority which at the end of the war had been designed to ensure that West Germany's vast coal and steel resources in the Ruhr could no longer be utilised for military purposes. It also provided at least a temporary resolution of the problem of what to do with the Saar territory (another vital area of coal reserves and steel production), placed under French control at the end of the war. The ECSC was the first of the European post-war institutions which possessed supranational sovereignty; the Basic Law of the Federal Republic (Article 24) explicitly empowered the federal government to transfer sovereignty to supranational authorities. It introduced an unrestricted free market for coal and steel products among the six participant states: the Federal Republic, France, Italy and the Benelux states (Belgium, Netherlands, Luxembourg). The fact that the Federal Republic was to be a full and equal partner in the ECSC was another reason for its enthusiastic participation; it represented an affirmation of the identity and the acceptance of the Federal Republic in the sphere of international politics.

The next major development was in the realm of European defence. The intensification of the 'cold war' and the outbreak in June 1950 of the Korean war, the growing unlikelihood of a German peace treaty to end the occupation and to reunify Germany, and growing pressure on budgets and on politicians in the USA and the United Kingdom because of the ongoing costs of occupation, encouraged the western powers to contemplate in 1952 what even a few months previously would have still been unthinkable – the rearmament of the Federal Republic. This development certainly was not popular within the Federal Republic itself, and provoked considerable opposition at the time. A first effort (the creation of a European Defence Community, EDC) came to nothing because the French National Assembly (which contained over one hundred Communist Party legislators) refused in August 1954 to approve the treaty which would have brought the EDC into being. Instead, the London Conference of September–October 1954 recommended that the Federal Republic should become a member of NATO. This recommendation was realised by the Paris Treaties in October 1954, which also lifted many restrictions on the sovereignty of the Federal Republic and created the Western European Union, with the Federal Republic as a member, to foster further European integration.[2]

The undoubted success of the ECSC encouraged its member-states to develop a much more ambitious enterprise, a European Economic Community, which would extend the free trade arrangements beyond the iron and steel industries to cover all forms of production and commerce. The Federal Republic became a signatory to the Treaty of Rome (1957) which took effect on 1 January 1958, creating the institutional and contractual basis for the common market and other aspects of the EEC. The first president of the EEC Commission was a German, Walter Hallstein, who had been a civil servant in the Adenauer government; this was a further sign of the growing international acceptance of the Federal Republic. The EEC later developed into the European Community (EC) when the ECSC and another institution of European integration (EURATOM, the European Atomic Energy Community) to integrate nuclear energy policies), merged their institutions with those of the EEC in 1967. Following the Maastricht Treaty (1992), the EC became the core of the European Union. In all these developments, as well as the more detailed innovations along the way (such as the creation of the single market, the various expansions of membership of the EC and EU, the single currency project) the Federal Republic has been a key actor.

The status of the German Democratic Republic in relation to the EC has always been a special one. The Federal Republic, because of its claim concerning its status as the only democratic, legitimate successor-state to the pre-war German republic, refused to regard the GDR as a 'foreign' country. So when the Federal Republic became a member of the EEC it claimed the right not to impose tariff barriers against the GDR, a claim which it asserted in a protocol to the Treaty of Rome. This meant that, in some ways, the GDR was almost a 'secret' member of the EEC. When the communist regime in the GDR collapsed and the prospect of reunification became likely, the EC had rapidly to adjust to a swiftly changing situation. Economic and monetary union between the Federal Republic and the GDR, then reunification itself, all meant that special arrangements had to be put in place concerning trade, agricultural subsidies, membership of the European Parliament and other matters. The fact that the GDR had always had a special status *vis-a-vis* the EC (unlike, say, Hungary or Poland) made this adjustment simpler. Adaptation was made smoother by a set of special transitional arrangements for the continuation of subsidies and the adjustment of East German agriculture, for instance, together with observer status for representatives in the European Parliament until the next scheduled elections in 1994.[3] Reunification also had repercussions for the relationship between the Federal Republic and NATO. The reunification agreements allowed newly reunified Germany to remain as a member of NATO, though with temporary special conditions attached, preventing the stationing of NATO military installations in the former GDR prior to the completion of the withdrawal of Soviet Union armed forces.

Parallel to these developments at the West European level, the Federal Republic also fostered a special relationship with France. Since the Franco-German rivalry had been at the centre of three wars since 1870, this was an important contribution to European security. Whilst relations between the

Federal Republic and the French Fourth Republic had been fairly amicable (despite diplomatic conflicts over the future status of the Saar, see chapter 1), when de Gaulle came to power as president of the Fifth Republic Adenauer found almost a kindred spirit. Both had a patrician and mission-oriented style of governing; both were Catholics with a keen sense of regional and national pride; both had a rather similar vision for the future of Europe; both were distrustful of American influence. The signing of the Treaty of Friendship on 22 January 1963 came in the final year of Adenauer's chancellorship, but has lasted to the present. As well as formalising the process of reconciliation between France and Germany, this treaty initiated regular consultations between the governments of the two states, from the French president and the West German chancellor downwards; it encouraged closer relations in the form of youth exchanges, educational collaboration and other means; it was the basis upon which later military co-operation in the form of a joint Franco-German brigade under French command could be created (in April 1991). Though within the Adenauer government there were disputes between those, such as Erhard, who wished to place more emphasis on the links with the USA (the 'Atlanticists'), and those who supported Adenauer's 'Gaullist' approach of placing priority on links with France, the general policy of fostering western integration can be seen as a keystone of the Adenauer era, and was, it can be argued, an essential precondition of any policy that would eventually produce German reunification.

Europe and the political system of the Federal Republic

Many aspects of the political system of the Federal Republic reflect Germany's relationship with institutions of European integration. The Basic Law itself, both in its original 1949 version and in its post-reunification edition, acknowledges the relationship between the Federal Republic and European integration. The preamble to the Basic Law now refers to the Federal Republic's intention to serve peace as a member of a united Europe. The principal Articles concerning European integration, however, are Arts 24 and 23.[4] Article 24 provides for the transfer of sovereignty from the Federal Republic to international organisations, including those which serve international security. Article 23 provides a constitutional basis for Germany's membership of the EU, including the right of the Federal Republic to pass laws transferring sovereignty to the EU with the consent of the Bundesrat. It requires the EU to operate broadly in conformity with the principles of civic rights contained in the Basic Law. The rights of the Bundestag, the Bundesrat and the Länder in relation to EU legislation and decision-making are protected by this Article.

Other Articles of relevance to the political relationship between the Federal Republic and the EU are Articles 32 and 73, which confirm that responsibility for relations with foreign states lies within the competence of the federation;

Article 45, which provides for the creation of a Bundestag committee for European Union Affairs; Article 52, which includes provision for the creation of a European Chamber (*Europakammer*) by the Bundesrat; and Article 88, which allows the rights and the functions of the Bundesbank to be transferred to a European Central Bank within the framework of the EU, provided such a bank is independent and is obligated to make the attainment of price stability its primary goal.

As occurs with other aspects of the Basic Law, the Federal Constitutional Court has the responsibility for adjudicating on issues where the interpretation or application of these Articles is challenged. There have been several cases where the relationship between the Federal Republic and international agencies related in some way to European co-operation has been the basis of cases brought to the Federal Constitutional Court. The SPD sought to use the Court to halt progress toward a European Defence Community in 1952, for instance, but the Court refused to grant the injunction which the SPD requested. A number of cases were brought to the Court relating to the constitutionality of German military participation in NATO and UN peacekeeping activities, culminating in a decision in 1994 upholding the right of the federal government to commit troops to 'out-of-area' activities in the Balkans and Somalia. A key decision relating to the European Union was the Maastricht Treaty case in 1993, which upheld the constitutionality of German assent to the terms of the Treaty, but imposed conditions concerning procedures for democratic legitimation of any future transfers of sovereignty, insisting that such further transfers must be expressly approved by the Bundestag (see Appendix 1, 1F). A case brought to prohibit German participation in the European single currency project was ruled as inadmissible by the Constitutional Court in April 1998.

The federal government is the principal actor in relations with the EU, NATO and other European organisations. The federal chancellor attends the 'summit' meetings of the European Council; the federal government is represented on the EU Council of Ministers, of course,[5] and negotiates changes in policy of the EU, from the budget to enlargement, from the single currency project to developments in the single market. The Foreign Ministry has primary responsibility for relations with other member-states and with the EU, and a junior minister in that department is given the task of dealing with European matters. The Finance Ministry also plays a co-ordinating role in relation to EU policy-making.[6] However, and especially because of the sectorisation of the German executive government under the *Ressortprinzip* (principle of departmental responsibility) included in Article 65 of the Basic Law, other ministries become involved depending on the policy area: the Economics, Agriculture and Transport Ministries are examples. There is little provision for central co-ordination of policy; the Cabinet, the coalition committee from time to time, and the Chancellor's Office undertake only a very limited degree of such co-ordination, and the treatment of European policy is more diffuse in the Federal Republic than in other of the large member-states. This pluralistic dispersal of policy responsibility has two disadvantages. First, so many EU policies have two or more sectoral dimensions. The Common Agricultural Policy (CAP) involves protection for farmers, but costs to the EU budget – and thus, indirectly, for the budget of the Federal Republic – and high prices for the consumer. Regional aid policies may affect the competences of the Economics and Environment ministries, for instance. Thus the development of a single, co-ordinated policy by the federal government is made more difficult. Second, since the EU itself is pluralistic in its operation, this makes for an amplification of problems of 'dealing with Brussels' to secure German interests, whether these interests are seen in terms of national advantage or the promotion of European integration. What is clear is that EU policies affect to an increasing extent the policy options available to many ministries. Aid to farmers, asylum policy, the imposition of taxes on heavy goods vehicles from other member-states using German roads, industrial policy, environmental protection standards, labour market regulation: these are just a few of the areas where EU policies constrain the options available to the federal government.

The legislature has come increasingly to concern itself with European policy-making. Both the Bundestag and the Bundesrat are kept informed of European policy developments by periodic reports from the federal government. The Bundestag now has a Committee for European Affairs, set up under Article 45 of the Basic Law following the 1994 Bundestag election (replacing an earlier Committee for EC Affairs). This committee has, in some ways, unusual formal powers; it is one of the very few Bundestag committees mentioned specifically in the Basic Law. Its powers and duties are regulated in some detail by a Law on Co-operation between the Federal Government and the Bundestag on EU Affairs (12 March 1993). Unlike other Bundestag committees, it can take decisions on behalf of the Bundestag if a party group or 5 per cent of MdBs request it to do so. It has, in conjunction with the President of the Bundestag, wide-ranging powers of allocation of legislation concerning the EU to other Bundestag committees. This Committee consists of thirty-six MdBs, together with eleven of Germany's Members of the European Parliament (MEPs) who have full rights except that they cannot participate in committee votes. However, this Committee for European Affairs lacks an equivalent ministry (which may affect its status) and has to accommodate the interests of other Bundestag committees (such as those for the budget and agriculture) which have 'European' concerns from time to time. The Bundesrat also has a Committee for European Affairs, which normally consists of Länder civil servants. This Bundesrat Committee for European Affairs co-ordinates the work of other committees of the Bundesrat on issues which have a European dimension. More significantly, as a result of a decision of the Bundesrat taken in November 1993 implementing provisions of Article 52 of the Basic Law, there is now a European Chamber, consisting of one representative from each Land, which has delegated powers to act on behalf of the Bundesrat on matters pertaining to the EU.[7]

    The Länder have acquired a much more explicit 'European' role within the
political system since the Maastricht Treaty. They have an obvious link to the
new Committee of the Regions created by the Maastricht Treaty. Germany has
twenty-four members, twenty-one of which represent the Länder (the other
three represent local government organisations). The Länder have acquired a
constitutionally anchored status in relation to both European policy within the
political system of the Federal Republic and the policy-making process in the EU
itself, when matters are discussed concerning the regions or affecting the policy
responsibilities of the Länder as set out in the Basic Law. Article 23 of the Basic
Law now requires the consent of the Bundesrat to any future transfers of sovereignty to the EU. It also provides for a delegate representing the Länder and
selected by the Bundesrat, to represent the Federal Republic in negotiations
where the Länder have exclusive powers under the Basic Law. Procedures for
implementing these new constitutional requirements are contained in a Law
on Co-operation of the Federation and the Länder on European Union Affairs
(12 March 1993). A Committee of Länder Ministers for European Affairs was
created in October 1992 to co-ordinate the views and strategies of the Länder
governments. Policies in the areas of education, transport, the environment
and regional aid are all either exclusively or jointly responsibilities of the
Länder, yet each is also a central policy concern for the EU. Where co-ordination with federal government policies is required, joint committees are created.
There is rarely much conflict between the two levels of government on such
issues, however. As in so many areas of German political life, progress tends to
be based upon consensus where possible.
    With regard to the political parties, since the 1970s there has been little con-
troversy or conflict between the Christian Democrats and Social Democrats
concerning the broader features of the relationship between the Federal
Republic and Europe, and the FDP (who, incidentally, provided the Foreign
Minister and hence had a significant role in shaping European policy from
1969 to 1998) is the most enthusiastic of all the parties on matters European.
The PDS and the Greens take a more critical view of progress towards European
integration; the PDS sees dangers of Europe being too capitalist and neglectful
of the social dimension, while the Greens focus on possible danger to the environment from an integration project focused on growth. Both also are critical
of German military involvement, as was demonstrated by the opposition of the
PDS and sections of the Green party to German military participation in the
NATO campaign against Serbia in 1999. The SPD briefly played with the idea
of opposing the development of the single currency project between 1995 and
1997, but soon found that there was little electoral advantage to be obtained
from such a policy stance. More recently, the CSU has taken a more sceptical
role concerning the European currency project. It has warned that a fragile
European currency can damage plans for further integration. The extreme
right parties oppose anything which, in their eyes, dilutes German national
identity, but this view generally finds little resonance in the electorate. Attempts

by the small party, Association of Free Citizens (*Bund freier Bürger*), in the early 1990s or *ProDM* (a small party opposed to German participation in the single currency project) in the 1998 Bundestag election, were failures; they attracted very few votes. The principal parties are represented in the European Parliament (though the FDP has failed to win seats there since 1994), and so play a role within the party alliances of that parliament, helping to shape responses to policy initiatives, to control the budget and – as events in 1999 demonstrated – to criticise the European Commission. To foster co-ordination on European matters, the parties include some of their MEPs on their party Executive boards.

For interest groups, the existence of the EU provides an additional arena for their attempts to influence policy in their own favour. There are numerous methods by which such groups attempt to secure advantageous decisions from EU institutions. Many German interest groups are members of appropriate European interest groups, such as the Committee of Professional Agricultural Organisations (for farming groups), the Association of European Automobile Manufacturers (for motor vehicle producers), the European Trade Union Confederation, and the various organisations which represent the free professions, such as lawyers, doctors and pharmacists. A number of German interest groups (and here one can include the Länder as interest groups, since they compete for EU structural funds, for example) maintain offices in Brussels, to be 'on the spot' for the receipt of information, the application of influence and co-ordination with representatives of the German government where government and interest group concerns coincide. The Länder had 140 staff in Brussels in 1998, more than the 120 staff of the German embassy itself. Subsidies from Brussels for economic development or tourism, for instance, constitute for some Länder between a third and a half of their budgets for those policy sectors (*Der Spiegel*, 3 August 1998, pp. 40–1).

The Council of Ministers is the arena in which policy decisions are taken, ranging from the introduction of a uniform withholding tax on savings to changes in the British 'claw-back' of a portion of its net contributions to the EU budget. However, though groups can attempt to persuade ministers from other countries of the justice or wisdom of their case, it is through their own minister that national groups may hope to exercise influence most effectively, and such persuasion is a process that is no different from persuading ministers of the merits of the group's case on domestic policy issues. The EU Commission is the principal target of European-level lobbying by interest groups, since the Commission initiates and then oversees the implementation of policy and because amendments of detail to such policy can be of the utmost significance to affected groups. However, with the recent accretion of powers to the European Parliament, interest groups also direct attention, in Brussels and Strasbourg, to the committee hearings and plenary sessions of the Parliament. Apart from opportunities to influence the outcomes of such hearings or debates, groups can benefit from the publicity associated with such approaches to the Parliament and from the aura of democratic legitimacy which the Parliament possesses, and which may benefit the campaigns of interest groups by a 'rub-off' effect. It must, though, always be kept in mind that the implementation of the greater part of EU policy is left to national governments, so German groups wishing to affect the implementation of such policy may be best advised to direct their attentions to persuasion of the federal or Land government (see chapter 9).

As European integration goes forward, so more and more policy issues are affected by EU decisions. Some are ongoing issues, such as the levels of quotas and price supports for agricultural products, changes of which can make or break farmers; rules on competition policy, which are of importance to firms contemplating mergers; implementation of the terms of the social chapter of the Maastricht Treaty, which can affect trade unions and employers; or environmental standards, which can affect the financial viability of transport firms, manufacturers, public utilities and retail shops. Other issues are of a 'one-off' nature, such as the conflict in which Germans brewers were defeated in the 1980s concerning importation of foreign beers which did not meet the traditional standards of German beer, the unsuccessful campaign to prevent the scheduled abolition in 1999 of 'duty-free' sales on ferries and at airports, or the transitional provisions made to accommodate the addition of the 'new Länder' of East Germany to the Federal Republic following reunification in 1990. This means that interest groups ranging from the German Chambers of Commerce and the German Farmers' Association to the member organisations of the German Federation of Trade Unions and the Association of Newspaper Publishers are increasingly likely to be affected by policy decisions at the EU level, and therefore need to devote increasing shares of resources to ensuring that such decisions are as favourable as possible to the interests of those whom such groups represent.

Germany and Europe: a symbiotic relationship

The relationship between the Federal Republic and Europe can be summarised in four short assertions: Germany needs Europe; Europe needs Germany; Germany has influenced Europe; Europe has influenced Germany.

The Federal Republic has benefited, and still does benefit, from its involvement in the institutions of European integration. The ECSC and then the EEC provided a path to international acceptance for the new Federal Republic, and, together with NATO and other European organisations such as the Western European Union (WEU) supplied a context within which the Federal Republic could protect its own interests and security without arousing the anxieties of its European neighbours. Without such a context, for example, it is difficult to imagine that German reunification would ever have received consent from France or the USSR. The institutions of European integration have provided scope for economic advancement by the Federal Republic; generally about 60 per cent of its exports have been directed to its partners in the EU. The North Atlantic Treaty Organisation has allowed the Federal Republic to found and then develop an effective, skilled and technologically advanced military capacity, and the industrial structure to supply weapons and military equipment to its own and other armed forces. Europe is also a kind of nationalist alibi for Germans. Some have said that it offers a 'substitute patriotism', in that Germans can safely take pride in saying that they are Europeans and can direct their enthusiasm towards European projects, but can also safely claim to be proud of being German as long as Germany is embedded in the schemes of European integration. Whereas the 'old nationalism' associated with the rise of Hitler is still taboo (and associated with right-wing extremism), 'new nationalism', symbolised by placing the EU flag next to the German flag, or by Kohl's phrase: 'Germany in Europe', seems safe and acceptable.

Europe has obviously benefited from Germany. First, there are benefits which are the mirror-image of those that Germany has received from Europe: the seemingly safe accommodation of what had been a pariah state within a multinational context. Any project of European economic integration would have been incomplete without the inclusion of the Federal Republic, simply because of the size of its economy and its important geographic position. The contribution of the Federal Republic in the 'cold war' to the defence of western Europe also cannot be ignored; again the size and the geographic location of the Federal Republic were of immense significance. But there have been other benefits as well. The Federal Republic has been a counterweight to France, and a more enthusiastic, committed European partner than France, so European integration has gained much from German membership in terms of lubrication of negotiations and in terms of balance among the partner-states, who otherwise might have found themselves under French hegemony. Several Germans have played a significant role in European integration: Adenauer, Carlo Schmid, Hallstein (the first president of the Commission), Genscher and Kohl, for instance. Manfred Wörner, a former Defence Minister, was appointed as NATO General-Secretary in 1988 – a symbol of how far the Federal Republic had progressed from its status at the end of the Second World War as a defeated and militaristic people. Nor can the financial contribution of Germany to the budgets of the EU and its predecessor institutions be overlooked. Though today a less prosperous Federal Republic is more cautious about its role as 'paymaster' of Europe, its aggregate and per head contributions remain high, constituting about 60 per cent of the EU budget. Germany makes a net contribution of DM264 (about £92) per head to the EU budget, second only to the contribution per head of the Netherlands. The United Kingdom, by comparison, contributes DM61 per head (about £21) (*Der Spiegel*, 14 December 1998, p. 23).

This symbiotic relationship can also be identified in terms of the mutual influence which Europe and the Federal Republic have exerted one upon the other. The Federal Republic has had influence on the development of European

integration through the policies of its leading politicians, which have, especially since the 1970s, pointed in the direction of closer economic and political
union, as reflected in the speeches of Helmut Kohl, for instance. The Federal
Republic has also been keen on the progressive enlargement of the European
Community. Its support of Britain's application was important in bringing
about the first enlargement, and it has been in the forefront of plans to widen
the EU and NATO by bringing in central and eastern European states. The political structures of the EU have been shaped in part by German influence.
Because Germany has experience with multi-level government and provision
for regional autonomy, it brings that experience to bear on discussions concerning the way in which a federal arrangement can accommodate regional,
national and supranational interests within the EU. The Bundesbank has
served as a model for the European Central Bank in the context of the single
currency project. Because of the sheer size and economic weight of the Federal
Republic, as well as its recent greater confidence in asserting its interests in
matters of foreign and security policy, Germany will necessarily be 'first among
equals' in all matters pertaining to greater integration within Europe.

The Federal Republic has been influenced in its political development and its
policy choices by its membership of European institutions. Obviously membership of NATO has enabled it to develop, with the agreement and co-operation of
its former enemies, a potent military capacity. Its economy has benefited from
the elimination of tariffs and the creation of a single European market, providing a degree of prosperity which has supported the costs of a comprehensive
welfare state, for instance. Industrial policy, agricultural policy and environmental policy, for example, have all been shaped and constrained by membership of the EC and EU. German reunification was facilitated by European
co-operation, and the generous structural aid from the EU to the 'new Länder'
helped relieve the financial burden of reunification after 1990.

What of the future? Despite the enthusiasm of political and economic elites
for a kind of 'permanent revolution' with regard to European integration, the
population seems neither enthusiastic about further integration nor particularly interested in it. European affairs are not regarded as especially important
by the electorate, and there is a definite decline in interest in matters European
in the 1990s. Surveys have also identified an increase in the numbers of
respondents rejecting further progress towards integration, with levels of rejection much higher than before reunification, and with East Germans showing
the highest levels of rejection.[8] Turnout in European Parliament elections (60
per cent in 1994, and only 45 per cent in 1999) is lower than for Bundestag or
Land elections, another indicator of the low level of interest which the electorate has for European matters. Should the constraints on national economic
and financial policy imposed by the single European currency become associated in the public's mind with economic recession, unemployment and reductions in welfare benefits, anti-European attitudes might harden, and European
policy could become an important issue of inter-party conflict. The political

elites wish to see progress towards European integration continue and become irreversible, but for them it is primarily a political project and less a matter of economic benefits and costs. The general public seems less convinced of the value which should be placed on integration as a political goal. The future development of the Federal Republic and, indeed, of the EU may depend on those in positions of political responsibility convincing the German public of the benefits for them of the symbiotic relationship between Germany and Europe.

Notes

1 Once the Federal Republic was created, it took its place in the Organisation for European Economic Co-operation, the institution which administered the distribution of Marshall Plan funds and coordinated plans for European reconstruction.

2 The Federal Republic actually became a member of NATO with effect from 9 May 1955.

3 For the 1994 elections a new allocation of seats in the European Parliament gave reunified Germany a larger number of seats (ninety-nine, instead of eighty-one) to accommodate eighteen additional East German representatives.

4 Article 23 was added after reunification, to meet the situation which had been created by the Maastricht Treaty. Article 23 previously had provided for the accession of territories of Germany outside the Federal Republic's borders to the Federal Republic, and had been used to bring first Saarland, and then the five 'new Länder' of the former GDR into the Federal Republic (see chapters 1 and 2). As no such territories any longer existed, Article 23 had lost its validity, so was available for this new purpose. Article 23 was then utilised for the constitutional reinforcement of the position of the Länder in relation to the EU following the signing of the Maastricht Treaty.

5 Though, under the post-Maastricht version of Article 23, a representative of the Länder may occupy the German seat when certain issues are under consideration for which the Länder are responsible.

6 Until the entry into office of the Schröder government in 1998, this role had been undertaken by the Economics Ministry.

7 Voting in the European Chamber is on the basis of one vote per Land, in contrast to the weighted voting in the plenary sessions of the Bundesrat itself (see chapter 8).

8 Levels of rejection (*c.* 25 per cent) are higher than the EU average (*c.* 20 per cent): data from Glaab et al. (1998, pp. 176, 178, 181). The same authors also note that in 1997 48 per cent of respondents were against the Euro replacing the Deutschmark, but that 85 per cent of elites questioned were in favour of the Euro (Glaab et al., 1998, pp. 186–7, 192).

References

Bulmer, S. and Paterson, W. (1987) *The Federal Republic of Germany and European Integration*, London, Allen & Unwin.

Glaab, M., Gros, F., Korte, K.-R. and Wagner, P. (1998) 'Wertgrundlagen und Belastungsgrenzen deutscher Europapolitik', in W. Weidenfeld (ed.), *Deutsche Europapolitik*, Bonn, Europa Union Verlag.
Stirk, P. (1996) *A History of European Integration since 1914*, London, Pinter.

Further reading

Bulmer, S. and Paterson, W. (1987) *The Federal Republic of Germany and European Integration*, London, Allen & Unwin.
Bulmer, S. and Paterson, W. (1996) 'Germany in the European Union: gentle giant or emergent leader ?' *International Affairs*, 72: 1, 9–32.
Katzenstein, P. ed. (1997) *Tamed Power. Germany in Europe*, Ithaca and London, Cornell University Press.
Paterson, W. (1996) 'Beyond semi-sovereignty: the new Germany in the new Europe' *German Politics*, 2: 167–84.
Stirk, P. (1996) *A History of European Integration since 1914*, London, Pinter.

11

Germany:
a 'normal' democracy?

Overcoming the past

Each one of the principal combatant states in the Second World War, the United States of America excepted, entered upon the post-Second World War period with a significant political legacy. France had to create a new Republic in the context of its recent history of military defeat, collaboration, occupation and resistance. Britain had its proud record of having 'stood alone' against Hitler's military threat, but had to come to terms with the record of the appeasement politics of the 1930s, the physical and economic damage caused by the war, and its much weakened hold on its empire. The Soviet Union had to undertake substantial physical reconstruction and consolidate its regime in a country that had proved once again to be vulnerable to invasion from the west.

Germany, though, had a far greater burden to carry, a burden that consisted of three distinct components. Like all the other European participants in the war, but more intensively than any except perhaps the USSR, it had to cope with enormous physical, demographic and economic damage. Second, in terms of international politics, it had to accept the status of an occupied state, totally lacking in autonomy, and blamed for a second time in four decades for causing the outbreak of a world war. Third, and most significantly, Germany had somehow to proceed into an uncertain future as a pariah people, held to have been responsible not only for aggression against its neighbours (in itself, nothing very new in European history), but also for its enthusiastic rush into acceptance of a totalitarian dictatorship which was responsible for many horrific developments, but most particularly for the Holocaust – the policy of genocide against the Jewish population of Europe. This material, this political, but especially this moral legacy of the war is the single most important factor which explains the historical course of politics in occupied, in divided and then in reunified Germany. It accounts for many of the special features of the institutions and processes of German politics in the Federal Republic, and for the difficulty which the Federal Republic itself and its neighbours have had with the achievement of the status of a 'normal' democracy in the Federal Republic, normal in the way that the democracies of France or Sweden, of the United Kingdom or the Netherlands can be regarded as 'normal'.

For East Germany, first under Soviet occupation, then as the German Democratic Republic, the burden of the past had somewhat different characteristics than in the Federal Republic. The economy suffered because heavy reparations were extracted by the Soviets, and the economy then rapidly became collectivised and run according to rigid socialist planning. Political and social development had to take place within the framework of communist ideology and Soviet self-interest. The separation of the GDR from the Federal Republic and, certainly after the erection of the Berlin Wall in 1961, its isolation from the West, constituted a special burden.[1] When the Berlin Wall was dismantled in 1989 and the GDR merged with the Federal Republic in 1990, East Germans found that there was a new and different 'burden of the past' for them: their history between 1945 and 1990, at first under communist occupation, then as a communist state. So the crimes of the GDR regime (including the shooting of would-be escapees at the border), collaboration of many of the population with the secret police, membership and especially office-holding in the SED or its auxiliary organisations such as the Free German Youth or the trade union organisation, and the economic backwardness of the East German economy were all aspects of this 'burden', and affect still, even more than a decade after reunification, the integration of East Germans into the society and polity of the Federal Republic.

The first two components of the Federal Republic's burden of the past were relatively easily transformed from negative to positive characteristics of the Federal Republic. Physical and social reconstruction on the one hand (see chapter 1), the acceptance of the Federal Republic as a semi-sovereign, then by a series of stages, a fully sovereign actor in the European and global political systems on the other hand (see chapter 10), came to be regarded as positive features. The idea of a 'model Germany' (*Modell Deutschland*) defined in mainly economic terms indicated the success of material reconstruction and of economic development by means of the 'economic miracle' of the 1950s and 1960s based on the social market economy. Sometimes the Federal Republic has been described as a 'Gulliver' in terms of its international relations, because its international obligations and its special status resulting from its past have meant that it has played a much less assertive role in international politics than its size, resources and capacity otherwise would have indicated (Paterson, 1992). Certainly the Federal Republic, if only because of its size and territorial location (especially since reunification), has become a significant and respected actor in international politics, during the 'cold war', in the processes of European integration, in relations since 1990 with former communist states in central and eastern Europe, and in its relations with third world countries, for example.

The third, the moral component, has been a much more enduring burden. It is one that, even in the 1990s, Germans themselves recognise differentiates them from the peoples of other states. When asked in 1992 if there was anything in Germany's history that distinguished Germany from other countries, 59 per cent of West Germans and 60 per cent of East Germans agreed that there was. When asked to identify what it was that distinguished Germany from other countries, 52 per cent of those West Germans who agreed that there was something distinctive (but only 11 per cent of the East Germans) mentioned the Third Reich and Hitler; 30 per cent of East Germans (but only 11 per cent of West Germans) referred to the Berlin Wall and divided Germany; 36 per cent of East Germans and 22 per cent of West Germans who agreed that there was something distinctive mentioned the Second World War or wars involving Germany; only 8 per cent of West Germans (3 per cent of East Germans) mentioned post-war reconstruction.[2] The majority of political institutions provided in the Basic Law, and the relations between them, have been profoundly affected by what the 'founding fathers' in Bonn in 1948–49 perceived to be those flaws in the Weimar democracy which directly contributed to the rise of the Third Reich. The concept of 'combative democracy' (see below) exists in the Federal Republic precisely because of this interpretation of the causes of the rise of Hitler and the Second World War. There are many examples one could find of this special legacy of Germany's twentieth-century history. They would include: the liberality of asylum provisions (and the political problems which such liberality has led to); the illiberal law forbidding reference to the 'Auschwitz lie' (*Auschwitzluge*);[3] the special sensitivity of the regime to extremism, but particularly right-wing extremism, though to communist infiltration also; tense relations with Germany's Jews and with Israel; the difficulties that many people had with West Germany's rearmament in the 1950s and with German military participation in UN or NATO peacekeeping missions in the 1990s; and Chancellor Kohl's emphasis on progress with European monetary union because, in his view, this would be a further step towards making war impossible between Germany and its West European neighbours. This history is thus special to an extent that is qualitatively different from the situation in either Italy or Austria, even though these countries also had been defeated in the Second World War.

This legacy is still troublesome. In autumn 1998, for example, nearly half a century after the founding of the Federal Republic, three very different responses to this moral legacy made headlines. None of these three illustrations was exceptional, in the sense that similar examples could be found from every one of the forty-eight previous years. They are important as evidence that still, after so long, the 'burden of the past' persists and is contentious. The first illustration was a march organised by the extreme right-wing National Democratic Party in Bonn, to protest against an exhibition which dealt with the crimes committed by the German military in the Second World War, and a counter-demonstration organised by left-wing 'anti-fascists' opposing the march.[4] The second illustration was a speech by President Herzog on 9 November 1998, marking the sixtieth anniversary of *Reichskristallnacht* ('crystal night'), when, with the encouragement of the Nazi regime and with the acclamation of many onlookers, Jewish property was destroyed and many synagogues burnt. The third illustration was the furore caused by the acceptance speech of the writer Martin Walser, when he was awarded a prestigious prize at the Frankfurt book fair. In that speech, he seemed to indicate that it was time to say farewell to the continuing need for each generation to feel responsible for the horrors of the Hitler regime. Criticism of his speech (or of their own interpretation of it, at any rate) came from a several sources, including from Igniz Bubis, the leading spokesman for Jews in Germany. For weeks afterwards, press and television discussion of that speech continued. In any other three-month period, one could no doubt identify a similar number of highly publicised events or statements to serve as indicators that *Vergangenheitsbewältigung* remains a potent ingredient in political life, which must cast doubt on the claim that Germany is now a 'normal' democracy.

Nevertheless, the political system and political activity in Germany at the end of the twentieth century are very different from those in the Federal Republic forty years ago. Some claim that the 'events of 1968' in West Germany (including West Berlin, one of the main centres of such radical political activity at the time) were a cause of the transformation of the Federal Republic from a 'special' and still in some ways a fragile democracy to a 'normal' and, many would assert, an extremely stable democracy.[5] This period of upheaval caused many people in the Federal Republic to be concerned about the lack of democratic procedures in the political system, but also in economic and social institutions (such as schools and universities). There are numerous indications that such a transformation has taken place. Almond and Verba, in their renowned study of political culture in five countries in the 1950s, found in the Federal Republic a passive, subject-oriented political culture in which democracy was accepted, if not enthusiastically supported, but where citizens neither felt able themselves to affect political outcomes nor had any great desire to become involved in politics (Almond and Verba, 1965, pp. 312–13, 362–3]) Analyses of the political culture of the Federal Republic more recently have found more positive acceptance of democracy, a high level of information about and interest in politics, and a readiness to take action (sometimes even illegal or at least unorthodox forms of action) to press for political ends. The Allensbach Institute, for example, reported that fewer than 30 per cent of respondents in the 1950s admitted that they were 'interested in politics' but since 1969 over 40 per cent have said that they were interested in politics (and at the time of German reunification well over 50 per cent said so).[6] The rejection of personal involvement in politics that was so widespread in the 1950s contrasts with levels of party membership in the Federal Republic in the 1970s and beyond that are very much in line with 'normal' West European levels of party membership. Other indicators: attitudes to authority, attitudes to the justifiable and legitimate use of German military force in peacekeeping missions, evaluations of Germany's past, for instance, all reinforce the argument that in many ways, though by no means in all, the democracy of the Federal Republic is now very much a 'normal' democracy, plagued by the 'normal' problems of West European democratic regimes.

The reunification of Germany has reinforced this tendency to normalisation, since it has removed the problem of 'the divided nation', a problem that was exacerbated by the fact that it was a nation that was divided between the two 'camps' of the 'cold war'. However, the process of integration since reunification of the two German societies which had developed so differently in West and East Germany has meant that a new set of challenges confronts the Federal Republic, challenges arising from the post-war division of Germany into a liberal-democratic state and a communist state. The GDR developed as a one-party state, lacking in most of the features that are associated with liberal democracy, possessing an economy that was planned, controlled and owned by the state, and which was debilitated by its close association with the Soviet Union to whose interests it had to pay tribute. So, once the formal aspects of reunification had been put in place, principally by means of the treaties first on economic and monetary union, then on political fusion, the long, difficult process of integration began. More than a decade has passed since the breaching of the Berlin Wall, yet surprisingly little progress has been made with such integration. Indeed, in some respects the gap between East and West Germany has grown larger. Two rather distinct systems of party competition seem to have developed, for instance (see chapters 4 and 5). Unemployment and lack of new investment remain at levels in the 'new Länder' which are way behind those in the rest of the Federal Republic. Attitudes towards democracy, at least towards democracy in the form in which it is incorporated in the Basic Law, are much less supportive in East Germany than in West Germany (Zelle, 1999). Violence against foreigners and support for extreme right-wing parties and organisations are – in relative terms – at higher levels in the 'new Länder' than in West Germany. A generalised feeling of resentment that the prosperity enjoyed in West Germany has not spread swiftly or sufficiently enough to East Germany is to be found in political rhetoric, in commentaries in the mass media, in responses in opinion polls and in private conversation in the 'new Länder'. On the other hand, West Germans regard East Germans as different from themselves, and resent the tax burden which subsidises East Germany and which – though liable to be paid by all Germans – falls much more heavily on West Germans (especially the temporary 'solidarity supplement' on certain taxes, including income tax). West Germans seem to lack understanding of the problems which East Germans have faced, both under communist rule and in adjusting almost overnight to the requirements of society in the Federal Republic (Roberts, 1991).

Other liberal democracies have problems of integrating two or more rather different sections of what could otherwise be regarded as a single political community; Belgium, Canada and Northern Ireland are obvious examples. So in one way this problem can be regarded as 'normal' in Germany's case. On the other hand, the problem is overlaid with special features dating back to the end of the war, and to the ideological conflicts of the 'cold war', so it, too, must be included in any survey of Germany's 'burden of the past'.

Defending democracy

According to many commentators from the 1930s to the present day, one contributory cause which led to the collapse of the democratic regime of the Weimar Republic and to its replacement by a dictatorship was a failure of the Weimar regime actively to defend democracy from its enemies. The Weimar constitution itself was relatively 'passive', lacking provisions that would deter anti-democrats from using the liberal nature of the constitution to attack democracy and the constitution itself. Few opinion leaders, whether from education, the mass media, the churches or interest groups, were prepared to support or defend the democratic ideal, and certainly not in the form in which it found expression in the Weimar regime. Most of the key institutions of society and the state, from the courts to the military, from the civil service and the universities to many of the political parties and commercial enterprises, were hostile to the Weimar Republic.[7] It was no wonder that the economic depression which began in 1929, the violent political activities of Nazis and communists, a weak and uncertain status for Germany in international politics, unstable governments and the absence of credible leadership from those democratic political parties which did support the regime brought about the downfall of Germany's first democratic republic so easily and so swiftly.

As was the case with so many other things, ranging from the electoral system to civic rights, from the constructive vote of no confidence to the indirect election of the federal president, the drafters of the Basic Law, when confronted by the need to create the conditions for a robust democracy which would not easily succumb to anti-democratic forces, tried to learn from the lessons of the Weimar Republic. It must be remembered that in 1948 the Weimar Republic had only been abolished fifteen years previously, and many of those sitting in the Parliamentary Council in Bonn had played an active role in the politics of the Weimar period, among them Adenauer and Heuss, soon to be the first chancellor and federal president respectively, so it was a very real and recent model for them. A series of innovations inserted into the Basic Law, together with a number of laws, court judgements, policies, administrative measures and political conventions, contribute to this purpose of ensuring that, this time, a democratic system in Germany would be able to defend itself against forces hostile to constitutional democracy. A special term has been coined in the Federal Republic to encapsulate this idea: *streitbare Demokratie* – combative democracy (sometimes also translated as: 'militant democracy'). This refers to a democracy that not only guarantees civic rights, free elections, limited government and the rule of law, but goes further, actively seeking to counter and overcome anti-democratic ideas, developments and organisations. The irremovable status of civic rights in the Basic Law (such as freedom of speech and of assembly); the provision in Article 21 that anti-democratic parties can be prohibited by the constitutional court; the right and duty of the Minister of the Interior to ban political and other organisations (other than recognised political parties) which endanger democracy (Article 9 of the Basic Law); the creation of official agencies to gather intelligence concerning potential threats to the democratic order (the Federal and Länder Offices for the Protection of the Constitution); emphasis on civic education, including the role played by the Federal and Länder Centres for Political Education and the Foundations associated with political parties (listed in chapter 5); the controversial 'radicals decree':[8] these all can be included as components of 'combative democracy'.

The Federal Office for the Protection of the Constitution (*Bundesamt für Verfassungsschutz*) was founded in 1950, and is an agency of the Interior Ministry. Its duties are to identify, investigate and report upon persons or groups who appear to pose a threat, or who potentially might be a threat, to the democratic order (including foreign intelligence agents) and to undertake the security clearance of those in the public service in sensitive positions. This Office adopts the term 'extremist' to refer to persons or groups whose aims or activities, in its opinion, threaten or might threaten the democratic order, as described in the Basic Law. Though the Office uses a variety of methods for its intelligence gathering, it has no powers of arrest. It must leave prosecution or other sanctions (such as imposing a prohibition order) to the relevant state authorities. The Office produces an influential annual report, analysing developments in the past year and providing tables showing, among other things, membership of various extremist groups of the left and the right (as well as those associated with foreign, often fundamentalist, political or religious groups), the number and types of criminal activities linked to extremism, and any other developments worthy of note. The Office also produces various publications on special themes, for public information. The Länder Offices for the Protection of the Constitution conduct very similar activities at Land level.

The activities of these agencies are sometimes controversial. In particular: (1) the structure and, some contend, the undemocratic methods used to gather intelligence could be regarded as quite as dangerous a 'cure' as the 'disease' of anti-democratic activity against which they are directed, and (2) in 'marginal' cases there will be differences of opinion, sometimes dividing the democratic parties themselves one from another, about whether a party or movement or group really has deserved to come under the official scrutiny of these agencies. Thus in recent years decisions concerning the democratic status of the Republican party on the right and the Party of Democratic Socialism on the left have been especially controversial, with some Länder Offices for the Protection of the Constitution taking different views from other Länder Offices and from the Federal Office itself.

It is important to understand that a party or other organisation may be classified as 'extremist' by the Office for the Protection of the Constitution, yet it does not follow that it will be prohibited. In the case of political parties which come under the provisions of the Party Law, they can only be prohibited by the Federal Constitutional Court. A case to ban a party can only be brought by the federal government, the Bundestag or the Bundesrat (or, for a party which operates only within that Land, by the Land government); a rival party, for instance, cannot initiate such a case. There are political reasons why the government or legislature may decide not to bring a case to the Court, even if the chances of securing a ban might be high. It might be considered to be unnecessary, since the party in question may be electorally insignificant; if the party does have a large membership or considerable electoral support, then it might well be regarded both as undemocratic to ban a party with so much support, and unwise, since such a ban might drive its membership 'underground', and even encourage members to undertake violent action on behalf of the prohibited party. So only two parties have been subjected to such legal prohibition: the SRP in 1952 and the KPD in 1956 (see Appendix 1, 1A and chapter 5). Serious consideration was given to trying to ban the NPD in the late 1960s, but it was thought to be politically unwise to bring such a case to the Constitutional Court. It is a further sign of the 'normalcy' of Germany's democracy that such prohibitions of parties are no longer thought necessary or appropriate.

Groups that do not enjoy the privileges of protection under the Party Law (because they do not contest elections or otherwise meet the definitional requirements of a party set out in the Party Law), even though they may label themselves as parties, can be prohibited by executive action under Article 9 of the Basic Law. That Article states that groups whose aims or activities run counter to the criminal law or are directed against the constitutional order or international understanding can be prohibited. The Interior Minister can ban such groups, and in the past few years a number of such groups (primarily those with a racist or ultranationalist bent) have been subject to such prohibition orders. For example, in 1995 three groups were banned: the Free German Workers Party, the Hamburg-based National List and the Direct Action/Middle Germany group. In total, these had no more than about 400 members.[9] Such bans may be accompanied by criminal prosecutions, as in these three cases, resulting in some members receiving prison sentences. Confiscation of property, publications and financial resources, and suspensions of certain civil rights (such as the right to make public speeches) can also be imposed on prohibited groups. Determined individuals try to get round such prohibitions by forming 'new' groups with new names, but these, too, may be banned and the process of imposing a ban may be disruptive, costly and, in terms of publicity, harmful to the image of the group.

The significance of such groups needs to be kept in perspective. Most are extremely small. Data from the Office for the Protection of the Constitution indicated that in 1998 there was a total of 53,600 right-wing extremists, an increase of 11 per cent on 1997. A disproportionate number of these resided in the 'new Länder'. Seven hundred and ninety acts of violence with a right-wing extremist background had been identified. On the far left, there were about 35,000 left-wing extremists, including some 2,000 supporters of the 'Communist Platform', a faction within the PDS. Seven hundred and eighty-three acts of violence with an extreme left-wing background were identified (*Frankfurter Allgemeine Zeitung*, 26 March 1999). However, even small groups may be intermittently and locally disruptive, and, anyway, the worst examples of racist violence in recent years have been the work of gangs of thugs who may or may not belong to such groups, and who are capable, in small groups or as a mob, of considerable violence without the benefit of the resources of formally organised associations.[10]

As well as these 'negative' weapons such as investigation by the Office for the Protection of the Constitution, prohibition of parties and banning of anti-democratic groups, combative democracy also has an arsenal of more positive weapons available to it. The most significant is political education. The term 'political education' itself is redolent of the ideological brainwashing which occurred in Nazi Germany and Stalin's Soviet Union; in that sense, it is under-stood as meaning 'indoctrination'. The term 'civic education' might be con-sidered preferable in a democracy. However, as used in Germany 'political education' does not imply 'indoctrination', but almost the opposite – readiness to debate and argue about politics, but from a basis of knowledge and in a spirit of toleration. This type of political education is to be found in school curricula, in adult education courses, in seminars offered by party Foundations, in activ-ities associated with churches and trade unions. It is promoted with the help of considerable public financing, which allows the Federal and Länder Centres for Political Education to commission, produce and distribute a range of publica-tions and media aids, ranging from copies of the Basic Law to quite complex studies of the party system, from periodical publications like *Das Parlament* (which reports weekly on themes and news associated with the Bundestag and Bundesrat, Länder parliaments, European Parliament and foreign legislatures and elections, as well as on special topics such as foreigners in Germany or the environment), to series such as Information for Political Education (*Informa-tionen zur politischen Bildung*) providing concise, textbook standard presenta-tions on themes such as the history of the Federal Republic or federalism. Ever since the start of the occupation period, the western allies, then the govern-ment of the Federal Republic, have placed great emphasis on political education as an antidote to totalitarianism (the Nazi as well as the communist variety) and as a method of strengthening democratic commitment in the Bonn Republic, a commitment that was so lacking in the Weimar Republic.

Extremism and prejudice: overcoming 'clear and present dangers'

Political education, the role of the Office for the Protection of the Constitu-tion, the 'radicals decree' and other measures associated with 'combative democracy' are not only put in place in order to prevent the re-emergence of Nazism. At the end of the twentieth century, few among the citizens of Germany can have played a personal role in either the misdeeds of the Third Reich or the aggressive war unleashed by Hitler. However, as was emphasised in the previous section of this chapter, the lesson from the Weimar experience was that a democracy must be alert at all times to all sorts of possible dangers to its survival, and that those dangers must be countered early and with vigour. It can be said of present-day Germany that:

- political extremism, racial violence and terrorist activities still exist, as they have done to a greater or lesser degree throughout the fifty-year history of the Federal Republic, and of course as they exist in Northern Ireland, England, France, Spain, Belgium and other areas of Western Europe;
- but that, because of Germany's special history, there is a special sensitivity towards such phenomena, and a special concern to combat and condemn them;
- and that perhaps a more pressing problem, again, not only in the case of Germany, is the more generalised, more widespread existence of prejudice and intolerance which may not involve any illegal or undemocratic activity, but which provides a degree of social acceptability to what otherwise would be seen as illegitimate and disgraceful activities.

There have been occasional upsurges in voting support for extremist parties: since 1990, and even before then. These upsurges have been exclusively on the right, unless one goes along with the controversial classification by some Länder Offices for the Protection of the Constitution, and some individual politicians, who regard the PDS as belonging to the category of extremist parties.

Studies of those elections demonstrate that many voters for extremist parties do not vote consistently, election after election, for such parties, and that upsurges tend to be the result of protest votes rather than expressions of support for the programmes of those parties. However, surveys also show a readiness to consider voting for these parties, which is more widespread than actual voting support, and they also reveal that many respondents sympathise with some of the demands of parties such as the German People's Union, the Republicans or the National Democratic Party, especially on issues relating to foreign residents and asylum-seekers, or concerning national pride and attitudes to the Third Reich and the war. Consequently, political education seeking to protect democracy against parties and political ideas inimical to the constitutional order as embodied in the Basic Law has to attempt to change attitudes at quite a deep level, as well as explain and clarify particular points such as the contribution which foreign-born residents and their German-born children and grandchildren make to the cultural life, to the prosperity and to the society of present-day Germany, or the actual costs of asylum-seekers and the measures taken to regulate their inflow. Reunification of Germany added a new

Table 11.1 *Electoral performance of extremist parties, 1990–99*[11]

Bundestag elections		
1990	Republicans	2.1 per cent
1994	Republicans	1.9 per cent
1998	Republicans	1.8 per cent
1998	German People's Union (DVU)	1.2 per cent

Land elections			
1992	Baden-Württemberg	Republicans	10.9 per cent
1996	Baden-Württemberg	Republicans	9.1 per cent
1990	Bavaria	Republicans	4.9 per cent
1999	Brandenburg	German People's Union (DVU)	5.2 per cent
1991	Bremen	German People's Union (DVU)	6.2 per cent
1993	Hamburg	Republicans	4.8 per cent
1998	Saxony-Anhalt	German People's Union (DVU)	12.9 per cent
1992	Schleswig-Holstein	German People's Union (DVU)	6.3 per cent

dimension to this problem of intolerance. It is indeed paradoxical that many of the worst cases of violent activity against foreigners have occurred in the new Länder, where the populations of foreign residents and asylum-seekers are much smaller, in relative terms, than in the western Länder. Hoyerswerda and Rostock are just two of the most notorious examples.[12]

Far less pervasive a factor in the politics of the Federal Republic, but much more dramatic, has been the incidence of terrorism. The most significant series of terrorist activities was undertaken by the Red Army Fraction, sometimes also called the Baader-Meinhof gang until the imprisonment and suicide of Meinhof in 1976 and Baader (along with two accomplices) in 1977. Terrorist crimes dating from 1968, and continuing into the post-reunification period, included arson, kidnapping, plane hijacking, and assassination of prominent personalities from political and commercial circles. Other terrorist activities included the kidnapping of Israeli athletes at the Munich Olympic Games in 1972 by Palestinian terrorists, terrorist attacks by IRA groups on British military installations in Germany, and various terrorist actions by Kurdish groups. There have also been attacks on politicians and apparent terrorist activities by individuals (the attempted assassination of Rudi Dutschke in 1968, the explosion of a bomb at the Munich October beer festival in 1980 and the shooting of Wolfgang Schäuble in 1990 among them). Whether confronted by a conspiracy of extreme left-wing terrorists, the lone actions of an individual, or the campaigns of foreign organisations against their enemies on German soil, the democratic system of the Federal Republic has adapted, responded and survived without in doing so losing its essential democratic qualities. This is another indicator of the success of 'combative democracy' in the Federal Republic.

New politics and old issues

In the immediate post-war period, the German people were primarily concerned with reconstruction of the economy, of their homes and towns and villages, of their family life and their culture. As in other countries, domestic politics was overwhelmingly concerned with 'bread-and-butter' issues relating to the division of wealth, the balance between levels of taxation and public expenditure, the creation and expansion of social welfare schemes, health services and education, and the provision of homes for all. Once the Federal Republic became prosperous through the 'economic miracle', once a social welfare system had been consolidated, an enviable health scheme was in place and educational provision was more than adequate, a novel set of issues started to acquire importance. These issues – environmental protection, equal opportunities for women, development aid for third world countries, disarmament and animal rights among them – were classified as 'new politics' issues, in contrast to the 'old politics' issues which had for so long dominated the political agenda. The extension of middle-class lifestyles and values was accompanied by a declining working-class share of the electorate. The dominance within this middle class of those in salaried employment, often in public sector occupations such as government administration, teaching, social work and university employment, rather than the self-employed or owners of family businesses, had created a sector of the electorate known as the 'new middle class', who proved to be especially interested in 'new politics' issues, and many of whom were ready to participate in organisations or movements whose political activity focused on such issues.

From the 1970s onwards, this wave of 'new politics' activity increased in significance. Local and regional 'citizen initiative groups' (*Bürgerinitiativen*) took action to block projects likely to damage the local environment or to promote projects to provide better public amenities, such as play areas or cycle paths. In particular, the expansion of nuclear power plants and the difficulties surrounding the safe disposal of radioactive waste from those plants encouraged activists to co-ordinate regional demonstrations and protests on a nation-wide basis. From such activities the Green party developed, which came to offer a political home not only to those obsessed with environmental concerns, but to all for whom 'new politics' constituted their political focus and for whom an alternative, unorthodox political style was a refreshing change from the orthodoxies of the established political parties.

The Federal Republic was not the only country to experience the advent of 'new politics'; the USA and Scandinavian countries, for example, also had to experience such a challenge to the standard political agenda and the 'old way of doing things'. But nowhere else has a new party, espousing 'new politics' with such enthusiasm, so swiftly, so successfully – and now, it seems – so permanently established itself in the party system and national electoral politics. Germany is the first country in which the Greens have become a significant partner in a national governing coalition.

Again there is a paradoxical situation. The Greens came to share government power just at a time when the political agenda was dominated by 'old politics' issues, especially concerning unemployment, tax reform and social welfare. The chosen instrument of the Schröder coalition formed in 1998 to tackle these issues has been termed an 'ecological tax reform', but this label cannot disguise the fact that there was much political argument concerning who would lose and who would gain from such a reform; in other words, redistributive politics was again dominant. In fact, 'old politics' issues never really disappeared from the political agenda but in the 1990s globalisation, developments in the EU and the world economic crisis, as well as the economic consequences of reunification, made more pressing the need to address these issues and allowed less time and opportunity to debate problems of environmental improvement or development aid strategy.

Nevertheless, 'new politics' has had its successes in the Federal Republic. Environmental concerns are given prominence in every party's manifesto at election time, and the federal government and all Länder governments have a minister responsible for environmental policy. The termination of nuclear energy provision in Germany is a key feature of the coalition agreement negotiated between the SPD and the Greens in October 1998 and of the 'government declaration' of Chancellor Schröder. More attention is given – in political parties and in other organisations – to ensuring that women are given more equal opportunities to fill elected and appointed offices, and to encouraging their fuller participation at all levels of public life. Some parties have formal gender quotas; others have alternative means of monitoring gender balance and encouraging women to seek party and public office. In this, Germany is ahead of most of its West European neighbours.

The prominence of 'new politics' has also drawn attention to the reluctance of young people to join parties and participate in 'orthodox' politics, though, as in Britain or France for example, many of them are eager to engage in exciting, unorthodox, rebellious forms of political activity (such as trying to block rail transport of nuclear waste, boycotting Shell petrol stations in protest against the dumping at sea of the obsolete Brent Spar drilling platform, or joining demonstrations against racial discrimination and violence) through association with movements or groups outside the ambit of the parties. The parties have responded, though with little success, by trying to be more open to new ideas and to inputs from non-members, by inviting young people to consider becoming party members, and by adopting more democratic measures such as membership ballots.

New Germany and the world order

Germany itself symbolises the post-'cold war' era, since it is now composed of what were formally separate states, one from each side of the 'iron curtain'. The removal of the problem of divided Germany and the consequent changes in Germany's relations with other countries (such as the conclusive settlement of the Oder-Neisse border dispute with Poland, the removal of Soviet troops from German territory and the termination of the remaining formal rights of the occupation powers within Germany) have meant that Germany itself has become a more self-confident, politically a more weighty and economically a more potent agent in international affairs. The role of Germany during Helmut Kohl's long chancellorship in promoting closer unity in the EU, and his enthusiastic, if dour, promotion of monetary union, have been mentioned in chapter 10, as has Germany's growing unease about the distribution of net payments to the EU. In politico-military terms, Germany's potential for contributing to peacekeeping and 'police' actions in trouble spots outside the NATO area is obviously considerable. The crucially important decision of the Constitutional Court in 1994, which confirmed the constitutional validity of government decisions to deploy military personnel for United Nations and NATO peacekeeping activities, paved the way for German military (and not just financial) contributions to such actions in future – opportunities which are likely to increase over the next few years. Nevertheless, as chancellor-candidate Gerhard Schröder stated in a press interview during the election campaign in 1998, referring to Israel and Yugoslavia: 'there are some areas of conflict where Germans have to be especially circumspect or sensitive because of history' (*Newsweek*, 27 July 1998, pp. 24–5).

Trends towards the globalisation of the economy are both a threat and an opportunity for Germany. They are a threat, in as much as high costs of production in Germany, due to generous social benefits, costly environmental policies and a high standard of living supported by high wage levels, may reduce Germany's competitiveness in its traditional markets, and may lead to investment by German businesses migrating to lower-cost countries. These developments have become very visible as the turn of the century approaches. Globalisation trends are an opportunity, because German technical know-how, a skilled and educated workforce, and a range of high-quality institutions especially in the financial, media, telecommunications and education sectors allow Germany to offer services to other countries – particularly in eastern Europe, Africa, Latin America and Asia – as they seek to develop their economies. These two features, threat and opportunity, are relevant to the continued health of Germany's democratic political system, since where the economic threat has already become most apparent in terms of unemployment (in the 'new Länder', for instance), run-down urban areas (parts of Berlin and Hamburg, for instance), and lower-quality schools and social services, political discontent has revealed itself in various ways. These manifestations of political discontent include demonstrations by coal-miners from the Ruhr, fearful of redundancy and the collapse of their communities if the heavy subsidies paid to the mining industry are reduced or withdrawn; attacks on asylum-seekers; voting support for extreme right-wing parties (as in Saxony-Anhalt in 1998) or, in the 'new

Länder', for the PDS; and decline in party membership. Where change has brought opportunity, political participation is stronger, orthodox parties gather more support (as is the case with the CSU in Bavaria, for instance), and political life is less dramatic and more stable.

The Federal Republic has always been concerned about its image in other countries, so its promotion of the work of the Goethe Institute, *Internationes*, the German Academic Exchange Service and the party Foundations has supplemented more orthodox diplomatic activity.[13] Relations with the USA have always been a priority (though often contending with the priority accorded to relations with France and other countries within the European partnership), partly of course because of the protective role which the USA of necessity adopted with regard to Germany at the end of the Second World War. Relations with Israel and with countries invaded by German armed forces during the war (such as Poland) have been important – though very sensitive – as well. The Federal Republic has played an active role in assisting developing countries in Africa, Asia and Latin America to improve their economies, by aid as well as by trade. The Ministry for Economic Co-operation, though a 'minnow' in the federal government, nevertheless has made a significant contribution over the years to the improvement of the situation of these countries; its assistance to flood victims in Nicaragua in 1998 was an example. Political Foundations made a notable contribution to Spain and Portugal as those countries made the transition from dictatorship to democracy in the 1970s, then in the 1990s turned their attention to the former communist states of central and eastern Europe, as they, too, underwent political, economic and social transformation. Having successfully, if painfully, transformed itself from being ruled by a dictatorial tyranny to becoming a highly successful market economy and liberal democracy, the Federal Republic has been well placed to pass on its experience.

A balance sheet: Germany's democracy at the end of the twentieth century

It is ironic that, after Germany's unhappy experiences with democracy in the inter-war period, the Federal Republic should now be classed as one of the most stable and successful of West European democracies. This democratic political system has been designed, developed and protected in a fifty-year period during which the Federal Republic has reconstructed its economy, integrated its society, including, in the 1940s and 1950s, large numbers of refugees and displaced persons, and secured its place in a West European community of nations during the trials and tensions of the 'cold war'. Its recent and, in some ways, most potent challenge was to adapt its institutions and political procedures to accommodate the 'new Länder' as a result of German reunification.

The democratic political system of the Federal Republic is not perfect – but then, neither is any other democratic political system elsewhere. Criticism can be levelled at many of its institutions and procedures, from the 'radicals decree' to the overwhelming political and social dominance of the established political parties. From time to time some sections of the electorate seem tempted by extremist parties and movements: but the same can be said of France, Belgium, Italy, Northern Ireland and many other places. There is a conservatism with regard to institutional change, economic adaptation and social reform that reveals itself in large matters such as the defence of subsidies for uneconomic coalmines, farms and shipyards, and in smaller matters such as limitations on shopping hours, but British unwillingness to reform its electoral system or the French propensity to erect barricades periodically in defence of trade union or professional interests could be cited as parallels.

Four claims can justifiably be asserted with regard to the political system of the Federal Republic. It is, first, a democratic political system, which enjoys an great deal of acceptance by, and support from, its citizens and indeed admiration from other countries, as demonstrated by institutional imitation in Austria, Spain, Italy, New Zealand and Scotland, among other examples.

Second, it is a stable system, with an arsenal of weapons with which to defend its democratic constitutional order ('combative democracy'). At the governmental level, ruling coalitions have tended to last for long periods, compared either to those of the Weimar Republic or to those of other democracies today. Chancellor Kohl's government replaced SPD-FDP coalitions which had lasted thirteen years; Kohl was replaced after sixteen years in office. No serious attempt has been made to replace the democratic regime, either by peaceful or violent means. In 1968 the radicalism of the student movement and intellectuals brought a swift response from the authorities, including passage of legislation and constitutional amendments to protect the regime in an emergency situation. The terrorism of the Red Army Fraction was met by generalised public revulsion, not mass revolution, and by swift and effective government counter-measures, including more rigorous legislation to combat terrorist threats. Hopes on the part of radical Greens and 'post-materialists' that a more open form of government could replace the orthodox and elite-based procedures of the Federal Republic were met by adaptation and reform, but not by change of regime. So when German reunification occurred in 1990, there was but little support for the idea of replacing the tried and tested Basic Law by a new constitution, even though the Basic Law itself had allowed for precisely that possibility in its Article 146.

The third claim is that German democracy has proved itself to be compatible with efficient government. One very simple comparison is between the central planning and single-party autocracy of the GDR and the liberal democracy of the Federal Republic before reunification. Whether in terms of productivity, trade, technological advances, standard of living or levels of satisfaction with social and political institutions, the Federal Republic 'delivered' more effectively than the GDR. Even allowing for the complications arising from the federal structure of the state (see chapter 7) the Federal Republic is generally responsive to the demands of its citizenry and sufficiently adaptable when faced with internal or external pressures for change.

Fourthly, this democratic system was founded and then developed in a very challenging context. The traumatic effects of the overthrow of the Hitler regime and defeat in the war, the restrictions and obligations imposed on the Germans by the occupation authorities, and the pressing requirements of physical and economic reconstruction all meant that the fostering of democratic politics was a special challenge. In many ways, the southern European dictatorships of Greece, Spain and Portugal, the formerly communist states of central and eastern Europe, and especially the 'new Länder' that used to comprise the GDR, have all had to handle the transformation process to democracy under much more favourable – if nevertheless still difficult – conditions than those which confronted the people of West Germany from 1945 onwards.

So yes, Germany is now a 'normal' democracy, a stable and efficient democracy which was developed, and which has since proven itself, in challenging times. Its development since 1945 is fascinating as history. That history also explains why it functions as it does today. Whatever the future course of European integration and however much the process of globalisation increases, Germany and its political system will assuredly continue to be of great importance in the future.

Notes

1 On the occupation period, see the excellent account by Naimark (1995).
2 Allensbach survey, cited in Greiffenhagen (1997, p. 413). For respondents who agreed that there was something distinctive, multiple answers were permitted.
3 Illiberal because it restricts freedom of speech and, potentially anyway, freedom of academic inquiry. The Basic Law provides an irrevocable right to free speech and to freedom of intellectual inquiry in Article 5. The 'Auschwitz lie' consists in the attempt to prove either that Jews were not murdered in Auschwitz concentration camps, or that their numbers were much smaller than is generally accepted in the literature on the Holocaust. Such claims are almost exclusively associated with extreme right-wing groups or organisations.
4 During the autumn of 1998, two television series dealing with the military in the Hitler period were broadcast: one called 'Hitler's Generals' dealt with a number of controversial high-ranking military personalities, such as Admiral Canaris; the other was a history of the army in the Second World War, including its activities in relation to the 'final solution' – the murder of Jewish populations in countries conquered by the German military. Both dealt with sensitive issues, and aroused controversy.
5 The 'events of '68' is the term applied to the protests, demonstrations and other activities in 1968 associated with the student movement and radical left-wing political activitsts. These 'events' occurred in many western countries, and included student protests at universities in Britain, France and the USA, as well as in the Federal Republic and other countries, street battles with police, sit-ins, strikes and

other forms of unorthodox political activity. The government of President de Gaulle was threatened by such events in Paris. The US presidential election that year was affected by street demonstrations and protests. It should be remembered that the Vietnam war was occurring at the time, and many students demonstrated against US military policy there. The 'Prague Spring' (attempts by Czechs to introduce a more liberal kind of 'reform communism') also took place in 1967–68, but was crushed early in 1969 by the intervention of the USSR and other communist bloc states.

6 *Allensbach Jahrbuch für Demoskopie*, 10, cited in Gallus and Lühe (1998, pp. 138–9).

7 For example, Hitler was given a light sentence and opportunities to publicise his views in court by Bavarian judges following his attempted *coup* in 1923; he was then given pleasant prison conditions and an early release on parole after serving one year of a five-year sentence.

8 This set of administrative arrangements was agreed by the federal and Länder governments in 1972. It is designed to ensure that applicants for public service positions (and those already at the time in such positions) should be able to demonstrate a wholehearted commitment to the principles of constitutional democracy as laid down in the Basic Law. It was very controversial at the time, and seemed to be directed more against those associated with extreme left-wing parties and groups than with those on the far right. It was sometimes called a 'career prohibition' (*Berufsverbot*), since it effectively closed some careers such as the civil service, the judiciary and teaching to those with even a relatively harmless previous association with, say, a Marxist student group. The principle of such a decree was also challenged, as being in itself anti-democratic. A history of the controversy can be found in Braunthal (1990).

9 *Freiheitliche Deutsche Arbeiterpartei, Nationale List, Direkt Aktion/Mitteldeutschland.* The first two of these organisations sought a declaration from the Constitutional Court that they were parties, and were thus not subject to executive prohibition, but the Court ruled against them, because they did not contest elections or meet other defining criteria of political parties.

10 There is evidence that at least some of these activities are planned and co-ordinated, and are not as 'spontaneous' as they may at first appear. The Internet and mobile phones make such co-ordination much easier.

11 For the purposes of this table, (1) the Republican party is classified as 'extremist', though it is acknowledged that there is controversy about this classification; (2) the PDS is not included in this table. For Bundestag elections, only party vote-shares of 1 per cent or more have been included; for Land elections only party vote-shares of 4 per cent or more have been included.

12 In Hoyerswerda, in Saxony, right-wing extremists attacked a residence for asylum-seekers in September 1991, resulting in some thirty people being injured. The inhabitants were driven to safety in buses, to the accompaniment of jeers from some of the local population. In Rostock, in the northern Land of Mecklenburg-Vorpommern, in August 1992 groups of right-wing extremists set fire to a hostel where Vietnamese lived, unhindered by the local police and urged on by cheering crowds.

13 The Goethe Institute promotes German language and culture abroad. *Internationes* provides German-language teaching resources and research materials for educational institutions and individuals outside Germany. The German Academic

Exchange Service fosters academic exchanges of university teachers, students and researchers, whether Germans wishing to study, teach or conduct research in other countries or residents of other countries wishing to study, teach or conduct research in Germany. The party Foundations have undertaken a range of activities concerned with political education (broadly defined) in countries outside Germany.

References

Almond, G. and Verba, S. (1965) *The Civic Culture. Political Attiutudes and Democracy*, paperback edn, Boston, MA, Little, Brown.

Braunthal, G. (1990) *Political Loyalty and Public Service in West Germany*, Amherst, University of Massachusetts Press.

Gallus, A. and Lühe, M. (1998) *Öffentliche Meinung und Demoskopie*, Opladen, Leske & Budrich.

Greiffenhagen, M. (1997) *Politische Legitimität in Deutschland*, Gütersloh, Verag Bertelmann Stiftung.

Naimark, N. (1995) *The Russians in Germany: A History of the Soviet Zone of Occupation, 1945–1949*, Cambridge, MA, Harvard University Press.

Paterson W. (1992) 'Gulliver unbound. The changing context of foreign policy', in G. Smith, W. Paterson, P. Merkl and S. Padgett (eds), *Developments in German Politics*, London, Macmillan.

Roberts, G. (1991) '"Emigrants in their own country"? German reunification and its political consequences', *Parliamentary Affairs*, 3: 373–88.

Zelle, C. (1999) 'Socialist heritage or current unemployment? why do the evaluations of democracy and socialism differ between East and West Germany?', *German Politics*, 1: 1–20.

Further readings

Betz, H-G. (1991) *Postmodern Politics in Germany. The Politics of Resentment*, Basingstoke, Macmillan.

Chapin, W. (1997) 'Explaining the electoral success of the New Right: the German case', *West European Politics*, 2: 53–72.

Roberts, G. (1991) '"Emigrants in their own country"? German reunification and its political consequences', *Parliamentary Affairs*, 3: 373–88.

Roberts, G. (1994) 'Extremism in Germany: sparrows or avalanche?', *European Journal of Political Research*, 4: 461–82.

Zelle, C. (1999) 'Socialist heritage or current unemployment ? why do the evaluations of democracy and socialism differ between East and West Germany?', *German Politics*, 1: 1–20.

Appendix 1: Court cases

1 Constitutional Court cases affecting the political system

A The prohibition of unconstitutional parties cases (1952 and 1956)

Situation

The federal government in 1951 asked the Constitutional Court to ban two parties: the extreme right-wing Socialist Reich Party and the Communist Party of Germany – on the grounds that they breached Article 21 of the Basic Law by seeking to combat the basic democratic order embodied in the constitution. The activities, organisation and publications of the SRP seemed to show clearly that it was a neo-Nazi party. Similarly the publications and pronouncements of the Communist Party, together with its organisational structure, demonstrated that it had the firm intention of replacing the constitutional order by a communist form of state.

Verdict

The Court ruled against both parties: against the SRP in 1952; and, after long deliberation, against the KPD in 1956. Both parties were dissolved and their property confiscated. In later years, when the government might well have initiated similar cases against the successor party to the KPD (the German Communist Party – Deutsche Kommunische Partei (DKP)), the extreme right-wing National Democratic Party, the German People's Union or the Republican party, it has not done so, indicating a preference for non-judicial methods of combating what some might consider to be anti-democratic or anti-constitutional parties: a sign that the Federal Republic has become a more established and self-confident regime. It should be noted, though, that non-party organisations, subject to the provisions of Article 9 of the Basic Law rather than Article 21, have frequently been banned by the Minister of the Interior as being anti-democratic. Such bans do not require the use of the Constitutional Court.

B The second television channel case (1961)

Situation

In an attempt to counter what he saw as an anti-government bias on the part of the television channel Arbeitgemeinschaft der öffentlich-rechtlichen Rundfunkanstalten der

200

Bundesrepublik Deutschland (ARD, supervised by the Länder, many of which had governments led by the SPD), Adenauer set in train a scheme to create a second television channel to be supervised by the federal government. Several Länder governments initiated a complaint to the Constitutional Court, on the grounds that the federal government had no powers under the Basic Law to engage in broadcasting activities. The federal government claimed in its defence that the Basic Law bestowed such power under Article 73, which gave the federation exclusive powers over the post and telecommunications.

Verdict

The Court ruled that the federal government under Article 73 only had authority to regulate the technical aspects of broadcasting. Other aspects of broadcasting were cultural matters, and therefore come within the constitutional powers of the Länder. This judgement emphasised the federal basis of the state, and the fact that the federal government is restricted in its authority to those areas specifically listed in the Basic Law, though the use of concurrent powers provided in the Basic Law has allowed the federal government to extend considerably its range of authority (see chapter 6).

C   The party financing cases (1966 and 1968)

Situation

Relying on their constitutional status under Article 21 (a status that the Constitutional Court had emphasised in its judgements in other cases, including the party prohibition cases) the parties in the Bundestag had passed legislation which allowed them to benefit financially from a range of privileges, such as the tax deductibility of donations. This included the 1959 Party Finance Law, which was a response to an earlier decision of the Constitutional Court concerning appropriate ways of giving political parties subsidies from public funds. The Land government of Hesse and three small parties which did not qualify for public funding under the existing law complained to the Constitutional Court.

Verdict

Though public funds could not be given to parties to defray costs of 'political education' (the basis of the 1959 legislation), the Court ruled that they could be supplied to offset costs of election campaigns, since election campaigning could be implicitly read in the Basic Law as a constitutional duty for the parties. However, if that were to be so, then all parties would have to be treated fairly. Though legislation providing for such funding need not allow *all* parties, however small, to qualify for subsidy, the qualifying level should be considerably lower than the 5 per cent share of list votes which had been the basis of the 1959 Party Finance Law. The Bundestag passed the Party Law of 1967 to incorporate, *inter alia*, provisions for party funding by the state in line with the Court's ruling (and also used that Law to include a variety of other matters concerning parties, some of which were the result of other decisions of the Constitutional Court). However, a complaint by several small parties led the Court to scrutinise the Party Law. In a decision in 1968 the Court ruled that the proposed barrier of 2.5 per cent of list votes as a qualification for state funding was still inappropriately high, and declared that 0.5 per cent should be the qualifying figure. Further revisions to the law concerning party financing occurred in 1983 and 1988, in each case resulting in a challenge by the Green party being taken to the Constitutional Court. Though the Court in 1986 upheld the constitutionality of the 1983 legislation (with minor exceptions), in 1992 it produced a radical decision which not only declared many of the aspects of the 1988 legislation unconstitutional, but, in doing so, also reversed many of the Court's previous decisions on the subject of party financing. New legislation was produced in 1994 to take account both of the rulings of the Court and a report of an expert commission set up by the federal president.[1]

D *The Bundestag dissolution case (1984)*

Situation

The success of the constructive vote of no confidence on 1 October 1982, by which Helmut Kohl replaced Helmut Schmidt as chancellor, meant that a change of chancellorship from one main party to the other had occurred between elections for the first time in the history of the Federal Republic. Since the next Bundestag election had been scheduled for autumn 1984, nearly two years later, it was thought by all the parties in the Bundestag to be essential to receive electoral legitimation for this mid-term change of government as soon as possible. However, the premature dissolution of the Bundestag by the federal president is permitted under the Basic Law only under the most exceptional conditions: either when a newly elected Bundestag cannot produce a majority to elect a chancellor, or when the chancellor loses a majority (as demonstrated in the rejection of a vote of confidence) and when no alternative chancellor is able to secure a majority (Article 68). Chancellor Kohl – like Chancellor Brandt in 1982 – contrived to lose a vote of confidence, thus enabling him to ask the president to dissolve the Bundestag. A number of former MdBs from the dissolved Bundestag complained to the Constitutional Court, on the grounds that the constructive vote of no confidence had clearly demonstrated that a majority was available for Chancellor Kohl, and that therefore the premature dissolution arose out of a deception, and was thus unconstitutional.

Verdict

The Court refused to nullify the federal president's decision, holding that it had to take at face value the good faith of the actions of the chancellor (in requesting a vote of confidence), the Bundestag (in voting on it) and the president (in granting the dissolution request), though the Court did regard the whole issue as controversial and by no means straightforward. Anyway, it would have been near impossible to reinstate the Bundestag once the federal president had legally dissolved it. Many continued to have doubts concerning the constitutionality of the situation (though the premature election was in fact held as planned on 6 March 1983). A number of politicians have suggested that a more definitive right to premature dissolution ought to be inserted into the Basic Law. It is important to note that any future successful employment of the constructive vote of no confidence is likely to give rise to a similar situation as that in 1982, since there would again be a demand for legitimation of the new government by an early election, though now the 1983 decision of the Constitutional Court has set a precedent.

E *The Bundestag committee membership case (1989)*

Situation

A Member of the Bundestag, Thomas Wüppesahl, had been elected on the Green party list in 1987. Like other MdBs, he was given assignments on Bundestag committees as a representative of the Green parliamentary party. He resigned from the party in 1988, and the Greens replaced him on all of the committees to which he was assigned. Wüppesahl claimed before the Court that his constitutional rights as a Member of the Bundestag had been infringed by the actions of the Green parliamentary party.

Verdict

The Constitutional Court confirmed the right of the Bundestag to design its own rules of procedure (Article 40 of the Basic Law). Such rules had to take account of the rights of individual Members of the Bundestag, but the Bundestag could determine the ways in which MdBs and parties would participate in the work of the Bundestag. The Greens were entitled to replace Wüppesahl once he had put himself in a position where he no longer could represent that party's views. However, the equality of all MdBs had to be protected and, as a consequence of this verdict, independent MdBs must now be granted at least one committee assignment. In 1991 the Court rejected a claim by the PDS to be granted the status of a parliamentary party, even though it failed to meet the requirement of the Bundestag's own regulations concerning the minimum number of representatives for allocation of such status. The Court again upheld the right of the Bundestag to create its own regulations on such matters.

F The Maastricht Treaty case (1993)

Situation

Manfred Brunner, a former FDP politician and a former employee of the European Commission, together with several other citizens, complained to the Constitutional Court that the provisions of the Maastricht Treaty on European Union would, if implemented, detrimentally affect several constitutional rights of the complainants, and that the transfer of sovereignty involved in the Treaty went beyond what was permitted in Article 24 (which allowed transfer of powers to supranational bodies), since the EU was a state-like entity. They further claimed that the Treaty involved the removal or amendment of unamendable features of the Basic Law, including the federal basis of the state and the principle of popular sovereignty.

Verdict

All the complaints were held to be without foundation except for the issues of democracy and the right to vote. Despite the term 'European Union', the organisation of the European Community remained inter-governmental, therefore any further developments had to be approved by the Bundestag before implementation in Germany. Further, the Bundestag continues to exercise control over the federal government, including that government's European policy. The Court also noted that the new version of Article 23 of the Basic Law provided assurances that progress in developing the EU would be subject to the principles of the rule of law, the federal principle and subsidiarity which informed the Basic Law itself. The judgement did insist that any transfer of powers to a supranational body be specific and limited, not general. The verdict was regarded as permitting German membership of a common European currency, but only if the criteria set out in the Maastricht Treaty were met fully. Brunner went on to form a new party, the Alliance of Free Citizens, which opposed the Maastricht Treaty, but this had no perceptible success. In January 1998 a number of individuals complained to the Court that, since Germany had failed to meet in full all the Maastricht criteria for membership of the common monetary system, German participation should not be allowed, relying on the Court's decision in 1993. The Court decided that there was no valid case upon which it could give a ruling.[2]

G *The electoral system cases (1997)*

Situation

The federal election 1994 produced an exceptionally large number of 'surplus seats' (*Überhangmandate*) (see chapter 4). These seats had the consequence that the majority for the governing coalition amounted to ten seats, rather than the two-seat majority that would have existed had there been no such surplus seats. Indeed, it could easily have been the case that the coalition would have had no majority at all but for that number of surplus seats. Additionally, for the first time since 1957, a party succeeded in bypassing the 5 per cent qualification for the allocation of list seats: the PDS with only 4.4 per cent of list votes nevertheless won four constituency seats, and thus qualified for a distribution of list seats also. The complainants who brought the case claimed that both these aspects of the electoral system were unconstitutional, in that they breached the requirement that the electoral system should protect the equality of votes (Article 38 of the Basic Law).

Verdict

The electoral system used in 1994 was constitutional, with regard to surplus seats and the three constituency seats alternative to the 5 per cent qualification. However, changes should be made to the boundaries of constituencies to minimise the possibility of surplus seats arising in future. If the number of such surplus seats should exceed narrow limits (5 per cent of all seats was indicated as such a limit by the Court) then that would no longer be in conformity with the constitution. However, this leaves an ambiguity – as with the Bundestag dissolution case, D above – as to what steps could then be taken concerning a federal election where that percentage was exceeded. The Bundestag in 1996 rejected proposals by the Greens that compensatory seats should be introduced to offset the disproportional effect of surplus seats, a system that exists in several of the electoral systems used for Land elections. This decision was in conformity with that in an earlier case before the Court. In 1963 the Court rejected a challenge to the validity of 'surplus seats' arising from revision of constituency boundaries in Schleswig-Holstein in the Bundestag election of 1961, on the grounds that these extra seats affected the equality of elections under Article 38.

2 Other cases

A *Cases concerning freedom of speech and opinion*

These include two cases in 1994 and 1995 concerning the right to make statements that 'soldiers are murderers' (echoing the claim made in the 1930s by the anti-Nazi and pacifist, Kurt Tucholsky). The Court upheld the right to make this claim under Article 5 of the Basic Law. However, in a ruling in 1994, the right to deny that the Holocaust occurred was held by the Court to be invalid as, claimed the Court, it is denial of a 'fact', not an expression of opinion.

B Protection of freedom of religious belief

The controversial 'crucifix case' in 1995 concerned parents who objected to their children being compelled to attend classes in Bavarian schools where a crucifix was on display in each classroom. The Court held that the complaint should be upheld, under the provisions of Article 4 of the Basic Law, protecting freedom of belief. This decision aroused considerable protest from the Catholic church, Christian Democratic politicians and sections of the press, in which the legitimacy of the Court's decision was challenged.

C A series of cases concerning the law on abortion, from 1975 onwards

The Court generally imposed restrictive conditions on the right to have an abortion outside the scope and sanctions of the criminal code, upholding the constitutionally guaranteed 'right to life' principle of Article 2 of the Basic Law. The controversy over abortion was revived with reunification, since the law in the GDR had been much more liberal; indeed, the attempt to reach a compromise on abortion law was the final issue which delayed agreement on the terms of the treaty of reunification. A temporary compromise, by which separate laws would apply in the old Federal Republic area and in the 'new Länder', lasted until the end of 1992. A new law was passed in 1992, but CDU Members of the Bundestag and the Land government of Bavaria complained to the Constitutional Court that the new law was unconstitutional. The Court ruled that several aspects of the new law needed revision to comply with the constitution, and in 1994 a revised law was passed (Prützel-Thomas, 1993).

D Cases concerning property rights, especially when such rights are affected by state action

These include a decision of the Constitutional Court in 1991. This upheld the constitutionality of a clause in an Annex to the Reunification Treaty (1990), which barred former owners of land which had been confiscated during the Soviet occupation in East Germany and prior to the establishment of the GDR from claiming restitution of their property.

E Rejection in 1986 of a complaint by the Green party that the Bundestag refused to place a representative of that party on the Bundestag committee which controlled the secret service

The Greens claimed that this violated several parts of the Basic Law, including Article 38 (that Members of the Bundestag represent the whole people). The Court confirmed the right of the Bundestag to regulate its own procedures in such matters (see also above, 1E, the Bundestag committee membership case (1989)).

F The Christian Democrats complained that the SPD–FDP coalition government had improperly issued government brochures and placed government advertisements in the press as part of the 1976 election campaign, to the benefit of the ruling parties

The Constitutional Court in 1977 upheld the complaint, stating that such activities violated the principle of democracy (Article 20), the equal status of parties (Article 21) and the equality of the electoral process (Article 38). A dissenting opinion claimed that such a view of the constitution had not been applied in the past, and that it should not now be applied without prior notice. Certainly previous governments (including Christian Democrat-led governments) had made electoral use of government-funded propaganda to a considerable extent.

G Upholding a complaint by the Greens, PDS and Republican party that the electoral system accepted by the legislatures of the Federal Republic and the GDR for the 1990 post-reunification Bundestag election was unconstitutional

This system proposed the application of the 5 per cent qualification for the enlarged Federal Republic, but permitted parties in East Germany to combine their lists with partner parties in West Germany for purposes of calculating their share of second votes. The Court ruled that this system was in contravention of Articles 21 and 38 concerning the equality of parties and of votes, since East German parties not fused with West German partners would find it difficult to obtain 5 per cent of votes in the whole of the enlarged Federal Republic, and the arrangements for combining lists of different parties would militate against parties without a suitable West German partner. The Court proposed instead that, given the special circumstances of this first post-reunification election – and for the 1990 election only – the possibility of joint lists of parties together with the application of the 5 per cent rule separately in West and East Germany would satisfy constitutional requirements. This system was then adopted by legislation, and was applied to the 1990 Bundestag election.

H Complaint about a NATO decision

This case was a rejection in 1983 of a complaint that a NATO decision (involving the consent of the Federal Republic's Foreign and Defence Ministers) to station Cruise and Pershing missiles within the territory of the Federal Republic violated the complainant's 'right to life' (Article 2) by making a counter-attack on the Federal Republic by the Soviet Union more likely.

J A complaint that government decisions to utilise German troops on UN missions in the former Yugoslavia and in Somalia were in breach of the limitations on the deployment of troops laid down in Article 87(a) of the Basic Law

Though the Court was very divided on the constitutionality of the government's actions, it finally upheld them in a decision in 1994, with the proviso that use of German troops outside the NATO area required the prior consent of the Bundestag.

Notes

1 On the various stages of the development of state funding of political parties in the Federal Republic, see Gunlicks (1995).
2 A more detailed study of the Maastricht Treaty case can be found in Ress (1994, pp. 56–69).

References

Gunlicks, A. (1995) 'The New German Party Finance Law', *German Politics*, 1: 101–21.

Prützel-Thomas, M. (1993) 'The abortion issue and the Federal Constitutional Court', *German Politics*, 3: 467–84.

Ress, G. (1994) 'The Constitution and the Maastricht Treaty: between cooperation and conflict', *German Politics*, 3: 47–74.

Appendix 2: Economic, social and political profiles of the Länder

Note For purposes of comparison, the unemployment rate for Germany on 31 December 1997 was 12.7 per cent. Non-German residents constituted 8.9 per cent of the population at the end of 1997. The composition of Land governments refers to the situation in June 1999.

Baden-Württemberg

The economy is a mixture of tourism (especially in the Black Forest area), agricultural activities (especially wine production) and industries – many based on advanced technologies – including computer-related industries and automobile production. Baden-Württemberg has the highest level of average income of all the Länder. The unemployment rate in 1997 was 8.7 per cent. The Land has an above average share of non-German residents (12.3 per cent in 1997). Catholics and Protestants are approximately equally represented in the population.

The Land was formed by a fusion (following referenda) in 1952 of the three southwest Länder of Württemberg-Baden, Württemberg-Hohenzollern and Baden. The Land legislature is elected for a five-year term. The Land constitution permits the use of the referendum. Baden-Württemberg was governed by a CDU prime minister since 1953, though sometimes coalitions of the CDU with the SPD or FDP were necessary. Occasionally extreme right-wing parties have had some success in Land elections, such as the Republicans, who won seats in the Land parliament in 1992 and 1996. The Land government in 1999 was a coalition of the CDU and FDP.

Bavaria

The economy, earlier predominantly rural, has become increasingly one based on manufacturing and service industries, especially in Munich, Nuremburg, Würzburg and Erlangen. The aeronautical, automobile and machine-tool industries are among those which predominate. The unemployment rate in 1997 (8.7 per cent) was, with that of Baden-Württemberg, the lowest of any Land. The percentage of non-German residents is about average (9.2 per cent). Catholics outnumber Protestants by nearly 3:1.

Bavaria had a long history of independent status as a kingdom (and retained its monarch until the end of the First World War), and is still very protective of its rights within the Federal Republic. It was the only Land to vote against acceptance of the Basic Law in 1949. This concern is demonstrated by the fact that its Christian Democratic party, the Christian Social Union, has preserved a separate existence within the party system, though it has always campaigned in Bundestag elections alongside the CDU, has always formed a joint parliamentary party with the CDU after each Bundestag election, and has always been a member of governing coalitions when a CDU chancellor has been in office. The Land legislature is elected for a four-year term. The Land constitution permits referenda to be held. Apart from the period 1954–57, the CSU has always been the governing party in Bavaria since 1946, and after 1960 had a sufficient majority to govern without the need of coalition partners. The Land government in 1999 was formed by the CSU.

Berlin

The economy is undergoing intensive development following the termination of the division of the city by the Berlin Wall and the reunification of Germany. The transfer of most of the institutions of government which were formerly in Bonn to Berlin has served as an economic stimulus, and its reacquired status as undisputed capital city of reunified Germany has attracted many firms and other institutions to locate head offices in Berlin. Tourism, congresses and service industries also contribute to the economy, though manufacturing industry, especially in East Berlin, is declining. Berlin has the highest number of university students of any city in Germany. The unemployment rate at the end of 1997 was 17.3 per cent. The city has an above average level of non-German residents (13.9 per cent). Protestants outnumber Catholics among the population by about 4:1.

Until 1990, East Berlin was governed by the communist SED, then, briefly in 1990 until reunification, by an SPD-led coalition. West Berlin was governed usually by an SPD lord mayor, though CDU lord mayors governed in 1953–54 and 1981–89. Coalitions formed either from one of these two governing parties with the FDP, or of the SPD and CDU together, have been necessary from time to time. A coalition of the SPD and the Berlin 'green' party (called the Alternative List) was formed in 1989 and lasted for several months. The successor party to the SED, the Party of Democratic Socialism (PDS) is very strong in East Berlin (and in 1994 and 1998 won four Bundestag constituency seats there). The Land legislature is elected for a four-year term. The Land government in 1999 was a coalition of the CDU and SPD.

Brandenburg

A thinly populated Land, Brandenburg since reunification has been trying to decrease its reliance on agriculture and attract investment for manufacturing and service industries. It remains, like all the East German Länder, one of the poorest of the Länder. The unemployment rate at the end of 1997 was 18.9 per cent. It has a below average share of non-German residents among its population (only 2.3 per cent in 1997). Among those in the population with a religious affiliation, the large majority are Protestant. As it surrounds Berlin, parts of Brandenburg serve as 'dormitory areas' for people who commute to Berlin to work or study.

Since reunification, Brandenburg has been governed by an SPD prime minister: 1990–94 in coalition with the FDP and Greens, but from 1994 as a one-party government. As in all East German Länder, the PDS is very strong in Brandenburg, and in the 1994 Land election had almost the same share of the vote as the CDU. The Land parliament is elected for a five-year term. In 1999 the Land was governed by the SPD.

Bremen

By far the smallest Land, in terms of area and population, Bremen is also distinctive because it is the only Land whose territory is divided by another Land (Bremen and Bremerhaven are separated by territory belonging to Lower Saxony). Formerly dependent upon shipping using its harbours and on shipbuilding, the economy of the Land of Bremen has diminished with the decline of those industries, though specialised shipping and container shipping remain significant. It still derives some benefit from food-related production, such as coffee-roasting and brewing, but otherwise is dependent upon service industries and some high-technology industries which have moved into Bremen. The unemployment rate at the end of 1997 was 16.8 per cent. It has an above average non-German share of the resident population (12.2 per cent in 1997). The religious affiliation of the population is overwhelmingly Protestant.

The SPD has always provided the lord mayor since the re-establishment of city government in 1947, though until 1971 as head of a governing coalition with the FDP or, for a time, with the CDU and FDP. In 1991 a 'traffic-light' coalition of the SPD, Greens and FDP formed the Land government. In the 1995 Land election, a split within the SPD led to a new party grouping, Arbeit für Bremen ('Work for Bremen'), winning a substantial number of seats, and forcing the SPD to enter a coalition with the CDU in order to continue governing. Arbeit für Bremen failed to win seats in the 1999 Land election. The extreme right-wing DVU (German People's Union) has won seats in the Land parliament: in 1987 one seat as 'List D', in 1991 six of the one hundred seats, and in 1999 one seat. The Land constitution allows for referenda to be held. The Land legislature is elected for a four-year term. The Land government in 1999 was a coalition of the SPD and CDU.

Hamburg

A city whose economy has depended in the past very much on its port and shipbuilding facilities (and today ranks second in size to Rotterdam as a Western European container port), Hamburg has increasingly come to rely on the service sector, including press and broadcasting, to supplement its shipping-related economy. Hamburg is Germany's second largest city. The unemployment rate at the end of 1997 was 13 per cent. It has the highest non-German share of resident population of any of the Länder (18.2 per cent in 1997). The religious affiliation of the population is predominantly Protestant.

Apart from a brief period (1953–57) when an anti-SPD right-wing alliance governed the city, the SPD has always provided the lord mayor and – alone or in coalition – has formed the Land government. The Greens have enjoyed particular success in Hamburg elections. Though the extreme right has not managed to win seats in the Land legislature, the extreme right-wing vote, divided among two or three parties, has been significant in the 1990s, and the DVU secured 4.9 per cent in the 1997 Land election. Since 1996, the Land constitution allows for referenda to be held. The Land legislature is elected for a four-year term. The Land government in 1999 was a coalition of the SPD and Greens.

Hesse

Hesse has an economy based on the service sector (especially in Frankfurt, where the Bundesbank and the head offices of numerous other banks are located), together with chemical, machine-tool, electrical goods and motor manufacture, as well as wine production. The unemployment rate at the end of 1997 was 10.4 per cent. It has an above average share of residents who are non-German (13.9 per cent in 1997). Though Protestants are in a majority, there is a substantial minority of Catholics among the population.

The SPD, alone or in coalition, formed the Land government uninterruptedly until 1987, when the CDU was able to form a government in coalition with the FDP. From 1991 the SPD again provided the Land prime minister, at the head of a coalition with the Greens, until the Land election in 1999. Hesse was the first Land to experience a coalition which contained the Greens – in 1985. Though the Land constitution allows for referenda to be used, there have been very few cases of a referendum being held. The Land parliament has a four-year term. In 1999 a CDU–FDP government was formed after the Land election.

Lower Saxony

Though large areas of the Land are devoted to agriculture, Lower Saxony also has important centres of motor manufacture (Wolfsburg is the 'home' of the Volkswagen company), steel production, and electronics-related industries. The unemployment rate at the end of 1997 was 12.9 per cent. It has a below average share of non-German residents (6.1 per cent in 1997). The population is largely Protestant.

The SPD formed the Land government until 1976, with the exception of the period 1955–57, when a prime minister from the DP led a coalition of right-wing parties. In 1976, the CDU was able to form a coalition with the FDP, and led the government until 1990. However, until 1994 (other than the period 1970–74, when the SPD could govern alone) a coalition was always necessary to ensure a majority for the government, whether led by the SPD or CDU. From 1990 the SPD formed the government, first in coalition with the Greens, but from 1994 with a sufficient majority to govern alone. The Land parliament is now elected for a five-year term (since 1998). The new Land constitution (1993) provided for the possibility of referenda. The Land government in 1999 was formed by the SPD.

Mecklenburg-Vorpommern

A very flat, thinly populated and rural Land in the north-east of the Federal Republic, Mecklenburg-Vorpommern relies on agricultural production, shipbuilding, food manufacture and construction-related industries, together with its important Baltic Sea port of Rostock. It had an unemployment rate of 20.3 per cent at the end of 1997. Non-German residents constitute only 1.4 per cent of the population (1997).

The Land legislature is elected for a four-year term. The 1990 Land election produced a coalition government between the CDU and FDP, led by a CDU prime minister. After the 1994 Land election a 'grand coalition' was formed between the SPD and CDU, with an SPD prime minister. The Land government in 1999 (formed following the 1998 Land election) was a coalition of the SPD and PDS, the first such coalition at Land level.

North Rhine-Westphalia

The Land with the largest population, North Rhine-Westphalia was formed after the Second World War almost entirely from parts of Prussia. Because of its extensive coal-mining and steel-producing industries of the Ruhr region, it has always been a very important region economically for Germany. It contains the important industrial cities of the Ruhr (such as Essen and Dortmund); the city of Düsseldorf is the Land capital, and Munster, Cologne and Bonn (the former seat of government of the Federal Republic) also lie within the Land borders. Though the heavy industries of the Ruhr have declined in importance, the Land contains numerous other important areas of economic activity, such as the chemical industry, banking and finance (especially in Düsseldorf and Cologne), and media-related enterprises. The unemployment rate at the end of 1997 was 12.2 per cent. Non-German residents constituted 11.2 per cent of the population at the end of 1997. Catholics are in a majority in the Land, though there are also areas where the Protestant church is dominant.

The Land has always been important politically, because of its size, economic importance and the proximity of Düsseldorf to Bonn. The relocation of the Bundestag, Bundesrat, party head offices and many of the government ministries to Berlin has meant that the city of Bonn has had to develop a strategy to attract new forms of economic activity to the former seat of government. The Land legislature is elected for a five-year term. Until the 1980s, North Rhine-Westphalia was regarded as a 'marginal' Land in electoral terms. A CDU-led coalition formed the government from 1947–56; then a coalition of the SPD and FDP governed until 1958. The CDU – alone or with the FDP – formed the government from 1958 to 1966, after which the SPD governed, first in coalition with the FDP (1966–80), then alone (until 1995), and since 1995 in coalition with the Greens. The Land government in 1999 was a coalition of the SPD and Greens.

Rhineland-Pfalz

Located in the west of the Federal Republic, bordering France and Luxembourg, Rhineland-Pfalz depends on agriculture (especially wine production; about two-thirds of all German wine comes from this area) for a large part of its prosperity. However, it also has important chemical industries and many small local businesses producing a variety of articles ranging from leather goods to semi-precious stones. The Land capital, Mainz, is home to two large television broadcasting concerns (ZDF and SAT-1). The unemployment rate at the end of 1997 was 10.3 per cent. It has a below average share of non-German residents (7.5 per cent in 1997). There are rather more Catholics than Protestants in the population.

The Land government was led by the CDU until 1991 (though from 1947 until 1971 always in coalition with other parties). Helmut Kohl was prime minister from 1969 until 1976. Since 1991, the SPD has provided the prime minister at the head of a coalition government with the FDP. The Land legislature is now elected for a five-year term. The Land government in 1999 was a coalition of the SPD and FDP.

Saarland

A small Land in the south-west of the Federal Republic, the Saarland – because of its proximity to France and its importance as a coal-mining and steel-producing region – was given to France to administer at the end of the Second World War, pending a terri-torial settlement in a peace treaty. In 1957, after a plebiscite in the Saarland on its future status, the area became a Land of the Federal Republic under the terms of Article 23 of the Basic Law. The decline of its basic industries has led to high unemployment rates (13.6 per cent at the end of 1997). The Land is trying to encourage research-oriented enterprises to locate in the region, with some success. It has a below average share of non-German residents (1997, 7.4 per cent). The population is largely Catholic.

The Land legislature is elected for a five-year term. Until 1985, the Land government was always led by a CDU prime minister, though sometimes a coalition was necessary. Oskar Lafontaine, formerly lord mayor of Saarbrücken, became prime minister in 1985, heading a government formed by the SPD alone until he entered the Schröder govern-ment as Finance Minister in 1998. In 1999 the SPD formed the Land government.

Saxony

Located in the east of the Federal Republic, and with borders shared with Poland and the Czech Republic, as well as with four other Länder, Saxony is the most prosperous of the 'new Länder' which formerly constituted the GDR. Its unemployment rate at the end of 1997 was the lowest of the 'new Länder', at 18.4 per cent. Saxony's economy depends on modernised industries (such as motor manufacture), research-related industries and service sector enterprises such as banking, advertising and publishing. Dresden, Leipzig and Chemnitz are the main business locations not just for Saxony, but for the whole of East Germany (apart from Berlin). Non-German residents constitute only 1.9 per cent of the population (1997).

The Land parliament is elected for a four-year term. The Land constitution allows for referenda to be held. The Land government since reunification in 1990 has been formed by the CDU under the leadership of the prime minister, Kurt Biedenkopf, who, though born in Chemnitz, came from West Germany and has been regarded as the most success-ful of the West German politicians who migrated to the 'new Länder'. In 1999 the CDU formed the Land government.

Saxony-Anhalt

The economy of Saxony-Anhalt depends on agriculture to a considerable extent, but also on manufacturing industry (including foodstuffs, motor vehicles and machinery), as well as chemical products, energy production and various forms of mining activity. At the end of 1997 the Land had the highest unemployment rate in the Federal Republic – 21.7 per cent. Non-German residents constitute only 1.8 per cent of the population.

The first Land government formed after reunification was a coalition between the CDU and FDP. After the Land election in 1994, controversially the SPD decided to form a minority government in coalition with the Greens, supported by votes of the PDS in the Land parliament. The Land election in 1998 produced a minority SPD government, again supported by the votes of the PDS. That 1998 election was remarkable for the extraordinary success of the extreme-right wing German People's Union party (12.9 per cent of the vote), who won sixteen of the 116 Land parliament seats. The Land legislature is elected for a four-year term. In 1999 the Land government was formed by the SPD.

Schleswig-Holstein

Located in the north of the Federal Republic, between the North Sea and the Baltic Sea, Schleswig-Holstein is a relatively small, flat and chiefly rural area. The emphasis in the economy is shifting from farming and fishing to modern industry and services. The Land capital, Kiel, still retains a significant shipbuilding industry. The unemployment rate at the end of 1997 was 11.2 per cent. Non-German residents constituted in 1997 only 5.2 per cent of the population. The population is overwhelmingly Protestant.

Though the SPD provided the prime minister in the period 1947–50, the Land was regarded as a CDU stronghold from 1950 until 1988. Governments in that period consisted either of the CDU alone, or the CDU in coalition with the FDP and, in the period 1950–58, with other small parties as well. From 1988 the SPD formed the government, without the need for coalition partners, but in 1996 had to form a coalition with the Greens. The Land legislature is elected for a five-year term. In 1999 the SPD–Greens coalition was the Land government. The Minister-President is Heide Simonis, the only female Land prime minister.

Thuringia

In addition to a substantial agricultural sector, Thuringia's economy depends on modernised manufacturing enterprises (such as motor manufacture and optical products), industries dependent upon new technologies (including computers), and research-related enterprises. The unemployment rate at the end of 1997 was 19.1 per cent. The Land has the lowest proportion of non-German residents – 1.2 per cent (1997).

The Land parliament is now elected for a five-year term. The Land constitution of 1994 allows for referenda to be held. Since 1990 the CDU has led the Land government first in coalition with the FDP, then from 1994 in a grand coalition with the SPD. In 1999 the Land government was a coalition of the CDU and SPD.

Index

Adenauer, Konrad 13–14, 17–19, 21, 22, 47, 56–7, 62, 73, 79, 81, 91, 95, 113, 114, 116, 118–21, 123–4, 127, 129, 168, 171, 177, 186, 201
All-German People's Party 117
Alliance '90 30, 65, 80, 84, 95
'Alliance for Germany' 25–7
Alliance for Jobs 164
Association of Free Citizens 175, 203–4
'Auschwitz lie' 197

Baden 6, 21, 58, 99, 110, 131, 208
Baden-Württemberg 10, 33, 58, 70, 79, 80, 83, 84, 87, 99, 100, 103, 104, 106, 107, 108, 110, 191, 208
   see also Baden; Württemberg
Barzel, Rainer 128, 137
Basic Agreement see Basic Treaty
Basic Law 12, 18, 19, 28–9, 35–9, 48, 74, 76–8, 81, 86, 88, 91, 93, 97–104, 108–9, 110, 112–13, 115–16, 117–18, 128, 131, 138, 142, 145, 149, 152, 155, 158, 165, 169, 171–4, 179, 183, 185, 186–9, 190, 196, 198, 200–6, 209
   amendment of 39, 48–9, 50–1, 127, 138, 142, 149, 196
Basic Paper (SPD-SED) 20
Basic Treaty 17, 18, 20, 42

Bavaria 3, 6, 10, 11, 21, 33, 42, 48, 58, 68, 70, 74, 80, 81, 87, 97, 131, 191, 195, 198, 205, 208–9
Bavarian Party 11, 80
Berlin 10, 26, 29, 30, 33, 46, 81, 83, 86, 87, 95, 99, 103, 104, 106, 107, 157, 184, 194, 209
   blockade and airlift 10, 12, 18
   Berlin Wall 17, 18, 25–6, 85, 126, 182, 183, 185, 209
   East Berlin uprising (1953) 17
Biedenkopf, Kurt 213
Bismarck, Otto von 3–4
Bizonia 11, 98
   see also Economic Council
Bonn 12, 30, 98, 212
Brandenburg 80, 87, 99, 108–9, 110, 157, 191, 209–10
Brandt, Willy 14–15, 18–19, 45, 46, 63, 107, 115, 118–20, 124, 128, 129
Bremen 33, 58, 70, 80, 82, 83, 87, 98, 99, 103, 104, 106, 108, 131, 157, 191, 210
budget 126
Bundesbank 43–4, 122, 172, 178
Bundesrat 30, 38, 39, 40, 98, 100–1, 104–7, 109, 113, 127, 137–40, 149, 150, 140–6, 145–6, 171–3, 179, 188, 189
   committees 140, 141
   composition 138–9
   veto power 105, 121, 127, 141–3
   see also Mediation Committee

215

Bundestag 30, 38, 40, 41, 54–5, 63, 78,
    93, 105, 107, 113, 115, 118,
    119–20, 121, 122, 123–4, 127,
    128, 129, 132–7, 157, 161,
    171–3, 188, 189, 206
  committees 135–6, 144, 146, 148,
    149, 161, 202–3, 205
  Council of Elders 133–4
  dissolution 15, 115, 202
  interest group register 161–2
  legislation 135, 140–3, 150
    see also Mediation Committee
  praesidium 133–4
  president 133
  reform 149
  rules of procedure 132–3, 143, 145,
    152, 203, 205
  social composition 147–8
Bundestag elections
  1949 election 13, 52, 62, 81
  1953 election 13, 62, 74, 79,
  1957 election 13, 62, 71, 72, 91,
    121
  1961 election 14, 62, 71, 73
  1965 election 62–3, 71, 73
  1969 election 14, 63, 71, 73, 79, 87,
    118
  1972 election 15, 63, 71, 82, 129,
    142
  1976 election 15, 63–4, 71
  1980 election 15, 64, 73, 79, 82, 84
  1983 election 15, 64, 71, 79, 84,
    202
  1987 election 16, 64, 84, 147
  1990 election 26, 28, 53–4, 64–5, 68,
    72, 73, 74, 84, 85, 87, 94, 191,
    206
  1994 election 26, 57, 59, 61, 65, 68,
    71, 72, 82, 84, 86, 87, 91, 94,
    115, 120, 191, 204
  1998 election 51, 52, 58, 59, 65–6,
    71, 72, 73, 82, 84, 86, 87, 91,
    94, 147, 175, 191
    see also candidate selection; election
    campaigning; electoral behaviour;
    electoral system
Bund freier Bürger *see* Association of Free
    Citizens

cabinet 81, 113, 118, 120, 125, 129,
    141, 172
candidate selection 58–60, 74, 107
Carstens, Karl 117
Centre party 5, 11, 78, 80, 91, 124,
    153
chancellor 38, 62–6, 107, 112–13,
    115–16, 117–26, 128–9, 143,
    172, 202
  deputy 124, 125
  Richtlinienkompetenz 38, 117–18
    see also chancellor democracy;
    Chancellor's Office; constructive
    vote of no confidence
chancellor democracy 13, 112, 128
Chancellor's Office 120, 125, 129, 133,
    172
Christian Democratic Union 11, 13, 14,
    15, 16, 45–6, 56, 57, 58, 59, 61,
    62–6, 68–74, 78–85, 90–2, 95,
    106, 107, 117, 113–14, 116,
    117, 118–19, 120, 121, 122–5,
    128, 136, 137, 139, 144, 147,
    148, 149, 155, 159, 160, 168,
    174, 205, 206, 208–14
Christian Democrats *see* Christian
    Democratic Union; Christian
    Social Union
Christian Social Union 11, 13, 14, 15,
    42, 45–6, 56, 57, 58, 61, 62–6,
    68–74, 78–85, 87, 90–2, 95,
    107, 113–14, 116, 118–19, 121,
    122–5, 128, 136, 137, 144, 147,
    148, 149, 159, 160, 168, 174,
    195, 205, 206, 209
churches 3, 12, 35, 69, 81, 92, 153–4,
    156, 159, 163, 205
citizen initiative groups 44, 84, 192
civil service 8, 32, 35, 126
coalition committee 125, 126, 130
coalition formation 122–4, 130
cold war 12, 17, 45–6, 168, 177, 182,
    185, 186, 195
combative democracy 45, 183, 186–91,
    196
Commissioner of the Armed Forces 122,
    144
communism 10, 11, 85

Communist Party 11, 16, 21, 45, 77, 78, 82, 86, 95, 153, 188, 200
communists 7, 16, 186
Concerted Action 164
Constitutional Court 38, 39–42, 49, 73, 74, 78, 87, 90, 93, 94, 95, 98, 101, 104, 106, 110, 115, 116, 117, 122, 127, 128, 138, 142, 145, 163, 172, 187, 188, 194, 198, 200–6
constructive vote of no confidence 15, 38, 46, 63, 118–19, 128, 131, 143, 186, 202
corporatism 164
Council of Economic Advisers 44, 122, 128–9, 144
Council of Europe 13
currency reform (1948) 12
    see also economic and monetary union (Germany)

Dehler, Thomas 116, 124, 128
Democratic Farmers' Party of Germany (GDR) 16
denazification 10–11
deputy chancellor *see* chancellor: deputy

Ecological Democratic Party 159
economic and monetary union (Germany) 26–7, 33, 43, 170, 185
Economic Council 11, 43
economy of the Federal Republic 15–16, 30–31, 33, 43–5, 88, 122, 168, 177, 178, 185, 192, 196, 208–14
    see also social market economy
election campaigning 60–1, 92, 120, 123, 146, 159, 201, 209
electoral behaviour 48, 66–7, 81–6, 88–9, 190
    turnout 66–8, 74–5, 94, 96, 178
electoral system 29, 38, 39, 42, 50–6, 67, 71–2, 78, 79, 86, 145, 186, 204, 206
    reform of 56–7, 74, 157
    Weimar Republic 5, 53, 54,

Engholm, Björn 110
Erhard, Ludwig 12, 13, 21, 43, 44, 47, 62–3, 119–20, 124–5, 129, 171
European Coal and Steel Community 13, 169–70, 176
European Community 170, 178
European Economic Community 13, 22, 37, 169–70, 176
European Union 30, 42, 49, 100, 101, 106, 122, 126, 138, 142, 156, 167, 170–9, 193, 194, 203
'events of 1968' 184, 197–8
extra-parliamentary opposition 47
extremism 87–8, 143, 177, 183, 187, 188–90, 196, 197, 198
    see also parties: extreme
extremist parties *see* parties: extreme

Federal Constitutional Court *see* Constitutional Court
federal government 38, 41, 56, 93, 100, 101–5, 113, 121–6, 139, 143–5, 152, 162–3, 172, 173, 176, 188, 198, 200–1
    see also cabinet; coalition committee; Ministries; parliamentary state secretaries
Federal Office for the Protection of the Constitution 86, 157, 187–9
federal president *see* president of the Federal Republic
Federal Republic of Germany 10
    development of 13–16
federal system 32, 37–8, 121
    constitutional basis 100–4
    development 97–100
    reform of 108–9, 110
First World War 4
Fischer, Joschka 124
Flick affair 136, 144, 163
Fraktion 81, 90, 93, 120, 124, 125, 128, 129, 132–3, 135, 136–7, 140–1, 143, 144, 146, 148, 161, 203
Frankfurt Parliament 2, 131
Free Democratic Party 11, 13, 14, 15, 21, 47, 56, 57, 60, 61, 62–6, 68–71, 73–4, 78–80, 82–4,

Free Democratic Party (*cont.*)
    90–2, 94, 95, 106, 107, 113–16,
    118–19, 121, 122–5, 127, 128,
    130, 136–7, 139, 144, 147, 160,
    161, 165, 174, 175, 196,
    208–14
Free People's Party 125
fundis *see* Green party

Genscher, Hans-Dietrich 15, 60, 64, 83,
    121, 123, 129, 146, 177
Gerhardt, Wolfgang 66, 107, 130, 136
German Democratic Republic 10, 13, 14,
    16–20, 22, 32, 42, 45–6, 85–6,
    93, 108, 117, 126, 170, 182,
    185, 196, 205
  downfall of 23–5
German Federation of Trade Unions
    154–5, 159, 160, 164
German Party 11, 13, 55, 62, 79, 95,
    121, 125, 211
German People's Union 80, 87–8, 107,
    190–1, 200, 210, 211, 214
German reunification (1990) 12, 13,
    17–19, 20, 22, 23, 26–8, 32–3,
    35–7, 39, 47–8, 64, 70, 79, 83,
    84, 85, 86, 88, 90, 92, 99, 108,
    117, 122, 136, 167, 168, 170,
    171, 176, 178, 182, 184, 185,
    190–1, 195, 196, 205, 209
German Social Union 82
Germany
  division of 45–6
  regimes, list of 1
  Second Empire 3–4, 76, 97
  unification of (1871) 2–3
Godesberg congress *see* Social Democratic
    Party
Godesberg Programme *see* Social
    Democratic Party
'grand coalition' 14, 19, 38, 44, 47, 56,
    57, 62, 63, 66, 73, 82, 91, 116,
    119, 121, 122, 123, 129, 139,
    142, 157
Green party 47, 54, 57, 60, 61, 64–6,
    68–71, 74, 78–80, 82, 84–5,
    90–2, 94, 95, 96, 106, 107, 114,
    121, 122–5, 129, 137, 145, 147,

    149, 157, 159, 160, 174, 192–3.
    196, 201, 202–3, 204, 205, 206,
    209, 210, 211, 212, 214
  see also Alliance '90
'Greens' *see* Green party
Guillaume, Günter 119, 136, 144
Gysi, Gregor 25–6, 60, 137

Hallstein, Walter 170, 177
Hamburg 70, 80, 82, 83, 87, 94, 95, 98,
    99, 103, 105, 106, 108, 131,
    140, 191, 194, 210–11
Hare-Niemayer formula 72
Heinemann, Gustav 113–17, 123
Heitmann, Steffen 114–15
Herzog, Roman 113, 115, 117, 128,
    183
Hesse 10, 59, 73, 80, 82, 83, 84, 99,
    100, 103, 104, 106, 107, 108,
    131, 150, 201, 211
Heuss, Theodor 13, 107, 113, 116–17,
    186
von Hindenburg, Paul 7–8
Hitler, Adolf 6–9, 20, 21, 49, 88, 93, 98,
    112–13, 116, 183, 190, 197,
    198
Holocaust 181, 204–5
d'Hondt allocation system 72
Honecker, Erich 17, 20, 25–6, 32, 34

individual rights 36–7, 41
integration of Germany 3–4, 29–33,
    47–8, 79, 114, 185, 195
interest groups 12, 35, 60, 92, 126, 141,
    145, 148–9, 175, 176
  see also: Bundestag: interest group
    register
  history of 152–4
interests *see* interest groups

Joint Constitutional Commission 36,
    109, 136, 149
judiciary 38, 39–40, 49

Kiesinger, Kurt Georg 14, 19, 63, 107,
    119–20
Kohl, Helmut 15, 31, 34, 59, 63–5, 83,
    107, 113, 114–15, 118, 119–20,

121, 122, 123–4, 127, 128, 129,
136, 139, 167, 177, 178, 183,
194, 196, 202
ten-point plan for reunification 26, 28
Krenz, Egon 25–6

Lafontaine, Oskar 64–6, 107, 120, 136,
213
Lambsdorff, Otto Graf 60, 129
Land elections 11, 15, 29, 80, 87, 88,
131, 144
Länder 3, 5, 12, 35, 37–8, 97, 98,
100–1, 104, 105, 121, 127,
138–9, 141–2, 145, 171, 174,
175, 201
see also under individual Länder
financing 38, 100–3, 109, 110
in the German Democratic Republic 29
see also 'new Länder'
Land governments 36, 41, 84, 85, 93, 97,
98, 124, 138–9, 146, 174, 176,
188, 193, 198, 201, 208–14
'coalition treaty' 139
Land parliaments 11, 12, 26, 29, 36, 79,
80–1, 84–5, 86, 87, 90, 93, 97,
100, 101, 108–9, 113, 126, 131,
146, 150, 157, 189, 208–14
legislature 105, 173
functions 140–6
see also Bundestag, Bundesrat, Land
parliaments
Liberal electoral alliance (GDR) 27
liberal parties 83
German Democratic Party (Weimar
Republic) 5, 153
German People's Party (Weimar
Republic) 153
Liberal Democratic Party of Germany
(GDR) 16
see also Free Democratic Party; Liberal
electoral alliance (GDR)
local government 102, 103, 104
Lower Saxony 59, 66, 70, 82, 87, 98, 99,
107, 108, 163, 211
Lübke, Heinrich 113–14, 116–17

Maastricht Treaty 42, 48–9, 170, 172,
174, 176, 179, 203–4

de Maizière, Lothar 27
Marshall Aid *see* Marshall Plan
Marshall Plan 10, 12, 168, 179
Mecklenburg-Vorpommern 59, 71, 86,
99, 106, 140, 198, 211–12
Mediation Committee 105, 136, 139,
142–3
Mende, Erich 123, 137
military, German 5–6, 8–9, 38, 49, 127,
144, 155–6, 168, 171, 174, 177,
178, 183, 194, 206
Ministries:
All-German Affairs *see* Ministries:
Inter-German Relations
Agriculture 114, 124, 164, 172
Construction, Town Planning and
Transport 129
Defence 122
Economic Cooperation 195
Economics 13, 123–4, 164, 172, 179
Finance 105, 123, 172, 213
Foreign Affairs 14, 15, 83, 118, 120,
121, 123, 124, 129, 172, 174
Inter-German Relations 46, 118
Interior 88, 95, 123, 187, 188, 200
Justice 105, 115, 116, 123, 141
Labour 124, 164
Transport 172
Mischnick, Wolfgang 137
Modrow, Hans 25–6

National Democratic Party 14, 44, 47,
54, 63, 78–80, 87–8, 183, 188,
190–1, 200
National Democratic Party of Germany
(GDR) 16
Nazis 6–9, 20–1, 82, 153, 183, 186
nazism 8, 10, 11, 80, 86, 88
New Forum 24, 26
'new Länder' 29, 30, 31, 32, 33, 36, 48,
56, 70, 80, 82, 85, 86, 94, 103,
104, 108, 114, 126, 139, 178,
179, 185, 188, 191, 194–5, 197,
205
see also Brandenburg; Mecklenburg-
Vorpommern; Saxony; Saxony-
Anhalt; Thuringia
'new politics' 79, 192–3

North Atlantic Treaty Organisation 13,
21, 37, 45, 122, 127, 145,
167–8, 169, 170, 172, 176–9,
183, 194, 206
North Rhine-Westphalia 33, 57, 59, 64,
70, 73, 78, 80, 83, 98, 99, 103,
104, 106, 107, 108, 117, 161,
212

occupation of Germany 10–12, 16, 21,
73, 76, 80, 82, 87, 93, 98, 104,
109, 153–4, 168, 194, 197, 205
Oder-Neisse border 19, 20, 28, 33, 194
Ostpolitik 14, 20, 63, 83, 118
overcoming the past 31, 181–6

parliament, history of 131
Parliamentary Council 12, 35, 48, 52,
81, 97, 98, 186
parliamentary state secretaries 125, 129,
146, 150
parties 47, 116, 193, 201, 205
see also under individual parties
extreme 44, 48, 78, 86–9, 94, 174,
185, 187, 190–1, 194, 200,
210–11
financing of 41, 42, 61, 74, 77, 85,
90–1, 92, 93–5, 128, 201–2
Foundations 92–3, 95–6, 187, 189,
195, 199
functions 91–3
organisation of 89–91, 106–7,
119–20
unconstitutionality of 41, 45, 200
party government 76, 78, 92
Party Law 77–8, 88, 89, 90, 91, 93,
188, 201
Party of Democratic Socialism 25–6, 30,
48, 54, 60, 61, 65–6, 70–1,
72–3, 79–80, 82, 84–6, 90–2,
94, 106, 114, 128, 133, 137,
139, 147, 160, 174, 187, 189,
190, 195, 198, 203, 204, 206,
210, 212, 214
party system 30, 37, 76–96, 112
German Democratic Republic 16, 25,
33, 90
Länder 80, 81, 97

policy process 126–7, 128
political culture 41, 46–8, 61, 67, 87,
167, 184
political education 10, 88, 92–3, 189,
190, 199, 201
political integration *see* integration of
Germany
Potsdam Agreement 10, 131
president of the Federal Republic 38, 40,
63–4, 112–17, 118, 132, 133,
142, 145, 149, 186, 202
election of 100, 113–14, 128
functions 115–16
Prussia 2–3, 97, 98, 99, 109, 168

radicals decree 45, 125–6, 187, 196,
198
Rau, Johannes 64, 107, 113–14, 115,
117, 128
realos *see* Green party
rearmament 13, 45, 117, 183
Rechtsstaat *see* rule of law
Red Army Faction 15
Refugee Party 62, 79, 125, 159
Reichstag 3, 5, 82, 112
fire 7–8, 20–1
Republicans 65, 79–80, 87, 187, 190–1,
198, 200, 206, 208
reunification of Germany *see* German
reunification
Rhineland-Pfalz 21, 58–9, 65, 70, 84,
99, 104, 106, 107, 108, 212–3
Round Table 25–6
Ruhr 6, 10, 83, 99, 168, 169, 194,
212
rule of law 37, 101, 203

Saarland 21, 29, 37, 64, 70, 73–4, 80,
83, 95, 99, 103, 107, 140, 169,
171, 213
Saxony 3, 33, 59, 80, 97, 99, 105, 114,
198, 213
Saxony-Anhalt 33, 66, 71, 87, 88, 99,
107, 108, 191, 213–4
Scharping, Rudolf 65–6, 107, 136,
Schäuble, Wolfgang 65, 124, 136, 146,
191
Scheel, Walter 14–15, 63–4, 114, 117

Schleswig-Holstein 42, 70, 80, 87, 157, 191, 194, 204, 214

Schmidt, Helmut 15, 63–4, 83, 119, 122, 125, 129, 137, 145, 146, 202

Schröder, Gerhard (CDU) 114, 118, 124

Schröder, Gerhard (SPD) 65, 107, 119–20, 125, 130, 136, 145, 179, 193, 194, 213

Schumacher, Kurt 62, 82, 168

Second World War 7–9, 22, 181, 183, 195, 197

Social Democrats (*see* Social Democratic Party)

Social Democratic Party 4, 5, 7, 10–11, 13, 14, 15, 16, 20, 45–6, 47, 56, 57, 58–9, 62–6, 68–73, 78, 80, 82–6, 89, 90–2, 106, 107, 110, 114–15, 118–19, 121, 122–5, 127, 129, 136, 137, 139, 144, 145, 147, 149, 153, 155, 159, 160, 172, 174, 193, 196, 208–1

   Bad Godesberg congress 13

   Bad Godesberg programme 62, 70, 83

Socialist Reich Party 11, 77, 78, 87, 188, 200

Socialist Unity Party 16, 20, 25–6, 32, 82, 85, 126, 149, 182, 209

   see also Party of Democratic Socialism

social market economy 43, 86, 182

Solms, Hermann-Otto 134, 137

Soviet Union *see* USSR

Spiegel Affair 21, 121, 129

split voting 54–5, 71

Stalin Note 18, 19

STATT-party 80, 94, 95

Strauss, Franz Josef 15, 21, 64, 81–2, 107, 121, 123, 146

Strück, Peter 136

Superwahljahr 68

'surplus seats' 52, 65, 66, 72, 74, 132, 204

Süssmuth, Rita 59, 124

terrorism 191

Thierse, Wolfgang 128, 133–4

Thuringia 68, 87, 99, 105, 106, 214

trade unions 7–8, 12, 31, 35, 58, 69, 82, 84, 92, 124, 129, 152–6, 159, 160, 163, 176, 182

Treuhandanstalt 27, 30

'two plus four' talks 28

Überhangmandate see 'surplus seats'

USSR 9, 10, 11, 12, 13, 14, 16–20, 24, 27, 45, 46, 79, 82, 93, 95, 170, 176, 181–2, 185, 189, 194, 205, 206

Vergangenheitsbewältigung see overcoming the past

Versailles Treaty 5–6, 8

Vogel, Hans-Jochen 64, 107

Volkskammer election (GDR) 25–7

voting behaviour *see* electoral behaviour

Wehner, Herbert 137

Wehrbeauftragter *see* Commissioner of the Armed Forces

Weimar constitution 5–6, 36–7, 39, 76, 113, 153, 186

Weimar Republic 4–7, 97, 112–13, 118, 183, 186, 189, 196

   parties in 76, 82

von Weizsäcker, Richard 93–4, 116–17

Württemberg 3, 21, 58, 97, 99, 131

Württemberg-Baden 98, 131, 208

Württemberg-Hohenzollern 98, 208